Reluctant Imperialists

Reluctant Imperialists

CALHOUN, THE SOUTH CAROLINIANS, AND THE MEXICAN WAR

Ernest McPherson Lander, Jr.

Louisiana State University Press
BATON ROUGE AND LONDON

Design: Dwight Agner
Typeface: VIP Sabon
Composition: LSU Press

A grant from the Clemson Faculty Research Committee aided the publication of this volume.

Some of the material herein has appeared previously, in slightly different form, in the following, to whom grateful acknowledgment is made: "The Palmetto Regiment Goes to Mexico," in *Proceedings of the South Carolina Historical Association, 1973* (Anderson, S.C.: South Carolina Historical Association, 1974); "General Waddy Thompson, a Friend of Mexico During the Mexican War," in *South Carolina Historical Magazine*, LXXVIII (January, 1977); "The Reluctant Imperialist: South Carolina, the Rio Grande, and the Mexican War," in *Southwestern Historical Quarterly*, LXXVIII (January, 1975).

Maps have been redrawn with permission of Macmillan Publishing Co., Inc., from *The Mexican War, 1846–1848* by K. Jack Bauer, copyright © 1974 by K. Jack Bauer.

LIBRARY OF CONGRESS CATALOGING IN PUBLICATION DATA

Lander, Ernest McPherson, Jr.
    Reluctant imperialists.

    Bibliography: p.
    Includes index.
    1. South Carolina—History—War with Mexico, 1845–1848. 2. United States—History—War with Mexico, 1845–1848—Regimental histories—South Carolina Infantry—Palmetto Regiment. 3. South Carolina Infantry. Palmetto Regiment, 1846–1848?—History. 4. Calhoun, John Caldwell, 1782–1850. 5. United States—History—War with Mexico, 1845–1848—Public opinion. I. Title.
E409.5.S7L36   973.6'2   79–16879
ISBN 0–8071–0594–5

To Tish

Contents

Illustrations and Maps

Preface and
Acknowledgments

SOME YEARS ago I noted that Senator John C. Calhoun had abstained from voting on the war resolutions against Mexico in May, 1846, and that he became a severe critic of President James K. Polk's war policy. I wondered how his stand affected his political influence within South Carolina, especially in view of the patriotic but tragic role played by the Palmetto regiment in Mexico. There seemed to be no open opposition to the senator, and the South Carolina General Assembly unanimously reelected him to the Senate in December, 1846.

More recently, as I began to delve into the subject, I soon learned that South Carolinians had mixed feelings about the war and that several prominent leaders were more outspoken opponents of conquest than was Calhoun. Although there was general elation over American victories and pride in the Palmettos' bravery, there was a feeling among some that the war was unjust or unnecessary, that the recent Seminole conflict had shown the folly of sending an army far into guerrilla territory, that the Mexican climate was hostile to Americans, and that the war would be too costly.

In January, 1847, Calhoun spoke out against sending American troops deep into Mexico. Instead, he called for a defensive strategy, a string of forts along the Rio Grande to El Paso and westward to the Pacific. As the struggle continued and the Mexicans refused to come to terms even after the loss of their capital city, Calhoun's "line policy" gained increasing support.

The situation was further confused by the Wilmot Proviso, first introduced into Congress in August, 1846. South Carolinians, like other southerners, were awakened gradually to the danger to their "peculiar institution" by the addition of territory wrested from Mexico. A few wanted no extra territory at all. Yet, the nation's honor demanded an indemnity from the stubborn republic beyond the Rio Grande. This was the slaveholders' dilemma. Within these pages I have noted the vicissitudes of South Carolinians' views at home, in Congress, and in Mexico toward the war, and I have also followed the course of the ill-fated Palmetto regiment to Mexico City and back.

I am indebted to numerous persons for aid in the research, preparation, and publication of this monograph, especially my wife, Sarah Shirley Lander, and colleague, Professor Robert S. Lambert, for their critical reading of the manuscript. I am also grateful to Betty L. Barrett for finding time amid pressing duties to type it, and to Olivia J. McGee for her able preparation of the maps.

Chronology of Important Events

1846

Jan. 13	General Taylor ordered to Rio Grande
Apr. 25	Mexicans attack Captain Thornton's dragoons
May 8–9	Battles of Palo Alto and Resaca de la Palma
May 13	Polk signs bill declaring war on Mexico
May 29	South Carolina officials issue call for volunteers
June 29	Pierce M. Butler elected commander of the Palmetto regiment
Aug. 8	Wilmot Proviso introduced in Congress
	Congress adjourns
Sept. 14	Santa Anna returns to military command in Mexico
Sept. 21–24	Taylor captures Monterrey
Nov. 16	War Department orders Palmetto regiment to active duty
Dec. 7	Congress convenes in Washington
Dec. 26	Palmetto regiment leaves Charleston for Mexico

1847

Feb. 9	Calhoun presents defensive-line policy in Senate speech
Feb. 22–23	Taylor defeats Santa Anna at Buena Vista
Mar. 4	Congress adjourns

Mar. 9	General Scott's army (with Palmetto regiment) lands below Vera Cruz
	Calhoun issues his call for southern unity
Mar. 29	Vera Cruz surrenders
Mar. 31	Expedition to Alvarado (with Palmettos) begins
Apr. 18	Scott defeats Santa Anna at Cerro Gordo
Apr. 20	Scott occupies Jalapa
May 15	Scott's advance units (with Palmettos) occupy Puebla
Aug. 7	Scott begins march toward Mexico City
Aug. 19–20	Scott defeats Mexicans at Contreras and Churubusco (Palmettos participate)
Sept. 13–14	Scott assaults and captures Mexico City (Palmettos participate)
Sept. 16	Santa Anna resigns as Mexican president
Oct. 6	Polk orders diplomat Nicholas Trist recalled
Dec. 6	Congress convenes in Washington

1848

Jan. 2	Trist illegally begins peace negotiations
Jan. 4	Calhoun speaks in Senate against "All-Mexico" movement
Jan. 13	Polk orders Scott relieved
Feb. 2	Treaty of Guadalupe Hidalgo signed in Mexico
Feb. 23	Polk sends treaty to Senate
Mar. 10	Senate approves treaty with amendments
May 25	Mexican Congress approves amended treaty
May 30	Palmetto regiment evacuates quarters near Mexico City to return to the United States

Abbreviations Used in Footnotes

CU   Clemson University, Clemson, S.C.
DU   Duke University, Durham, N.C.
LC   Library of Congress, Washington, D.C.
SHC   Southern Historical Collection, University of
      North Carolina, Chapel Hill.
SCL   South Caroliniana Library, University of South
      Carolina, Columbia.

Reluctant Imperialists

CHAPTER I *We Have the War and Must Fight It Out*

WHEN CONGRESS passed a joint resolution in February, 1845, calling for annexation of Texas, the entire South Carolina delegation voted approval. During the congressional battle several South Carolinians played important roles, but the work of Secretary of State John C. Calhoun was of more significance. Earlier, in the spring of 1844, Calhoun, resentful of English abolitionist schemes in Texas, had privately lectured Richard Pakenham, the new British minister to the United States, on the benefit of slavery to both races. When this polemic was leaked to the press, it antagonized the antislavery forces in the North and was partly instrumental in the Senate's defeat of an annexation treaty in June.

Later in 1844, Calhoun's counsel to President John Tyler helped to guide the annexation movement on proper course again. Working through William R. King, the American minister to France, Calhoun sowed doubts in French minds about the value of joint British-French efforts to support Texas independence. He appointed capable Andrew J. Donelson as American chargé d'affaires to Texas, and he worked behind the scenes to marshal support for a joint resolution of annexation. Finally, he wisely counseled the president against delay. The relative importance of each of the secretary's actions is difficult to determine, but taken together they may well have furnished the margin for success.[1]

1. The vote in the Senate for annexation was 27 to 25, in the House 132 to 76. For Calhoun's role see Charles M. Wiltse, *John C. Calhoun: Sectionalist, 1840–1850*

In general, South Carolinians looked with favor on bringing Texas into the Union, and they hoped its annexation would not create insurmountable difficulties with Mexico. However, relations between the two countries became strained, and by early 1846 war seemed more than remotely possible. Several notices in the South Carolina press speculated with concern about the fate of John Slidell's peace-seeking mission to Mexico. Turmoil in Mexican politics cast a shadow over Slidell's chances for success. There was news that General Mariano Paredes had overthrown President José Herrera and that former President Antonio López de Santa Anna was about to return from exile.[2]

In the confused political situation south of the Rio Grande, Slidell was unable to gain recognition, much less negotiate the difficulties between the two nations. Back home there were frequent rumors of impending war, of British intervention. Most Palmetto editors probably felt as Frederick W. Symmes, of the Pendleton *Messenger*, did. He hoped that war could be "honorably" avoided and that the American government would "remain quiet." In his opinion Mexico's refusal to receive Slidell was insufficient cause for war. The Georgetown *Winyah Observer*, as late as March 25, likewise urged "great caution" in dealing with Mexico. However, most editors reserved comment. They were generally more concerned with the Oregon controversy during the early months of 1846.[3]

Meanwhile, in early March chances for Slidell's reception by the newly installed Paredes government seemed momentarily to brighten. On receiving promising news, President James K. Polk considered asking Congress for $1 million or $2 million to be paid immediately to Mexico upon the signing of a treaty. Polk's optimism may have been further buoyed by a visit from General

(New York, 1951), 199–216; Gerald M. Capers, *John C. Calhoun, Opportunist: A Reappraisal* (Gainesville, Fla., 1960), 217–20; Margaret Coit, *John C. Calhoun: American Portrait* (Boston, 1950), 361–81.

2. Abbeville *Banner*, February 18, 1846; Pendleton *Messenger*, January 9, 1846; Charleston *Courier*, January 22, 1846; Anderson *Gazette*, February 6, 1846; Edgefield *Advertiser*, January 7, 1846.
3. Pendleton *Messenger*, February 13, 1846; Georgetown *Winyah Observer*, March 25, 1846; Charleston *Courier*, February 5, 1846; Anderson *Gazette*, February 13, 1846.

Waddy Thompson, Jr., on March 27. Thompson, an outstanding Whig party leader in South Carolina, had served as minister to Mexico in 1842–1844. He was sympathetic with Mexico, comprehended that country's problems, and had advised General Paredes on matters of reform. He desired patience on the part of the American government.[4]

The president secured approval from several prominent senators for his financial scheme, but they warned that Calhoun's support was likewise needed. The former secretary of state, now back in his old Senate seat, demurred. He feared that Polk's proposal would somehow hamper a peaceful settlement of the Oregon question. Ever the pessimist in all but his presidential ambitions, Calhoun had earlier expressed the view that there was "a very intimate connection" between the Oregon and Mexico questions. In his opinion a war with one "would almost certainly involve a war about the other." In any event, Polk received disheartening news on April 6 of Slidell's final rejection in Mexico. The president had already sent General Zachary Taylor's army into the disputed territory between the Nueces and the Rio Grande, a move that worried Calhoun. But for the moment Polk declined to take further action.[5]

The news of Slidell's rejection brought forth a flurry of editorial comment in South Carolina. The Charleston *Courier* and the Pendleton *Messenger* expected war momentarily, while the *Winyah Observer* devoted almost its entire front page to Paredes' bellicose address to the Mexican people on March 21. The hawkish Abbeville *Banner* rhetorically asked: "And why should we tamely submit to her insults? . . . As for the result of a war with imbecile Mexico, who for a moment would fear it?"[6]

4. See Ernest M. Lander, Jr., "General Waddy Thompson, a Friend of Mexico During the Mexican War," *South Carolina Historical Magazine*, LXXVIII (January, 1977), 32–42; Milo M. Quaife (ed.), *The Diary of James K. Polk: During His Presidency, 1845 to 1849* (4 vols., Chicago, 1910), I, 302, 305.
5. John C. Calhoun to B. Tucker, February 2, 1846, in John C. Calhoun Papers, SCL; Calhoun to T. G. Clemson, March 23, 1846, in John C. Calhoun Papers, CU; Charles G. Sellers, *James K. Polk: Continentalist, 1843–1846* (Princeton, N.J., 1966), 403–404.
6. Abbeville *Banner*, April 22, 1846; Charleston *Courier*, April 14, 20, 1846; Pendleton *Messenger*, April 17, 24, 1846; Georgetown *Winyah Observer*, April 26, 1846.

Few of the Palmetto weeklies devoted as much attention to the Mexican problem as did the Edgefield *Advertiser*, under the editorship of William F. Durisoe. The *Advertiser* noted that Mexico had sunk into such a degree of "madness and anarchy" that only "an iron-willed despot" could save the country from "certain extinction." The man for the position was Santa Anna, a suggestion the Abbeville *Banner* had made earlier. As for war with the United States, the *Advertiser* believed the Mexican general's inflammatory speeches were no more than "Mexican bravado." Unfortunately, the poor Mexican people had become "perfectly confused, dispirited, and unprincipled." They, nevertheless, deserved American pity and compassion. True, America had suffered from serious Mexican provocations and indignities, but the editor sincerely desired no war if there was any "honorable way" to avoid it. Should the president be determined on war, the editor proposed war with Great Britain instead of "impotent" Mexico.[7]

The outstanding South Carolina newspaper critic of Polk's Mexican policy was the Charleston *Mercury*, under the editorship of J. Milton Clapp, a native of Ohio, a graduate of Yale, and said to be "a man of independence and ability." Financial control of the paper rested with the politically powerful Rhett family, supporters of Calhoun. Even after Slidell's rejection by Mexico, the *Mercury* saw no reason for hostilities. Instead, it urged a settlement with Britain over Oregon. That was the same advice Senator Calhoun offered Polk on April 18, at which time the president agreed to delay action toward Mexico for "a reasonable time."[8]

Before making some irrevocable decision about Mexico, Polk wished to consult Slidell personally. As the latter slowly made his way toward Washington, a satisfactory Oregon settlement loomed in the offing. Polk decided the time was near to deal firmly with

---

ton *Messenger*, April 17, 24, 1846; Georgetown *Winyah Observer*, April 26, 1846.
7. Edgefield *Advertiser*, April 15, 29, 1846; Abbeville *Banner*, February 18, 1846.
8. Laura A. White, *Robert Barnwell Rhett: Father of Secession* (New York, 1931), 22, 89n; William L. King, *The Newspaper Press of Charleston, S.C.: A Chronological and Biographical History, Embracing a Period of One Hundred and Forty Years* (Charleston, S.C., 1872), 151–52; Charleston *Mercury*, April 16, 1846; Quaife, *Diary of James K. Polk*, I, 337–38.

Mexico. Thus, on April 28 he instructed Secretary of State James Buchanan to begin drafting a war message. The cabinet concurred. When Slidell finally saw Polk on May 8, the president decided to act promptly and energetically.[9]

Meantime, tension heightened between opposing armies on the Rio Grande with the disappearance on April 10 of Colonel Trueman Cross, General Taylor's chief quartermaster. First accounts reported his capture by a Mexican patrol. This was a "high-handed outrage" according to the Charleston *Courier*, which demanded his prompt release and punishment of his captors. On April 21 Cross's body was found stripped of all valuables. By then Major General Pedro de Ampudia had arrived in Matamoros with reinforcements. Four days later Captain Seth Thornton's scouting patrol of eighty dragoons rode into a Mexican ambush. Most of the Americans were either killed, wounded, or captured.[10]

The news of the Mexican attack on Thornton's dragoons reached Charleston on May 7, and the following day the *Courier* devoted about two and one-half columns to the reports. On the ninth the *Courier* published a scathing editorial about Mexican insults, atrocities, and invasion of "our territory." The editor, William S. King, attributed Mexican boldness to the "passive manner" in which Americans had borne injuries and insults. He now issued a call for war and an invasion of Mexico "up to the very gates of her Capital." For the next week the *Courier*'s news columns were filled with reports of activities along the Rio Grande and of excitement in New Orleans and Mobile. Yet, Charleston remained relatively calm, although curious crowds gathered daily at the city's newspaper offices.[11]

The Charleston *Mercury*, likewise reporting the hostilities, presented a different viewpoint. Its editor was highly critical of Polk for having sent General Taylor to the Rio Grande. "This position is the worst possible," he declared, "whether for peace or war—

9. Quaife, *Diary of James K. Polk*, I, 354, 363, 375–77; Sellers, *Polk: Continentalist*, 404–405.
10. Charleston *Courier*, April 28, 1846; K. Jack Bauer, *The Mexican War, 1846–1848* (New York, 1974), 46–48.
11. Charleston *Courier*, May 8–14, 1846.

under the very nose of Mexico, and separated by an impenetrable country from his supplies." Taylor's exposed position reflected "the least possible credit on the War Department." [12]

News of the Mexican ambush reached Washington late on Saturday, May 9, the very day that Polk's cabinet had considered war. Over the weekend the capital buzzed with excitement as the president prepared to ask Congress for a declaration of war. Congressman Isaac E. Holmes, the veteran from the Charleston district, was indignant. Privately expressing views similar to those of the *Mercury*, he accused the administration of numerous blunders "consummated by the greatest of all blunders—sending our Army two hundred miles from civilization or rather population to occupy the banks of the extreme River . . . evincing a spirit of aggression [or] if you choose annexation, which must startle Europe—especially England."

Holmes fully expected the administration, having created a war "without the advice of Congress," to endeavor to shift the responsibility to the legislative branch. He was willing, he wrote, to vote money and men to succor Taylor, and he hoped Congress would try to find some ground for negotiation. But he was not sanguine, for he feared the "Western boys" were ready to march on Mexico City. [13]

Besides Holmes the South Carolina delegation in the House consisted of Robert Barnwell Rhett of the Beaufort District, dean of the group; Armistead Burt; Richard F. Simpson; James A. Black; Joseph A. Woodward; and Alexander D. Sims, a Virginian who moved to Darlington in 1826. Burt, Simpson, Black, and Woodward first entered Congress in 1843 and Sims followed in 1845. Six of the seven were lawyers, and five had served previously in the South Carolina General Assembly.

In the Senate John C. Calhoun had resumed his former seat six months earlier, and he was particularly anxious to avoid a declaration of war against Mexico, at least for the time being. He

12. Charleston *Mercury*, May 8, 11, 1846.
13. Isaac E. Holmes to J. H. Hammond, May 10, 1846, in James H. Hammond Papers, LC.

expected little aid from his elderly colleague, George McDuffie, a veteran of many political battles but now failing rapidly in mental and physical vigor.

In the House Calhoun was to rely chiefly on Holmes and Rhett, two skillful parliamentarians, although Simpson, a Pendleton neighbor, and Burt, an Abbevillian who had married a Calhoun cousin, were also close supporters. Black, a Columbia banker, and freshman Congressman Sims were less inclined to follow Calhoun's lead.[14]

On Monday, May 11, the president's war message was read to Congress before packed galleries. The administration forces had carefully set the stage in the House for swift passage of a war bill. Debate was limited to two hours, part of which time was spent reading documents. A handful of Whigs, strongly aided by Holmes, tried to slow the current. Holmes was on the floor several times, yielding first to one congressman then to another. Speaking amid an uproar and confusion, the South Carolinian agreed to vote for supplies immediately to repel invasion, but he doubted the wisdom of a declaration of war. Instead, he preferred a calm and deliberate review. For all he knew, the Mexican government might disavow the acts of its general. Moreover, a declaration of war would expose American commerce to depredations of privateers. He recalled the *Leopard*'s attack on the *Chesapeake* in 1807 and asked, "Was that absolutely war?"

Rhett followed Holmes. After repeating some of his colleague's views, he noted that the president "does not recommend us to make war. Not a state of war exists, but a state of hostilities." Nevertheless, administration spokesmen were not sidetracked by legal niceties. They insisted on bringing to a vote Kentucky Congressman Lynn Boyd's amendment, which read: "Whereas by act of the Republic of Mexico a state of war exists between that Government and the United States." The crucial amendment passed

14. For sketches of the South Carolina members in the House, see *Biographical Directory of the American Congress, 1774–1971: The Continental Congress, September 5, 1774, to October 21, 1788, and the Congress of the United States from the First Through the Ninety-First Congress, March 4, 1789, to January 3, 1971. Inclusive.* (Washington, D.C., 1971), 597, 677, 1135, 1602, 1700, 1701, 1956.

8   *Reluctant Imperialists*
123 to 67. Of the seven-member South Carolina delegation, all nominally Democrats, only Black supported the administration.

Immediately following approval of Boyd's amendment, the administration supporters forced a vote on the entire war bill and thus placed the opponents of war in a dangerous political dilemma. The war bill included supplies for the army, and few were willing to deny aid to Taylor's force on the Rio Grande. Facing a sensitive political choice, the entire South Carolina delegation, however reluctantly, supported the war resolution, which easily swept through the House 174 to 14.[15]

It was in the Senate that Polk expected the strongest opposition. He believed the Whigs would probably oppose the war bill on partisan grounds if they could persuade Calhoun, Thomas Hart Benton, and two or three other Democratic senators to join them. The bill could be saved, the president believed, only through "the fear of the people by the few Democratic Senators who wish it defeated."[16]

Polk's analysis of the situation was essentially correct. As soon as his message was reported in the Senate and a call was made to print twenty thousand copies, John C. Calhoun arose and requested "high, full, and dispassionate consideration" of the volatile situation. Later in the deliberations Calhoun again pleaded for time to consider all points. As did Rhett, he noted a constitutional distinction between hostilities and war. Yet, he was prepared to do "all that the Constitution, and patriotism, and honor of my country" would require.

Calhoun felt his position strengthened when Benton, the veteran Democrat from Missouri, proposed dividing the president's message into two parts. Benton wished to send the part dealing with the Mexican attack to the Military Affairs Committee and the part calling for war to the Foreign Relations Committee. Benton's proposal, though adopted, encountered strong opposition

15. *Congressional Globe*, 29th Cong., 1st Sess., 792–94. The debates, with some elaboration, were reported in the Charleston *Mercury*, May 15, 1846, and the Charleston *Courier*, May 15, 1846.
16. Quaife, *Diary of James K. Polk*, I, 392–93.

from Senators William Allen (Ohio) and Lewis Cass (Michigan), administration spokesmen. Cass also took exception to Calhoun's constitutional interpretation of war, whereupon the South Carolinian reiterated that only Congress could declare war. It would be "a great abuse of language, in a constitutional sense," he continued, to say that the United States was already at war with Mexico. Thus, the first day's debate in the Senate on the war bill ended inconclusively.[17]

On Tuesday morning, the twelfth, both the Foreign Relations Committee and the Military Affairs Committee reported favorably on the sections of the war bill referred to them the previous day. A full-fledged debate followed, with Calhoun and Whig leaders John M. Clayton (Delaware) and John M. Berrien (Georgia) leading the opposition. Calhoun, while voicing no objection to voting supplies, again requested time to consult the documents carefully. In reply, Allen, chairman of the Foreign Relations Committee, insisted that "no time could be afforded for the least delay." In the following exchange Calhoun asserted that he was not prepared "to affirm that war existed between the United States and Mexico." Echoing Congressman Holmes's comments of the previous day, Calhoun asked Allen how did he know that the Mexican government would not disavow what had been done.

Speaking for a third time later in the day, Calhoun pleaded with his Senate colleagues to remove the war-declaring preamble from the army supply bill. A declaration of war would create new relations between the United States and other powers, including bringing a swarm of privateers upon American commerce. Why all the haste? The Senate's attitude had plunged him into "a state of wonder and deep alarm." His was a vain plea, for the administration forces clearly had the necessary votes.

The climax to the prolonged debate came when Whig Senator John M. Clayton's motion to strike out the preamble was defeated 25 to 20 and Whig Senator John J. Crittenden's (Kentucky) similar move lost 26 to 20. Calhoun, McDuffie, and eighteen Whigs

---

17. *Congressional Globe*, 29th cong., 1st Sess., 783–85.

made up the minority. When the war bill passed the Senate 40 to 2, the elderly, feeble McDuffie deserted his colleague and voted aye. Two Whig Senators and Calhoun abstained. Why could not the Whig minority block the war bill? They recalled what had happened to the Federalists for their resistance to the War of 1812, and they were also prisoners of fear of what would happen to their party if its action impeded reinforcement of Taylor and some disaster should fall.[18]

Privately, the frustrated Calhoun reported his version of how war had been "precipitately forced on Congress." He blamed Polk for "this sad state of things" whereby future presidents could create situations forcing similar action from Congress. He feared that hostilities with Mexico would jeopardize a peaceful settlement of the Oregon dispute. In fact, he later claimed that had the English delayed another five days before reaching agreement on Oregon, the news of the Mexican War would have prevented a settlement.

The president's message had been divided into two parts by the Senate, Calhoun continued, with the expectation of "deliberate discussion" on the part relating to war. Contrary to the order of the Senate, Benton, chairman of the Military Affairs Committee, reported a bill that included both the raising of an army and a declaration of war. But worse yet, Calhoun said, "our friends in the Senate had attended a Caucus and thoughtlessly agreed to it." He sadly noted that even McDuffie had gone along with the caucus. With this action, he saw that "all was lost." As for the opponents in the House, "they fell into disorder and yielded to the excitement of the moment."

Calhoun said that some six weeks earlier he had seen the peril of ordering General Taylor to the Rio Grande and had desired an inquiry. He had spoken to Whig leaders about the danger but explained why he himself could not offer a motion. He had regarded it his duty to remain on good terms with President Polk in order to aid in a peaceful settlement of the Oregon controversy. In retrospect he concluded:

18. *Ibid.*, 795–97, 799, 802–804; Frederick Merk, *Manifest Destiny and Mission in American History: A Reinterpretation* (New York, 1963), 94–95.

If it had been deliberately put to a vote, whether it was right to order Gnl Taylor to the del Norte [Rio Grande], or for him to take post opposite to Matamoras, & plant his cannon against it, or that Mr. Slidell should be sent to Mexico, when he was under the circumstances he was, or whether we should declare war on account of the claims against Mexico, most of which are without foundation, there would have been not a tenth part of Congress in the affirmative. . . . I fear what was done in a hurry will long have to be repented at leisure.[19]

Convinced that the war could have been easily avoided, Calhoun continued his private criticism of the Polk administration, regretted his own inability to have prevented the war, repeated fears of English interference, and admitted his stand had weakened him with the party and "the unthinking part" of the community. Before mid-June, however, he exhibited a brief spell of optimism. Looking back some months, he explained to his daughter Anna that the nation had been threatened with an English and Mexican war due to "great mismanagement" by the president. Now, the Oregon settlement, for which Calhoun claimed credit, coupled with American victories on the Rio Grande, would, he hoped, soon bring the Mexican War to a close. In the interim, he awaited "a fair opportunity" to present fully his views on the war —views he felt would gain more support than he had temporarily lost.[20]

Clearly the war resolution had not been fairly posed, and there was much greater opposition in Congress than the final votes indicated. Reaction in the South Carolina press was mixed. At the moment, the Charleston *Mercury* was Calhoun's chief defender

19. J. C. Calhoun to T. G. Clemson, March 23, May 12, 1846; to James E. Calhoun, July 2, 1846, in Calhoun Papers, CU; J. C. Calhoun to H. W. Conner, May 15, 1846, in Henry W. Conner Papers, LC; J. C. Calhoun to A. P. Calhoun, May 14, 1846, in J. Franklin Jameson (ed.), *Correspondence of John C. Calhoun*, Vol. II of *Fourth Annual Report of the Historical Manuscripts Commission of the American Historical Association* (Washington, D.C., 1900), II, 690–91; William M. Meigs, *The Life of John Caldwell Calhoun* (2 vols., New York, 1917), II, 382. Although Benton loyally supported Polk, he recorded in his memoirs that Mexico was justified in attacking Taylor. Thomas Hart Benton, *Thirty Years' View: Or, a History of the Working of the American Government for Thirty Years, From 1820 to 1850* (2 vols., New York, 1856), I, 678.
20. J. C. Calhoun to T. G. Clemson, May 28, June 11, 1846; to James E. Calhoun, May 29, 1846; to Anna Clemson, June 11, 1846, all in Calhoun Papers, CU.

and the most caustic Palmetto critic of the administration, which it claimed had committed the "enormous folly" of placing an army of 2,500 in the unfavorable position, far from its supplies, of facing 10,000 Mexicans. The War Department had provoked and invited an attack upon Taylor "by every possible means," the editor averred. Now, the administration proposed to commit "the still greater folly" of sending 90,000 men to save 2,500 from the consequences.

The *Mercury* happily noted a Charleston rally of May 15 that unanimously adopted resolutions thanking the South Carolina congressional delegation for the "noble and independent stand they have taken to avert the evils which have been precipitated on our land." The editor defended Calhoun's abstention from voting for war and added that "public opinion here warmly and proudly applauds the course of Mr. Calhoun on the war bill." In reporting Taylor's movements along the Rio Grande, the editor confidently predicted that within a few days the Mexicans would be routed and driven across the river, an event that could end the war "if Congress were not a little daft." [21]

However. following news of General Taylor's victories at Palo Alto and Resaca de la Palma in early May, the *Mercury* found no spirit of moderation in the press or at public meetings. The West was "getting wolfish" and the entire country seemed "fast coming to the cut throat mood." Deploring the "love of conquest," the editor touched a sensitive point destined to crop up repeatedly in months ahead. If America conquered Mexico, what would it do with seven million Indians who were "bigotted, ignorant, idle, lawless, slavish, and yet free?" Moreover, in trying to conquer Mexico the army would surely encounter a debilitating climate, bilious fevers, and the dreaded vomito—yellow fever. [22]

For the *Mercury* to maintain that there was no spirit of moderation in the press was an exaggeration. Several Palmetto newspapers defended Calhoun, voiced their opposition to war and

21. Charleston *Mercury*, May 14, 16, 18–20, 1846. The Charleston rally was chaired by Colonel James Gadsden, a close friend of Calhoun.
22. *Ibid.*, May 25, 30, June 8, 1846.

conquest, and criticized the president in some degree. Editor Frederick W. Symmes of the Pendleton *Messenger*, noted as a Calhoun organ, felt that America would have been "the gainers" had a declaration of war been avoided. The Anderson *Gazette* scored the administration for its "unwise move" of placing Taylor's army on the Rio Grande, and the Charleston *Evening News* repeated the *Mercury*'s warning of the physical dangers of invading Mexico. The *Winyah Observer* quoted, with apparent approval, a scathing New York editorial that asked: "Can he [Polk] put out the fire which he has kindled through the nation? . . . If we have the law of nations on our side, have we the law of God?"[23]

The Charleston *Patriot*, edited by Charles K. Bishop, pointed out the perils of invading and conquering a nation so different in race, customs, political institutions, and religion. "Is Mexico prepared to become one of us?" Bishop asked. "This thirst of conquest" boded ill for America's preservation and prosperity. The Edgefield *Advertiser* stated that, while critical of the rashness of the "insolent and pusillanimous" Mexicans, it was "always" opposed to the war. Yet, the editor apparently spoke for the majority when he added, "But the blow has been struck, and our citizens have been slain; and whether she be right or wrong, we go for our country." Even the *Mercury* ruefully admitted, "We have the war and must fight it out."[24]

On the other hand, President Polk received ardent support from the outset from several South Carolina papers. The prestigious Charleston *Courier* deplored criticism of the administration and strongly advocated conquest of Mexico and imposition of peace on "our own terms." The Abbeville *Banner*, edited by Charles H. Allen, issued the call to arms to repel the foreign foe who had invaded "our soil." The hawkish Greenville *Mountaineer*, under

---

23. Pendleton *Messenger*, May 22, 1846; Anderson *Gazette*, May 15, June 5, 1846, quoting Charleston *Evening News*; Georgetown *Winyah Observer*, May 29, 1846, quoting New York *Journal of Commerce*. Newspapers seldom gave dates of journals they quoted. Archibald Todd was editor of the *Gazette*, J. N. Cardozo of the *Evening News*, the Watermans, Elias Sr. and Jr., of the *Winyah Observer*. See William L. King, *Newspaper Press of Charleston*, 78–81.

24. Anderson *Gazette*, July 3, 1846, quoting Charleston *Patriot*; Edgefield *Advertiser*, May 13, 20, 1846; Charleston *Mercury*, May 15, 1846.

the editorship of Colonel G. F. Townes, praised Polk's war message, blamed the Mexicans with their "haughty pretensions" for starting the war, deplored American forbearance of Mexican "insults" and "outrages," and demanded an invasion up to Mexico City itself. From Columbia the *South Carolinian*, published by B. R. Carroll and A. G. Summer, cried for swift prosecution of the war, with fifty thousand volunteers to be sent to Mexico if necessary.[25]

The president's support increased when news arrived of Taylor's victories on the Rio Grande. The columns of the Charleston *Courier* were filled on May 22 with accounts of his "glorious achievement." Noisy victory demonstrations in the streets of the port city were accompanied with firing of cannon. Victory rallies were reported elsewhere in the state. In general, Polk and Taylor were praised, the Mexicans condemned, and offers made "to protect the interests and glory of our nation." While Polk remained under fire from some editors, the prowar rallies indicated that Senator Calhoun might well have jeopardized his political influence within his own state. This became glaringly visible when Colonel Franklin H. Elmore appeared as main speaker at the large Columbia rally. Elmore, one of Calhoun's chief lieutenants and president of the politically powerful Bank of the State of South Carolina, vehemently defended America's claims to land between the Nueces and the Rio Grande. It was American territory, he declared, "as clearly as the streets of Columbia."[26]

Calhoun's friend and a former governor, James Hamilton, Jr., feared that his abstention on the declaration of war would injure his political stature, and he mildly reproved the senator. "That on principle you were right in your objections to the War Bill I ad-

25. Charleston *Courier*, May 21, 1846; Abbeville *Banner*, May 20, 1846; Greenville *Mountaineer*, May 15, 1846; Columbia *South Carolinian*, May 14, 1846. H. A. Jones of Abbeville wrote that if the war "be properly managed, we can soon whip Mexico into a subjection that will teach her in the future to have some regard to the laws of Nations." To W. A. Townes, May 27, 1846, in Townes Family Papers, SCL.
26. Charleston *Courier*, May 22–23, June 4, 6, 1846; Charleston *Mercury*, May 23, June 4–5, 1846. It was privately reported that Elmore, also a friend of Polk, had promised the president to try to persuade Calhoun to support the administration. Sellers, *Polk: Continentalist*, 420.

mit, but whether it was *expedient* to be *rigorously right* is another Question." Charleston banker and railroad promoter James Gadsden also warned, "I believe your views are not properly understood, and that for the present you have not the public voice with you." But another Charlestonian, James Gregorie, wrote Calhoun that his position on the war had the approval "more unanimously here, than anything I ever saw."[27]

Division of opinion in neighboring Georgia likewise indicated a decline in Calhoun's political influence. True, he received praise from former Governor Wilson Lumpkin and many Whigs, who sought to use his position to divide the Georgia Democrats. The latter were not influenced. They simply read Calhoun out of the party. Nevertheless, no Palmetto journal directly censured Calhoun, and only one open meeting in South Carolina seemingly attempted to reprove him, that at Edgefield Court House on June 1.[28]

The Edgefield meeting, called to encourage volunteers for the war, began calmly enough. The usual sort of patriotic speeches were made, and Colonel Francis W. Pickens, a Calhoun kinsman, introduced five resolutions in support of the administration. When it appeared that they would be adopted without opposition, Colonel Louis T. Wigfall rose to take exception to resolution number 3, which read: "*Resolved*, That Mexico having made such intimations as induced us to send a Minister to settle our difficulties without appeal to arms, and then having rejected that Minister with contumely and threats, it became the duty of our government to occupy and defend the extreme frontier as defined and

27. James Hamilton, Jr., to J. C. Calhoun, May 25, June 21, 1846; James Gadsden to Calhoun, May 18, 1846; James Gregorie to Calhoun, May 23, 1846, all in Calhoun Papers, CU.
28. Wilson Lumpkin to J. C. Calhoun, May 20, 1846, *ibid.* From Georgia, W. H. Hull wrote, "Mr. Calhoun has killed himself about here as far as *Democratic* support goes." To Howell Cobb, May 22, 1846, in Ulrich B. Phillips (ed.), *The Correspondence of Robert Toombs, Alexander H. Stephens, and Howell Cobb*, Vol. II of *Annual Report of the American Historical Association for the Year 1911* (Washington, D.C., 1913), 78–79. See also Wiltse, *Calhoun: Sectionalist*, 284; Capers, *Calhoun*, 233–34; Royce C. McCrary, "Georgia Politics and the Mexican War," *Georgia Historical Quarterly*, LX (Fall, 1976), 211–27.

claimed by Texas, when she was received as an independent State into this confederacy." As an addendum Wigfall offered a resolution in support of Calhoun's conduct in the Senate. After a lively debate Pickens' resolutions were approved and Wigfall's addendum tabled.

First reports of the meeting gave little indication of a political squabble.[29] But Calhoun's Edgefield friends looked upon Pickens' resolutions as a concerted effort to undermine the senator's support. In a somewhat vague manner the *Mercury* soon began to publish "regular and irregular" proceedings of the rally. Pickens had assailed Calhoun "in sneering tone and contemptuous manner" and questioned his fidelity to the country, although the attack was more by indirection than direct confrontation, so the *Mercury* reported. Apparently, Wigfall had learned of the plot, if such it was, and was prepared to counterattack. However, by the time he had introduced his resolution, Pickens, claiming illness, had left the meeting. Wigfall spoke with such intense feeling that he upset some of the local politicians, who, in reply, disclaimed the slightest intention of censuring Calhoun. Wigfall was hardly the appropriate person to help Calhoun, for his political fortunes were at a low ebb in Edgefield. He was in deep financial trouble and had killed prominent young Tom Bird in 1840 in what could hardly be called a duel. Even so, the *Mercury* tried to dismiss the whole incident as insignificant.[30]

Exactly what Pickens had in mind may never be clear. A group of Calhoun supporters including Congressman Armistead Burt, who was in close touch with Wigfall, Thomas G. Key, editor of the Hamburg *Journal*, and Joseph Abney, junior editor of the *Advertiser*, believed the Brooks family—Colonel Whitfield Brooks and his sons Preston and Whitfield, Jr.—was in league with Pick-

29. Edgefield *Advertiser*, June 3, 10, 1846.
30. Charleston *Mercury*, June 9, 17, 23, 1846; J. Terry, in Edgefield *Advertiser*, June 10, 1846; Alvy L. King, *Louis T. Wigfall: Southern Fire-eater* (Baton Rouge, 1970), 44–46. Wigfall moved to Texas later in the year. See also C. W. Lord, "Young Louis Wigfall: South Carolina Politician and Duelist," *South Carolina Historical Magazine*, LIX (April, 1958), 96–112.

ens. This clique, which also included William F. Durisoe, senior editor of the *Advertiser*; Colonel Milledge L. Bonham; and possibly others, evidently believed that Calhoun had suffered a loss of popularity because of his antiwar position and that it would be judicious to identify with the Polk administration.

Wigfall warned that Pickens and his friends were politicking in town every day and quoting Burt as the authority that Calhoun was "flat" in Washington. Key understood that the Brooks family was piqued at Calhoun for ignoring some recent communications, but he could not account for Pickens' conduct. In any event, he was of the opinion that Pickens' hopes for political advancement would suffer as a result of the movement. If one can believe Key and Abney, the war was not popular in Edgefield District, Pickens' clique was but a handful, and the Edgefield people loved Calhoun "as they would love a father." One immediate result of the dispute was Abney's loss of position with the *Advertiser*.[31]

Although Pickens had long been a faithful ally of his kinsman Calhoun, his political ambitions could not always be best served by blindly following the elder statesman. In South Carolina, as elsewhere, political factions formed, feuded, split, and reformed. Since nullification days, Calhoun, the dominant leader in the state, had tried to maintain political harmony and unity in the face of grave national issues.

Some of Calhoun's chief support came from the Rhett-Elmore faction, headed by Robert Barnwell Rhett and Franklin H. Elmore. Pickens disliked that clique and blamed their "vilest intrigue" for denying him the speakership of the national House of Representatives in 1839. Pickens suffered further frustration when J. P. Richardson defeated his friend James H. Hammond for governor in 1840. In that instance Calhoun's silence had assured victory for ex-Unionist Richardson. There seemed, however, to be a lack of trust between Calhoun and the Rhett-Elmore group. Earlier, Congressman Sampson H. Butler had confided to Hammond:

31. L. T. Wigfall to A. Burt, July 7, 1846; Joseph Abney to Burt, June 6, July 9, 23, 1846; T. G. Key to Burt, June 15, July 16, 1846, all in Armistead Burt Papers, DU.

"They hate Calhoun and would denounce him, tomorrow, if they dared. I tell you, he does not agree with them . . . but like all politicians, he dont want to break with them." [32]

Pickens suffered further frustration in 1842 when both Calhoun and William C. Preston resigned their Senate seats. Pickens, among others, was anxious for one of the vacant positions. But he was bypassed as the legislature chose George McDuffie, a nullifier, for one position and ex-Unionist Daniel Huger for the other, seemingly with Calhoun's approval. Nevertheless, Pickens remained loyal to his chief.

However, Calhoun found it difficult to maintain political harmony among the various factions, and when he withdrew from the presidential contest of 1844, some of his restless followers were ready to kick over the traces. They were especially aroused over the Whig tariff of 1842, all the more odious because of low cotton prices. The entire cotton belt was suffering. The tariff disturbed South Carolinians more than any other issue except abolition. Immediately after Congress adjourned in March, McDuffie denounced the tariff, whereupon Pickens commented, "He will raise the banner of disunion if only they will follow him."

Calhoun, recently appointed as secretary of state, continued to favor a cautious policy. At his behest Pickens and Elmore attended the Baltimore convention as observers and worked for Polk, whom they considered safe on the tariff and Texas questions. They publicly pledged South Carolina's support for Polk. But the proceedings at the convention were hardly pleasing to some South Carolina radicals, who noted that the Democratic party was badly divided on both Texas annexation and the tariff. When the Senate on June 8 voted down the Texas treaty by more than two to one, the radicals were ready to revolt.

Led by Rhett, Holmes, Hammond, now serving as governor, and John A. Stuart, Rhett's brother-in-law and editor of the *Mer-*

32. F. W. Pickens to J. H. Hammond, December 15, 1839, February 1, 1840; S. H. Butler to Hammond, February 5, 1840, all in Hammond Papers, LC; Wigfall to J. L. Manning, March 10, 1840, in Williams-Chesnut-Manning Papers, SCL. See also Ernest M. Lander, Jr., "The Calhoun-Preston Feud, 1836–1842," *South Carolina Historical Magazine*, LIX (January, 1958), 24–37.

cury, the insurgents directly challenged Calhoun's leadership. They called for southern and state conventions to consider Texas and the tariff and to nullify the latter unless assured of relief. Their movement reached its climax on July 31 at a public dinner at Bluffton, Beaufort District, where the fiery Rhett reiterated their principles.[33]

One immediate result of the "Bluffton Movement" was a serious rift in the Rhett-Elmore clique, for F. H. Elmore remained loyal to Calhoun and worked with other conservatives to pressure the radicals to support Polk. Elmore staged a mass meeting in Charleston on August 19 that pledged South Carolina Democrats to the party ticket. At the same time, Pickens visited Tennessee, spent two days in Polk's home, and reported that the candidate was determined to reduce the tariff and "at all hazzards" to acquire Texas. Visiting Charleston twice in the fall, Calhoun himself worked to win back or isolate the insurgents. By late November he had been largely successful. When the state legislature convened, Governor Hammond's message urging nullification fell on deaf ears. Instead, the legislators approved a series of pro-Union resolutions introduced by state Senator Pickens, no longer a close friend of Hammond.[34]

In mid-November, 1845, Calhoun aroused new opposition to his leadership by his speech at the Memphis convention. Serving as chairman and bidding for a new South-West alliance, he called for a vast internal improvements program in the Mississippi Valley, to be financed in part at federal expense, a turnabout for him. Be that as it may, the South Carolina General Assembly on November 26 routinely elected Calhoun, 135 to 4, to the United States Senate to replace Huger, who had resigned specifically for that purpose. Later the same day, Frederick J. McCarthy of Beau-

33. John Boyd Edmunds, Jr., "Francis W. Pickens: A Political Biography" (Ph.D. dissertation, University of South Carolina, 1967), 105–108; Wiltse, *Calhoun: Sectionalist*, 178–82, 187–90. An account of the so-called Edgefield Junto is in James W. Gettys, Jr., " 'To Conquer a Peace': South Carolina and the Mexican War" (Ph.D. dissertation, University of South Carolina, 1974), 85–135.

34. Wiltse, *Calhoun: Sectionalist*, 190–95; Edmunds, "Francis W. Pickens," 112–13; Pickens to J. C. Calhoun, September 9, 1844, in Calhoun Papers, CU.

fort District, acting under Rhett's guidance, introduced resolutions in the House condemning Calhoun's Memphis position. The
senator's partisans handily sidetracked the resolutions, causing a
Courier correspondent to report, "The Bluffton Boys wanted to
apply the birch to Mr. Calhoun, but the majority was too strong
for them, and he is still the great unwhipt."

Discontent continued to smolder, but Rhett raised no further
opposition and temporarily sided with Calhoun when the Mexican War broke out. Nevertheless, Calhoun remained on his guard,
for H. W. Conner later warned him that Rhett's ambition was of
"so exceedingly selfish a character as to leave no doubt on my
mind that he would without hesitation sacrifice you and all the
world besides, if the least in the way to his own advancement."[35]

In this intrigue and shifting of political positions, Pickens' relations with Calhoun became strained. In September, 1845, Calhoun sought his opinion about the advisability of returning to the
Senate. Pickens replied that he ought to do so, but candidly advised him to have it "authoritatively announced that you would
under no consideration whatever allow your name to be *spoken*
of in *connexion with the Presidency*." Such a public renunciation,
Pickens believed, would strengthen Calhoun's influence in the
Senate. Perhaps Pickens also believed that his own political interests were poorly served by Calhoun's perennial presidential ambitions. The advice piqued Calhoun, who told his brother-in-law
that many persons from all over the nation had urged him to accept the presidency if offered and that Pickens was the only one
who had suggested that he renounce his candidacy. "I attributed
it in him to error of judgement," Calhoun added. "Nothing could
induce me to give such a pledge."[36]

Relations became more strained in early spring, 1846, when
the *Southern Quarterly Review* published an article entitled "Internal Improvements." Editor Daniel K. Whitaker made an invid-
ious comparison between Calhoun's stand at Memphis on internal

35. Conner to J. C. Calhoun, May 7, 1847, in Calhoun Papers, CU.; Charleston *Courier*, November 28–29, December 1–2, 1845; W. B. Fickling to J. H. Hammond,
June 26, 1846, in Hammond Papers, LC; Wiltse, *Calhoun: Sectionalist*, 237–41.
36. Pickens to J. C. Calhoun, September 29, 1845; J. C. Calhoun to James E. Calhoun,
January 16, 1846, in Calhoun Papers, CU.

improvements and Pickens' views expressed on the same subject in the national House of Representatives in 1840. Upon learning that Calhoun believed he had written the article, Pickens made a vehement denial. In a lengthy letter he explained that he had neither seen nor heard of the article until the editor showed it to him, about two days prior to publication. Pickens averred that he had objected to its tone and language and had requested omission of the most objectionable parts. Nonetheless, Calhoun remained skeptical.[37]

Then came the Edgefield meeting. If Colonel Pickens entertained hopes of generating support for President Polk at Senator Calhoun's expense, he was quickly disappointed. No one of prominence answered his call. Instead, several denials of any intent to reprove Calhoun were issued from Edgefield. Even such staunch supporters of Polk as the Abbeville *Banner* and the Greenville *Mountaineer* rushed to Calhoun's defense. And from Charleston, James Gadsden wrote: "Our Edgefield discontents have been unfortunate in their explosion. Even the steam of war has failed in sustaining them."[38]

For his part Calhoun remained silent, though privately regretting Pickens' "rude assault." He supposed the colonel was seeking an alliance with Tennessee and Pennsylvania "as a means of gratifying his badly regulated ambition." He would not raise a finger against Pickens, for there were those who had "old scores to settle with him, ready to seize the occasion to keep him employed in defending himself." It was Calhoun's opinion that the "wholly unprovoked" attack had "completely prostrated" his kinsman. Such an assessment was verified a few weeks later when James H. Hammond confided that Pickens was "utterly dead" in South Carolina.[39]

37. Pickens to J. C. Calhoun, April 17, 1846; Calhoun to Anna Clemson, June 11, 1846, *ibid.*
38. Gadsden to J. C. Calhoun, July 4, 1846, *ibid.*; Edgefield *Advertiser*, June 10, 24, July 1, 8, 15, 1846; Abbeville *Banner*, July 22, 1846; Greenville *Mountaineer*, July 3, 1846; Pendleton *Messenger*, June 26, 1846.
39. J. C. Calhoun to Anna Clemson, June 11, 1846; to James E. Calhoun, July 2, 1846, in Calhoun Papers, CU; J. C. Calhoun to James E. Calhoun, June 29, 1846, in Calhoun Papers, DU; Hammond to M. C. M. Hammond, September 18, 1846, in Hammond Papers, SCL.

If there was continued belief that Calhoun's popularity was waning in his home state, it was dispelled at numerous 1846 Fourth of July celebrations. These ceremonies were sparkling all-day affairs where music, speeches, noise, patriotism, whiskey, and food were equally mixed. At Abbeville, for instance, a procession began at 10 A.M., consisting of the local militia, the Abbeville company of Mexican volunteers ("McDuffie Guards"), a "youthful band of patriots" ages five to twelve, and a brass band. At the courthouse square the band furnished music, the Declaration of Independence was read aloud, and Hiram Tillman delivered a "very able and patriotic oration." Afterwards, the assembled throng attended a barbecue followed by thirteen regular and forty-nine volunteer toasts. The band played while cannon boomed. The Mexican volunteers were special guests and were repeatedly greeted with "hearty cheers." Most celebrations elsewhere followed a similar ritual and passed off in an orderly fashion, although the *Winyah Observer* complained of "a small sprinkle of fisty-cuffing and eye gouging" at the Sampit muster house.[40]

In the toasting ceremonies Calhoun came off well. At Abbeville he was "the champion of South Carolina," "the great conservator of peace." The *Mercury* reported six celebrations and the *Courier* eight where Calhoun was honored. He was "our Country's great master spirit," "too profound to be appreciated," "the statesman that weathered the storm," "as fearless as he is patriotic," "the wise and prudent statesman," and so on. After surveying accounts of Fourth of July celebrations, the Greenville *Mountaineer* concluded, among other things, that General Taylor and his army were great heroes, that the Oregon treaty was satisfactory, that the Mexican volunteers were gallant and patriotic, that the United States was the greatest nation in the world, and that Senator Calhoun was ranked as "the ablest in talent, foremost in wisdom, and of unquestionable purity and patriotism." And, according to John G. Bowman, editor of the *South Carolina Temperance Advocate*, the pro-Calhoun sentiments expressed on the

40. Abbeville *Banner*, July 8, 1846; Georgetown *Winyah Observer*, July 8, 1846.

Fourth of July had caused several noncommittal newspapers to give the senator's vote on the war bill "their tardy approval."[41]

Additionally, Calhoun received telling public support from an old Unionist antagonist, Joel R. Poinsett, formerly an American minister to Mexico and now in retirement. In a detailed but restrained article appearing in the July issue of the *Commercial Review of the South and West*, Poinsett exhibited considerable knowledge of Mexican history and politics and revealed a sympathy for the Mexicans. He regretted the necessity of the war and felt certain that the Mexicans, despite their bluster, were ready to negotiate the boundary before Taylor invaded the disputed territory. He asked his countrymen to show compassion and understanding and not to undermine the struggling republicanism in Mexico.

"In short," Poinsett continued, "while we war against a tyrannical military despotism, let us not forget that the Mexican people are brother Republicans. . . . No triumph of our arms, no accession of territory can ever compensate for having in any wise contributed to the establishment of kingly government in North America." Finally, he warned that if America persisted, the Mexicans would be "obstinate foes."[42]

Having skated on thin ice, Calhoun was gratified at the open support he now received. To a group of Georgetown citizens who commended him for his effort to avert war, he temporarily broke silence. Once the war had begun, further discussion could be of no avail, he wrote, "and might tend to retard its speedy termination—a consummation, which all, who love their country must desire." Calhoun knew he had to support the war effort, for there were obviously many in South Carolina who felt as Joseph Abney

41. Abbeville *Banner*, July 8, 1846; Charleston *Mercury*, July 13–14, 1846; Charleston *Courier*, July 8–9, 11, 15, 1846; Greenville *Mountaineer*, July 17, 1846; John G. Bowman to J. C. Calhoun, November 19, 1846, in Calhoun Papers, CU.

42. Joel R. Poinsett, "War in Mexico," *Commercial Review of the South and West*, II (July, 1846), 21–24. In 1850 the *Review* changed its name to *DeBow's Review*. Privately, Poinsett warned Senator Cass of the many dangers of invading Mexico. He wrote, "You are surely not serious when you talk of invading Mexico and marching upon the Capital with 50,000 volunteers," May 16, 1846, quoted in J. Fred Rippy, *Joel R. Poinsett: Versatile American* (Durham, N.C., 1935), 226–27.

of Edgefield did. Abney explained to Congressman Burt that as much as he admired "the immaculate purity" of Calhoun, "if he were to oppose the prosecution of the war now it has commenced, I would condemn him with all the power I have." [43] Meanwhile, a regiment of volunteers had been recruited in South Carolina and was awaiting the call for active service.

43. R. F. W. Allston to J. C. Calhoun, July 8, 1846, in Calhoun Papers, CU; Calhoun to Allston, July 19, 1846, reprinted in Georgetown *Winyah Observer*, August 5, 1846; Abney to Burt, June 6, 1846, in Burt Papers.

CHAPTER 2 *The Honor of Our State Is Pledged*

WHEN NEWS of the Mexican attack on Captain Thornton's dragoons reached Charleston on May 7, the city remained relatively calm; but upon learning of Congress' declaration of war, Charlestonians demanded immediate action. Led by Colonel James Gadsden, who was the railroad promoter, Dr. A. G. Mackey, Colonel R. Q. Pinckney, Major James Simons, and others, public rallies were held May 15 and 16 at the city hall. The audience was harangued with jingoistic oratory, after which resolutions were adopted pledging support to the president. In the midst of the fervid atmosphere about fifty young men volunteered to go to Mexico. The committee in charge also called upon Governor William Aiken to expedite any calls for volunteers from the federal government.[1]

Within a few days Governor Aiken announced that President Polk had requisitioned a volunteer infantry regiment from South Carolina, and on May 29 the state adjutant and inspector general, James W. Cantey, announced that applications would be accepted until June 10 at the executive office in Charleston. The table of organization called for ten companies of 77 soldiers each plus one colonel, one lieutenant colonel, one major, and several

1. Charleston *Courier*, May 16, 18, 20, 1846. It should be noted again (see p. 12) that the meeting also passed a resolution praising the South Carolina congressional delegation and suggesting no hint of disapproval of Calhoun's action on the war bill.

lesser personnel in the headquarters, making a regiment of 777 soldiers.[2]

Although the Charleston Company prided itself on being the first in the state to be received officially, many districts quickly busied themselves with raising companies. Events in Chester were typical of the excitement. After a preliminary but well-attended meeting on June 1, a call was issued for volunteers to gather on June 6. On that occasion Nathaniel R. Eaves, a militia major and state senator, made a chauvinistic appeal, the ladies sang an ode, and, while the Chester band played one of its "liveliest airs," the call for volunteers was issued. Sixty-seven young men immediately enrolled. Two days later another meeting was held amidst music and speeches, including another "patriotic harangue" by Major Eaves. As soon as the company reached its quota, it organized and chose R. G. M. Dunovant as captain. Major Eaves ceremoniously delivered the company to its new captain, who replied, "If I dishonor them let me be shot; not in the front, for I would not deserve to die as a soldier, but in the back."[3]

The same sort of emotionalism prevailed at Lexington. The Fifteenth Militia Regiment was mustered for a review, and its commander made "a feeling and irresistible appeal to their patriotism." He brought forth tears as he reminisced about marching to Florida during the Seminole War. Other officers supported his appeal. At the signal *march* a great cheer arose from the throng, while eager militiamen stepped forward to fill the company's ranks. The *Courier*'s correspondent proudly added, "Tell me not that chivalry of the age has passed."[4]

In Greenville District, where two companies volunteered, only one, the Saluda Company under Captain T. P. Butler, was accepted. In Abbeville, although the *Banner* was confident that the state could raise ten thousand volunteers, some difficulty was encountered before the local company reached its quota. Neighboring Edgefield also "caught the flame," and editor Durisoe uttered

2. Charleston *Courier*, May 25, June 1, 4, 1846.
3. Charleston *Mercury*, June 15, 1846.
4. Charleston *Courier*, June 15, 1846.

bold remarks about gallantry and bravery. If Edgefield failed to do its duty in the present crisis, he said, "we would never again acknowledge that it was she that gave us birth." Even so, recruiting was slow, and only by strenuous efforts was the Edgefield Company filled.[5]

Recruiting elsewhere was not always easy, and in some districts no attempts at all were made to raise a company. The Hamburg *Republican* scored the statewide apathy and asked: "Where is the boasted chivalry of our State? . . . We hold that no patriot will now stop to calculate whether the Executive of the United States has acted wisely or otherwise in ordering [the army] to their present position." The Edgefield *Advertiser* likewise upbraided the districts that failed to raise volunteer companies. And in Abbeville the *Banner*, so optimistic at first, pleaded with South Carolinians to be "less famous for windy resolutions and more notorious for action."[6]

The Anderson *Gazette* aptly summed up the problem:

We hear many with one accord making excuses. Some object to the length of time their services are required [twelve months], others to the season of the year in which the call is made, or the great distance to the seat of war; one has to attend to his merchandise and another his crop; and finally one has married a wife and therefore begs to be excused. Upon the whole, we are inclined to think, that to secure volunteers from this quarter, the fighting must be postponed till the coming of frost, or be brought nearer to us.[7]

Whatever the difficulties, the requisite ten companies were filled and accepted for twelve months' service. They came from the following districts: Abbeville, Charleston, Chester, Edgefield, Greenville, Kershaw, Lexington, Newberry, Richland, and Sumter. There were reports that companies were organized in Union,

5. Greenville *Mountaineer*, June 5, 12, 26, July 10, 1846; Abbeville *Banner*, May 27, June 17, 1846; Edgefield *Advertiser*, May 20, 27, June 3, 10, 1846.
6. Edgefield *Advertiser*, June 10, May 27, 1846, quoting Hamburg *Republican*; Abbeville *Banner*, June 10, 1846.
7. Anderson *Gazette*, June 5, 1846. Colonel John Cunningham of Abbeville, later editor of the Charleston *Evening News*, said he would like to volunteer, but he was a candidate for public office, had professional engagements, and was "bound to home by a young family and its responsibilities." To Burt, May 23, 1846, in Burt Papers.

Barnwell, Spartanburg, Fairfield, York, and Greenville districts but were refused, either because they offered their services too late or failed to meet requirements imposed by the War Department.[8]

The ten companies met in their respective districts on June 29 to ballot for regimental officers. While there was no dearth of candidates, Pierce Mason Butler of Edgefield emerged victorious as overwhelming favorite for the position of colonel and commander of the regiment. Winning against stronger competition were James Polk Dickinson of Camden, as lieutenant colonel, and Adley H. Gladden of Columbia, as major. Seemingly by common consent, the South Carolina volunteers adopted the name "Palmetto regiment."[9]

Butler, former governor, veteran of the Seminole War, ex-Indian agent in Oklahoma, planter, and banker, appeared to be a happy choice for colonel of the regiment, except that he now suffered from chronic rheumatism. However, he eagerly accepted the position and thanked the regiment for conferring upon him "the highest distinction" of his life. He reminded the volunteers of their duty to the nation and their duty to uphold the "ancient honor" of South Carolina. The newly chosen colonel then hurried to Washington to confer with the president and attend regimental business. Dickinson, second in command, was also a veteran of the Seminole War. He was tall and handsome, a lawyer and legislator, and a distant relative of the president. He was privately reported to have "squandered his estates by prodigal generosity and extravagance." Thus, deeply in debt, Dickinson welcomed an opportunity for military glory in Mexico. But publicly he was said to be ready "to sacrifice all private interests at the call of patriotism."[10]

8. Charleston *Courier*, June 12, 16, 20, 30, July 2, 1846; Greenville *Mountaineer*, June 19, 1846.
9. Greenville *Mountaineer*, July 3, 1846; Charleston *Courier*, June 16, 26, July 7–8, 1846.
10. Charleston *Courier*, August 3, November 28, 1846; Thomas J. Kirkland and Robert M. Kennedy, *Historic Camden: Part Two, Nineteenth Century* (Columbia, S.C., 1926), 131–35; *DAB*, III, 365–66.

Upon completion of the regimental organization, Governor Aiken informed Secretary of War William L. Marcy that the venturesome Palmettos were keen for service. Marcy's reply of July 14 disheartened the volunteers, for he advised the governor that the regiment was not needed at that time. The Charleston Company officers, impatient of delay, appealed directly to Marcy to receive their company into immediate active service. If their warlike fervor had been dampened by the secretary's earlier reply, it must have been chilled completely when he informed them, July 27, that he could foresee no need for the regiment then or later. He was of the opinion that a sufficient force had already been organized and "sent forward" to prosecute the war. Thus, for the moment the high hopes of the volunteers died. The regiment soon fell into disarray.[11]

While there was little action on the war front, in Washington Congress was busy on the political front. Its attention was centered on internal improvements, the independent treasury, and the tariff, an issue that had again inflamed South Carolinians since the Whigs raised duties in 1842. Senator Calhoun, having weathered the little squall from Edgefield in June, was likewise pleased with the favorable public reception of his Memphis report, published in early July. But the tariff worried him, for the administration's effort to revise rates downward was encountering strong opposition. Then, just before the vote was to be taken, Senator William Haywood (North Carolina) resigned without warning, thus placing the administration's bill in jeopardy. From Charleston, Elmore penned Calhoun, "The whole city is thrown into excitement beyond anything I have seen for a long while by the treachery of Mr. Haywood." Nevertheless, the Walker Tariff passed the Senate by 28 to 27 on July 28, and Polk signed the measure two days later.

In the end Calhoun seemed jubilant. Not only had the tariff been lowered, but the independent treasury was re-created, and Polk's veto of the rivers and harbors bill, would, in Calhoun's

11. Charleston *Courier*, July 21, August 1, 1846.

opinion, "bring about a rally on the [Memphis] report." The South
and West, he glowingly reported, had "never so strongly united
before," and, except for the Mexican War, events in the session
had been more to his liking than for many years. His biographer
C. M. Wiltse writes, "The South especially was in high spirits and
was inclined to give the credit not to Polk but to Calhoun."[12]

With domestic legislation settled, Polk sought congressional
support for a new approach to terminate the war. Secret negotiations with General Santa Anna, in exile in Cuba, led the president to believe that American aid and money could restore the
former Mexican ruler to power, where he would then conclude
peace on terms favorable to America. Polk sought to induce Congress to vote secretly for $2 million for his scheme but was forced
into the open. He thus requested the funds in a special message to
both houses on August 8, the last day of the session.

Many congressmen, including the South Carolina delegation
in the House, were favorably disposed to the president's request.
Rhett had already reassessed his position toward the administration, had paid his respects at the White House, and had defended
the president's veto of the rivers and harbors bill. He now declared that Polk had given a new lease of power to the Democratic party. Holmes also urged immediate and favorable action
on Polk's request, for "any man would hail with satisfaction any
prospect of the termination of a war which . . . involved the country in the expenditure of millions." During the lengthy and bois-
terous night session of the eighth, Sims hailed Polk's message "as
a propitious omen [of] the rainbow of peace."

Unfortunate for Polk's plan, several free-state congressmen,
noting the South's control of the Senate since the admission of
Texas and Florida, and fearing the $2 million would be used to
purchase territory that would eventually become slave states, induced David Wilmot of Pennsylvania to offer a proviso to prohibit slavery in any part of the territory that might be acquired
from Mexico. Sims believed that Wilmot's amendment was of-

12. *Ibid.*, July 29, August 1, 1846; Gadsden to J. C. Calhoun, July 10, 1846; F. H. Elmore to Calhoun, July 28, 1846; Calhoun to T. G. Clemson, July 11, August 8,
September 20, 1846, all in Calhoun Papers, CU; Wiltse, *Calhoun: Sectionalist*, 272.

fered expressly to defeat the $2 million appropriation, and, speaking for most southerners, he warned of his opposition to the president's request with the proviso attached. Wilmot's proviso was approved 83 to 64, and the appropriation bill passed the House 85 to 79, with the entire Palmetto delegation in opposition. Much to the South's relief, the bill was filibustered to death in the Senate as Congress hastened to adjourn.[13]

The Wilmot Proviso, which was to cause a storm of protest later, received little notice in the South Carolina press at the moment, probably because the Senate quickly killed it. The *Mercury* briefly commented that it did not regret the failure of Polk's "Mexican peace bill" and added that "with the absurd proviso of the House, it ought not to have passed, and at any rate it was of little consequence."[14]

Although the president's "peace bill" failed in Congress, his efforts aided Santa Anna's return from Havana to Mexico, where the former dictator soon overthrew General Paredes and resumed power. His return was met with general approbation in South Carolina. The *Courier* was of the opinion that the Mexican leader had agreed with American agents upon peace terms before leaving Havana. The Pendleton *Messenger* likewise believed Santa Anna desired peace, if he could manage it politically. He was probably the most talented of the Mexican leaders, said the *Messenger*, and possessed too much sagacity to prosecute a hopeless war against the powerful United States. The Abbeville *Banner* agreed.[15]

On September 19 the *Mercury* published a disturbing proclamation by Santa Anna, calling on the Mexican people for "the real regeneration of the Republic." Nevertheless, the editor noted that it was "more calm and dignified than revolutionary manifestations usually are." He consequently viewed Santa Anna as "peaceably inclined." The reasonably favorable press attitude in South Carolina toward Santa Anna was doubtless due in part to

13. *Congressional Globe*, 29th Cong., 1st Sess., 1187, 1211–18; Bauer, *Mexican War*, 77–78; White, *Robert Barnwell Rhett*, 88–89; Benton, *Thirty Years' View*, II, 681–82.
14. Charleston *Mercury*, August 14, 1846.
15. Charleston *Courier*, September 11, 1846; Pendleton *Messenger*, September 4, 11, 18, 25, 1846; Abbeville *Banner*, September 2, 1846.

General Waddy Thompson, a South Carolinian who had served as America's minister to Mexico in 1842–1844. In a recently published and widely circulated book, *Recollections of Mexico*, Thompson wrote that while Santa Anna was avaricious, he was cordial, able, patriotic, and "not the sanguinary monster" that some supposed him to be. The Mexican leader soon disabused Americans of any ideas of his peaceful intent; whereupon, the press began to castigate him. Privately, Calhoun's Cincinnati friend, Ellwood Fisher, suspected that "our jockey President has been outjockeyed by Santa Anna." [16]

With military and diplomatic operations at a standstill, some of Calhoun's informants foresaw utmost peril for the nation in general and the Democratic party in particular. Former Governor James Hamilton, Jr., who had recently talked with Polk, wrote Calhoun on August 12 that if the president failed to change his war strategy, the administration would lose public confidence before the next session of Congress. Hamilton feared the "enormous" expenses of the war. [17]

Calhoun was likewise concerned about the expense of a long war. He foresaw a large national debt, which would be used as a pretext to raise the tariff again. By early August he perceived that the administration and the country were tired of the war and were in "as great haste to get out of it, as they were to get into it." His course stood vindicated, he wrote, "in the opinion of all," without his having to defend himself. He was awaiting "a suitable opportunity" to propose a different policy toward Mexico. Meanwhile, he kept his own counsel. [18]

16. Charleston *Mercury*, September 19, 1846; Greenville *Mountaineer*, October 2, 1846; Waddy Thompson, *Recollections of Mexico* (New York and London, 1847 [1846]), 65, 80–81; Ellwood Fisher to J. C. Calhoun, September 24, 1846, in Chauncey S. Boucher and Robert P. Brooks (eds.), "Correspondence Addressed to John C. Calhoun, 1837–1849," in *Annual Report of the American Historical Association for the Year 1929* (Washington, D.C., 1930), 359–60.
17. Hamilton to J. C. Calhoun, August 12, 1846, in Calhoun Papers, CU. See also Fisher to Calhoun, September 24, 1846, and F. W. Byrdsall to Calhoun, August 4, 1846, in Boucher and Brooks, "Correspondence Addressed to John C. Calhoun," 357, 359–60; Anderson *Gazette*, August 21, 1846.
18. J. C. Calhoun to T. G. Clemson, July 11, 30, August 8, 1846; to James E. Calhoun, July 29, 1846, in Calhoun Papers, CU.

In the late summer Calhoun believed his popularity was rising. So did Congressman Burt and others. There was even an absurd rumor that he would return as secretary of state. What must have been especially pleasing to him was an unexpected visit by Colonel Pickens in Washington, while enroute with his family to the North. Pickens was anxious to clarify his position at the Edgefield meeting, but Calhoun received him coldly and refused to return his call until Pickens had made satisfactory explanations through mutual friends. In the presence of Congressman Holmes, Pickens, "in Strong language," repeated his disavowals of the reports emanating from the Edgefield meeting. Calhoun was civil to Pickens during the meeting but retained doubts about his veracity.[19]

What Pickens said specifically to Calhoun on that occasion is not known. Later he defended his conduct at some length. He had left the Edgefield meeting and did not know what was said about Calhoun until the next day, "and yet," he wrote, "I have been *made responsible for all that was said and done*." It was true that he frankly differed from Calhoun on the war bill but that was all. On the other hand, he noted that Elmore had expressed the same sentiments at a Columbia meeting without arousing complaint.

Pickens blamed Colonel Wigfall, who was "without a particle of principle or truth & has since left in disgrace for N Orleans being entirely sold out by the sheriff." Wigfall, for "the most malignant motives," had circulated false stories about the meeting. It was part of a concerted plot, in Pickens' opinion, to cause ill feelings between himself and Calhoun in order to deny him a Senate seat. At the time of the Edgefield meeting it was privately known that McDuffie would resign in the fall. Nonetheless, as Pickens made no public disavowal, Calhoun remained aloof.[20]

It is still not clear what Pickens did or said. That he was appre-

19. J. C. Calhoun to T. G. Clemson, August 8, 1846, in Calhoun Papers, CU; C. H. Allen to Burt, July 25, 1846, in Burt Papers; Edgefield *Advertiser*, July 22, 1846, citing Camden *Journal*.
20. Pickens to J. C. Calhoun, December 13, 1846; T. G. Clemson to Calhoun, March 28, 1847; Calhoun to Clemson, May 6, 1847, in Calhoun Papers, CU.

ciative of Polk's efforts in behalf of the South is understood, but to denounce Calhoun publicly made little sense. The two men had been on the closest terms and corresponded frequently; they had close ties by blood and marriage, and their families visited back and forth. Pickens had aided Thomas G. Clemson, Calhoun's son-in-law, in purchasing an Edgefield plantation and at the time of the unfortunate meeting was doing much to help manage the property while Clemson was serving as chargé d'affaires in Brussels. But whatever the truth of the matter, he was unable to convince Calhoun that he had no ulterior motives.[21]

Leaving Washington immediately at the close of the session, Calhoun arrived in Pendleton on September 10 after a few days of rest and politicking at the plush watering places in western Virginia, but he continued to maintain his silence about the war. He wrote his brother-in-law that the Polk administration had such "wild conceptions" about its Mexican policy that he had ceased to make an attempt "directly or indirectly" to influence them. From Charleston, I. E. Holmes praised Calhoun for his "bold stand" against the declaration of war. "There is no doubt that the administration are alarmd," he declared. "They can't back-out, and the prospect of peace retires from view like the Alps to Hannibal, the more the country is penetrated." The administration, he added, dreaded to lay the budget before Congress.[22]

What the administration needed was some decisive victory, a "Coup De Clat," Holmes called it, before Congress assembled.

21. See, for example, Pickens to J. C. Calhoun, November 24, 1843, March 30, July 30, 1845; Calhoun to T. G. Clemson, November 12, 1844; Clemson to Calhoun, July 19, 1846, *ibid*. Upon returning from visiting Polk in August, 1844, Pickens wrote Calhoun: "I think we have now every prospect of carrying the election. . . . I am sure a calm & dignified course in yourself will give you the complete command of the future, and you know I have generally spoken my candid sentiments to you." September 9, 1844, *ibid*.

22. Greenville *Mountaineer*, September 25, 1846; Charleston *Courier*, August 29, September 15, 1846; J. C. Calhoun to James E. Calhoun, September 15, 1846; Holmes to Calhoun, October 2, 1846, in Calhoun Papers, CU. Even supporters of Polk, such as James H. Hammond, were gloomy. Hammond wrote in late July that if mediation failed, "years on years may elapse before the war is closed." To M. C. M. Hammond, July 24, 1846, in Hammond Papers, SCL.

General Taylor obliged with the capture of Monterrey after a fierce and bloody three-day battle in late September. The South Carolina press had high praise for the gallantry of Taylor's volunteers under heavy Mexican fire. Rumors now filtered down from Washington that the administration would prosecute the war vigorously until Mexico came to terms. Polk, it was said, planned to call out a large number of volunteers from the South. Perhaps, the Palmettos would yet have their chance.[23]

A vigorous prosecution of the war is exactly what the *South Carolinian* advocated. Its editors, B. R. Carroll and A. G. Summer, declaimed against "faithless" Mexicans, who should be punished for their "treacherous dishonor." While praising Polk for "his skill and cautious foresight," the editors chided the American government for waiting "too long" and enduring "too patiently." They called for the annexation of Mexican territory as an indemnity. The president also found a champion in the recently organized Sumter *Banner*, under the editorship of William J. Francis. The *Banner* justified the war as "almost a political necessity" to prevent Mexico from becoming virtually a colony of Great Britain.[24]

Despite Taylor's triumph at Monterrey, some of the South Carolina press had second thoughts about his march into enemy territory. Suppose Monterrey provoked the Mexicans to "more bitter hostility," exclaimed the Pendleton *Messenger*. Noting heavy American losses in the victory, the Abbeville *Banner* feared that the war henceforth would be "no child's play." For its part the *Winyah Observer* berated President Polk for having sent Taylor to Monterrey in the first instance. His small and exposed army was situated in "a most precarious and dangerous predicament." The administration should never have ordered him so deep into Mexico with less than 25,000 men. As expected, the *Mercury* was the severest critic of all. "The question is asked at each step

23. Holmes to J. C. Calhoun, October 2, 1846, in Calhoun Papers, CU; Charleston *Courier*, October 24, 1846; Anderson *Gazette*, October 23, 1846. First news of Monterrey's capture appeared in the Charleston *Mercury*, October 10, 1846.
24. Columbia *South Carolinian*, October 29, November 11, 1846; Sumter *Banner*, November 18, 1846.

in the invasion of Mexico—what have we gained?" The editor
quoted a correspondent of the New Orleans *Picayune* who perceived that "our army, as now situated, can be compared to the
French in Spain, when Joseph [Bonaparte] was driven out." And
Armistead Burt told Calhoun that his friends in Washington informed him of "much solicitude" in the capital. He feared the
war would be "protracted and sanguinery," and only God knew
when it would end and at what cost. But most critics seemed inclined to agree with James Gadsden's view that nothing could be
done about "the folly which has governed" except "to permit
events to take their course." [25]

In answer to Polk's critics, editor G. F. Townes of the Greenville *Mountaineer* proposed an alternative to an invasion into the
Mexican heartland. He suggested holding New Mexico and California, already in American hands, and putting a few army garri-
sons there to drive back Mexican incursions. In Townes's opinion
such a policy would bring the Mexicans to terms as quickly as invasion and victories. As early as May 30, the *Mercury* had published a similar proposal by a New York paper but had made no
further mention of it. The idea of holding California and New
Mexico also appealed to others, and later Calhoun developed
Townes's proposal more fully as his "line policy." [26]

Meanwhile, during the late summer and early fall there were
frequent reports of Colonel P. M. Butler's activities. He was in
Washington attending business; he was at Virginia Springs because of poor health; and he was back in Columbia and then Edgefield, with his health "yet feeble." On September 15 he wrote the
South Carolinian that defeat of the Mexicans would only increase
their hatred of America, and not until "their domestic altars" were
in danger would they make peace. He also reported that Presi-

25. Pendleton *Messenger*, October 16, 1846; Abbeville *Banner*, November 4, 1846;
Georgetown *Winyah Observer*, November 18, 1846; Charleston *Mercury*, November 10, 1846; Burt to J. C. Calhoun, November 4, 1846, in Calhoun Papers, CU;
Gadsden to James E. Calhoun, October 29, 1846, in James Gadsden Papers, SCL.
26. Charleston *Mercury*, May 30, 1846, citing New York *Courier and Enquirer*; Greenville *Mountaineer*, October 30, 1846. See also Charleston *Evening News*, quoted in
Pendleton *Messenger*, November 20, 1846.

dent Polk had assured him personally that the Palmetto regiment would be the first called into service should the war become prolonged. In Butler's opinion the regiment would be needed about December 1. This was denied by Congressman Joseph A. Woodward, based on a recent letter from Secretary Marcy, who explained that it was "very improbable" that the Palmettos would be called at all.[27]

Privately, Butler disclosed to his friend Colonel B. T. Watts, personal aide to Governor Aiken, his fear of a long and unprofitable conflict. He believed Polk was "scared to death" lest the treasury "break down" and was thus "taking *extraordinary means*" to come to terms with Mexico. He expressed little confidence in the president's advisers. Nevertheless, he was gratified to lead the Palmettos and tried to persuade Watts to enlist, on the promise of a staff appointment. Ill health or not, the forty-eight-year-old Butler seemed eager for battle. He added: "It is said a young man for *war* or *love*—both you & myself can be young under the emergency—or in a crisis."[28]

In early October Butler was again in Columbia, "his flagging health" fast being restored, so it was reported. Later in the month Butler revealed to Congressman Burt that he had recently undergone surgery for hemorrhoids. Although the wound was still tender he felt confident that he had recovered sufficiently "to meet the enemy of my country or the enemy of my person." The latter was a reference to a quarrel and impending duel with Colonel Richard B. Mason of Virginia.

Ill feelings developed between the two men while serving their nation among the Cherokees in Oklahoma, Mason with the army and Butler as an Indian agent. Matters came to head when Mason in November, 1845, openly accused Butler of defrauding Cherokees in his care, a charge denied by Cherokee Chief John Ross and by Butler in a scathing denunciation of Mason. While in Wash-

27. Charleston *Courier*, August 21, September 11, 19, 1846; Greenville *Mountaineer*, October 2, 1846, quoting Columbia *South Carolinian* and Columbia *Southern Chronicle*.
28. P. M. Butler to B. T. Watts, September 21, 1846, in Beaufort T. Watts Papers, SCL.

ington in August, 1846, Butler agreed to meet Mason on the dueling ground as soon as he was sufficiently recovered from his rheumatism. In preparation for the confrontation Butler practiced daily with firearms, insofar as his physical condition permitted.

Some of Butler's friends, particularly ex-Governor Hamilton, tried unsuccessfully to compose the quarrel and prevent the duel. Still in "great pain" from rheumatism, Butler on November 10 requested Burt to inform Mason's friend, Colonel John McCarty, that he was ready to meet Mason "at the earliest practicable day." He wished no further postponement for he expected little improvement in his health over the next two or three months. A sudden turn of events prevented the duel. Colonel Mason was ordered to military duty in California, and Butler was soon on his way to Mexico. They never saw each other again.[29]

While the duel was still pending, Secretary of War Marcy notified Governor Aiken that the South Carolina Regiment was required for immediate service. His instructions, dated November 16, called for the regiment to rendezvous at Charleston as quickly as the companies could be assembled. In Charleston the regiment would undergo inspection by officers of the regular army, including a medical officer. Only men between the ages of eighteen and forty-five and in good "physical strength and vigor" would be accepted. The jubilant Edgefield *Advertiser* voiced the opinion of many: "The glorious News has come at last!—The brave and chivalrous sons of South Carolina will now bare their arms against the foe of Southern rights and Southern institutions."

There was one nagging obstacle. The terms of service had been changed from twelve months to the duration of the war. This legally released every volunteer and required each company to be reorganized. The Greenville *Mountaineer* foresaw some confusion but had no doubt that each "gallant" company would be

29. Charleston *Courier*, October 12, 1846; P. M. Butler to Burt, October 22, 28, November 10, 1846, in Burt Papers; *DAB*, XII, 373–74. On September 16, 1847, Hamilton wrote Senator A. P. Butler, an older brother, an account of the affair. Letter in Greenville *Mountaineer*, October 15, 1847. For Butler's activities as an Indian agent, see Carolyn T. Foreman, "Pierce Mason Butler," *Chronicles of Oklahoma*, XXI (Spring, 1952), 6–28.

speedily filled. The *South Carolinian* urged prompt compliance, saying, "this is no time for Soldiers to debate the merits of the Mexican War." The Charleston *Courier* noted the rising war spirit in the legislature, just convened, and felt certain the state would promptly furnish its quota of troops. Colonel Butler issued the necessary orders and appealed to all volunteers to accept the War Department's changed conditions because "the honor of our State is pledged." [30] From all appearances Secretary Marcy's call aroused the war spirit in South Carolina, despite doubts about Polk's war policy. The state bustled with renewed military activity. It would soon be seen whether the volunteers would rush to the colors.

30. Greenville *Mountaineer*, November 27, 1846; Edgefield *Advertiser*, November 25, 1846; Columbia *South Carolinian*, November 25, 1846; Charleston *Courier*, November 26, 1846; Pendleton *Messenger*, November 27, December 4, 1846. Unsuccessful efforts were made by the new governor, David Johnson, and others to have Butler promoted to brigadier general. Calhoun to Johnson, December 29, 1846, in Calhoun Papers, SCL; Anderson *Gazette*, January 8, 1847. During the fall congressional elections, South Carolina was in the doldrums. Only one incumbent, easily reelected, faced opposition. Greenville *Mountaineer*, October 9, 1846.

CHAPTER 3 *The God of Battles Be with You*

SECRETARY MARCY'S call for South Carolina troops reached the state just before the General Assembly convened in annual session. On November 24 Governor Aiken, addressing the legislature, deeply deplored the war, for which he blamed Mexico's "utter disregard of national obligations." He decried the necessity for its continuance and hoped American victories would not encourage a warlike spirit leading to conquests. Yet, he maintained, American honor demanded that Mexico be forced to feel the full strength of American power. The legislature, for its part, appropriated twenty thousand dollars to help outfit the South Carolina volunteers.

Within a few days the new governor, David Johnson, a former Unionist, in his inaugural followed a moderate line similar to Aiken's. While denouncing war "in its mildest form" as one of "the greatest scourges of mankind," he unhappily observed that American blood had been shed on the battlefield. "Let us not stop to enquire why this is," he advised, "but bring to the conflict all our energies, that the war may have a speedy termination." He was certain that South Carolina would do its duty, that its sons would sustain its honor and patriotism.[1]

In a not too subtle effort to encourage recruitment, the *Courier* reported that many legislators believed the war unlikely to con-

1. Greenville *Mountaineer*, December 4, 11, 25, 1846.

tinue for more than another twelve months. Such views were discounted by Joel R. Poinsett. Writing an article for the December issue of the *Commercial Review of the South and West*, the former minister to Mexico advised against the belief of an easy conquest of Mexico, which had become "an implacable, if not dangerous enemy." Each Mexican state would organize its own means of resistance, and American arms might capture the Mexican capital yet at the same time become surrounded by an armed populace. In Poinsett's opinion the war now required a larger American army than previously supported, an army of well-disciplined regulars. Volunteers were unsatisfactory; they were too rash. The bravest and the best would perish, he warned.[2]

In the meantime, Colonel Butler busied himself with organizing the South Carolina Regiment anew. In detailed instructions to each company commander he requested eighty effective privates, although the minimum allowable was sixty-four. When the requisite number was attained, the commander was to notify Butler and depart immediately for Charleston. The state government would pay all necessary expenses of transportation and subsistence to Charleston, where the War Department would then take charge. With regard to recruiting, Butler was determined to leave nothing to chance. For example, in accepting the Edgefield Company into service, he authorized its captain, Preston Brooks, to seek fifteen or twenty extra enlistees, provided they would be willing to serve in another company that might arrive at the rendezvous undermanned.[3]

The Charleston Company was among the first to be reorganized. On Saturday evening, November 21, the call was issued by a group of volunteers parading through the streets with a brass band. The enlistment roll remained continuously open at the armory. The city council voted a bonus of twenty-one dollars and a uniform for each man mustered into service. Although some of

2. Charleston *Courier*, December 3, 1846; J. R. Poinsett, "Our Army in Mexico," *Commercial Review of the South and West*, II (December, 1846), 426–30.
3. Edgefield *Advertiser*, December 2, 1846; P. M. Butler to Preston Brooks, December 6, 1846, in Preston Brooks Papers, SCL.

the original members refused to enlist again, within a week the company was filled with "brave spirits ready to risk all for the honor of the State, at the call of the country."[4]

Honor was the watchword at Sumterville too, as the *Banner* called for the volunteers of the previous June to step forward. Editor William J. Francis exhorted, "The honor of their native District and State requires that they should respond with alacrity to the summons." At a parade a few days later, some thirty-five to forty men enlisted under the new terms. The leaders scurried about and by December 5 had a sufficient number of volunteers to organize. The company elected as captain Francis Sumter, a young lawyer grandson of "The Gamecock," Thomas Sumter, and chose "the Sumters" for its name. Two days later the company assembled at the courthouse in readiness to depart for Charleston.[5]

The Abbeville Company, named the "McDuffie Guards" in honor of the district's eminent senator, was called upon to reorganize on December 3. Charles H. Allen, the local editor, boasted that after "a few more thunders from our cannon" the war would be left to the historians. Embarrassingly, only thirteen of the original enlistees volunteered to sign again. Apparently, Poinsett's views of a long and costly struggle were widely believed.

With time running out, the Abbeville Company seemed unable to attain its quota. The district's militia regiment was mustered several times and subjected to the usual chauvinistic oratory, accompanied with martial music. J. Foster Marshall, the company's captain, John B. Moragne, and other ambitious young war hawks stumped the district in search of volunteers. Their quota was achieved at a meeting on December 11. At the same time, Abbeville citizens pledged about two thousand dollars to help equip the company, which was described by H. H. Townes as filled with "nearly every rich & promising young man" in the district. The Abbeville *Banner* proudly announced that "Old

4. Charleston *Courier*, November 23, 28, 1846; Charleston *Mercury*, November 30, 1846.

5. Sumter *Banner*, November 25, December 2, 9, 16, 1846; Anne King Gregorie, *History of Sumter Country, South Carolina* (Sumter, S.C., 1954), 154–56, 159.

Abbeville is true to her ancient reputation." Townes scolded his younger brother for not enlisting and, as an afterthought, said, "Mother ought to have made you volunteer." [6]

A similar ritual took place in Edgefield. At a meeting on November 30, amid music and "most feeling and eloquent addresses," forty-three men agreed to sign up. The volunteers then marched to the courthouse square to the music of the "Star Spangled Banner." In the ceremony that followed, Susan Pickens, daughter of Colonel Francis W. Pickens, presented the company a banner with an injunction to "follow wherever it waves, and bear it aloft in triumph, or perish beneath it in glory." Accepting the standard, made by the Edgefield ladies, Captain Brooks pledged the company's honor "before high Heaven" to carry out her request.

Brooks reminded the assembly that the company's quota was yet to be met, and he issued a public call to any able-bodied man "who regards his personal comfort less than the honor of his country." It would be a "calamity," he emphasized, if the sons of Edgefield were destined "to *hear* and not to *tell* how fields were won." After witnessing the flag ceremony, the local editor, carried away with emotion, wrote, "Twas then we panted to throw down our quill and grasp the sword and die with her beautiful banner floating o'er us."

During the next week the company's roster met the minimum requirement, and on Sale Day, December 7, additional enlistees pushed the total over one hundred. The next day the town entertained the "Old '96 Boys," the company's adopted name, with a lavish banquet. The spirits must have flowed freely, because it required almost two full columns of the *Advertiser* to list the numerous toasts raised to Edgefield's heroes. Late the same day the volunteers raised a war whoop and marched—or staggered—out of town enroute to their rendezvous. [7]

Elsewhere, companies were organized in Richland (Colum-

6. Abbeville *Banner*, December 16, 1846; Anderson *Gazette*, December 18, 1846, quoting Abbeville *Banner*; Pendleton *Messenger*, December 11, 1846; H. H. Townes to W. A. Townes, December 8, 14, 1846, in Townes Family Papers.
7. Edgefield *Advertiser*, November 25, December 2, 9, 1846.

bia), Chester, Lancaster, Barnwell, Kershaw (Camden), Fairfield (Winnsboro), and Newberry districts, though the latter was too late to be accepted. As indicated, the call to colors met with a mixed reception. Earlier, when Joseph Abney of Edgefield enlisted, he solemnly declared, "I should have felt dishonored, if I had not volunteered to fight . . . when there is so much indifference about it, manifested in all parts of South Carolina." Later, when W. W. Adams eulogized Sergeant William Blocker, slain in Mexico, he recalled the difficulty of raising a company in Edgefield in June, 1846. Blocker and Whitfield Brooks, Jr., according to Adams, had spent several days riding over the district seeking volunteers. And when the War Department later changed the terms of service, it required "strenuous exertions" by Blocker and others to fill the company again.[8]

In Columbia the prospect had also been discouraging. It seemed as if the early "burning patriotism . . . had passed away." At first effort only twenty signed the roster. J. L. Clark, a local banker, wrote that Colonel Butler was in town aiding recruitment, and there was "marching & drumming thro the street all day & all night" for volunteers. In his opinion the company would be filled "after a good deal of drinking, chivalry and all that," but he observed "mighty little of the Real Chivalry in the Ranks." The Columbia press did its part, for three editors, including two veterans of the War of 1812, enlisted.[9]

In Greenville Captain T. P. Butler mustered out his volunteers on December 1, but only twenty-three of the original group reenlisted. All-out efforts were made on December 7 with a large rally at the courthouse, complete with music from two bands, a flag-waving parade down Main Street, and emotional speeches from

8. Abney to Burt, June 6, 1846, in Burt Papers; Edgefield *Advertiser*, May 8, 1848. The company commanders were as follows: Francis Sumter (Sumter), R. G. M. Dunovant (Chester), Keith Moffatt (Kershaw), Preston S. Brooks (Edgefield), J. Foster Marshall (Abbeville), William Blanding (Charleston), Joseph Kennedy (Fairfield), W. D. DeSaussure (Richland), Leroy Secrest (Lancaster), N. G. Walker (Barnwell), and James Williams (Newberry).
9. Charleston *Courier*, December 3, 1846; J. L. Clark to J. H. Hammond, November 28, 1846, in Hammond Papers, LC. The two veterans of the War of 1812 were Samuel Weir and D. E. Sweeney.

the district's leading orators. Only nineteen more were induced to volunteer. Thus, Greenville, which had raised two companies in the early days of the war, was unable to recruit one company six months later. Efforts in other northwestern South Carolina districts likewise failed.[10] In fact, not a single company was recruited in what is today the back country bloc of Anderson, Oconee, Pickens, Greenville, Laurens, Union, Spartanburg, Cherokee, and York counties. And, with the exception of Charleston, no company was recruited from the coastal districts.

As noted, recruiting encountered apathy everywhere except in relatively populous Charleston. But why were districts in central South Carolina more successful in raising companies than those elsewhere? One reason was the aggressive appeal issued by newspapers in the central districts: Sumter, Richland (Columbia), Kershaw (Camden), Edgefield, and Abbeville. Greenville seemed to be the only district with a strong prowar newspaper that failed to recruit a company in December. As for the low country districts, there was not a single newspaper within one hundred miles of the coast outside Charleston and Georgetown.

Recruiting in low country districts was also hampered by a relatively low white population. Georgetown, for example, had only 1,158 white males in 1850. But what of the back country districts with relatively large white population? Spartanburg, for example, had 9,118 white males in 1850. At the outset there seemed to be as much prowar sentiment in the back country as elsewhere in the state. The Whig party, once moderately active in northwestern South Carolina, was too weak by 1846 to generate antiwar rallies then or later. When the first call for volunteers was issued in late May, companies were organized in Spartanburg, York, and Union districts, and two were organized in Greenville. But back country ardor cooled when only one of five companies was received, probably because their services were tendered too late. The more centrally located districts, on or near railroads, had the advantage of faster communication. When the call for

10. Greenville *Mountaineer*, December 4, 11, 1846; Pendleton *Messenger*, December 11, 1846; Anderson *Gazette*, December 11, 1846.

volunteers was renewed in November, eight of the eleven companies accepted into service had originally been organized in June.

Editor Archibald Todd of the Anderson *Gazette* aptly noted reasons for the cooling fervor. The previous spring many had thought it would be "a mere frolic" to march to the city of Mexico and take possession of a golden treasure thought to be there. The military had been "so wretchedly managed" as to discourage many volunteers. It was now clear that there would be "some tall fighting" before the Mexican capital fell. Hence, when the War Department changed the terms of enlistment, it enabled the volunteers "to crawl out" if they wished, an option many exercised. That recruitment was difficult should not have been surprising, for, after all, many prominent figures had publicly or privately expressed grave doubts about the American venture. Francis W. Pickens generally agreed with Todd. On November 30 he wrote to Polk objecting to the change in the terms of service. He reported that while "many sons of our most respectable gentlemen" were ready to serve a year as privates, they were unwilling to pledge themselves indefinitely to the ranks as common soldiers, especially since experienced Mexican hands expected the war to be protracted for years. A loyal supporter of the president, Pickens ruefully admitted that "great apathy" prevailed in the state. For this he blamed Calhoun, whose "great name & popularity here utterly prostrated our early efforts." [11]

When the volunteer companies "took up the line of march" for the Charleston rendezvous, some were fortunate to be near the railway. Not so for companies from Abbeville, Lancaster, and Chester; they were forced to march many miles before entraining. The Chester Company arrived dusty and tired in Columbia

11. Anderson *Gazette*, November 27, 1846; Pickens to Polk, November 30, 1846, in James K. Polk Papers, LC. Ex-Governor Hammond, a friend of Polk, privately admitted that Mexico was "unconquerable," but, should the war continue, he favored using "fire & sword & doing them all the damage we can." J. H. Hammond to M. C. M. Hammond, November 21, 1846, in Hammond Papers, SCL. James L. Petigru, the staunch Unionist lawyer, in referring to a prominent planter who volunteered as a private, concluded that "he must be a little cracked." Petigru to Thomas Petigru, November 25, 1846, in James Petigru Carson, *Life, Letters and Speeches of James Louis Petigru: The Union Man of South Carolina* (Washington, D.C., 1920), 257.

Brigadier General James Shields, commander of the brigade in which the Palmetto regiment fought at Churubusco and Mexico City. Shields, an Illinois jurist before the war, later served as a United States senator from three states: Illinois, Minnesota, and Missouri. *Courtesy of the Illinois State Historical Library*

Pierce M. Butler, governor of South Carolina, 1836–1838, and colonel of the Palmetto regiment. Killed at Churubusco.   *Courtesy of the South Caroliniana Library*

Major General John A. Quitman, commander of the volunteer division in which the Palmetto regiment served. *Courtesy of the South Caroliniana Library*

General Waddy Thompson, Jr., Whig congressman, 1835–1841, and United States minister to Mexico, 1842–1844.
Courtesy of South Caroliniana Library

Joel R. Poinsett, United States minister to Mexico, 1825–1830, and secretary of
war, 1837–1841.   *Courtesy of the South Caroliniana Library*

John C. Calhoun. Taken from a daguerreotype made in 1844, while Calhoun was secretary of state.   *Courtesy of Clemson University*

on December 8. As they hobbled sore-footed down Main Street, lined with a curious crowd, Benjamin F. Perry did not observe "a dry eye" present among the spectators. The Chester Company was escorted by two local militia companies and South Carolina College cadets to the Statehouse and then to a nearby campground for an overnight stay. Lieutenant Colonel Dickinson addressed the company, and in a ceremony on the college campus the cadets presented a sword to Captain Dunovant, the company commander.

One of the best-liked members of the Chester Company was its standard-bearer, Nathaniel R. Eaves, the "Little Warrior," as the state senator was known. A bachelor and a major in the militia, Eaves had enlisted as a private. He too blistered his feet on the march and complained a week later that they were still "somewhat painful." The standard he carried bore the words DON'T STAY WITH ME—YOU HAVE WORK TO DO—GO AHEAD.[12]

When the McDuffie Guards marched away from the Abbeville courthouse, every spectator present shed tears, reported H. H. Townes. The company's route to the railroad passed through Edgefield. As they neared the village, on December 17, an Edgefield committee of fifty rode out to greet them, and General Milledge L. Bonham addressed them. The committee then escorted the "flower and stamina of Old Abbeville" to the town square for ceremonies and on to Goodman's Hotel for a banquet. The company was entertained until late in the evening with numerous toasts and speeches, including another by General Bonham. The next morning the committee escorted the Abbevillians for about a mile out of town, where they subjected their guests to another chauvinistic outburst. The company, still in good spirits despite a surfeit of oratory, loudly voted its thanks to Edgefield for its hospitality and resumed its march.[13]

The Sumter Company, upon leaving Sumterville, marched only two miles before camping for the evening. There they suffered

12. Edgefield *Advertiser*, December 16, 1846; Perry in Greenville *Mountaineer*, December 14, 1846; N. R. Eaves to Mrs. Esther Buford ("Sister"), December 14, 1846, in N. R. Eaves Papers, SCL.
13. Edgefield *Advertiser*, December 23, 1846; H. H. Townes to W. A. Townes, December 16, 1846, in Townes Family Papers.

their first casualty. One private was injured so badly by the kick of a mule that he had to return home. On the second day the company reached the vicinity of Stateburgh, where local citizens rounded up a sufficient number of wagons and carriages to transport the entire outfit to the nearest railhead.[14]

With companies rapidly converging on Charleston, regimental officers hastily erected quarters at Camp Magnolia and prepared to train the new recruits. By December 19, ten companies with almost nine hundred men had arrived "eager for action." Senator Eaves boasted that he would bring back Santa Anna's ears. However, in Newberry all was gloom. Its company, organized late, had marched forty miles through a cold rain in a single day to reach Columbia, only to be turned down.[15]

The Palmettos were described as being "noble and soldier-like" in appearance but "swarthy and smoked" from pinewood fires at Camp Magnolia. An observer noted that the volunteers complained of a cold reception in Charleston. This was due in part to the conduct of some who behaved badly, became drunk and impolite, and rowed with sailors and local citizens. In a drunken brawl with seamen on a "very disreputable street," an unidentified volunteer fired into a crowd and killed a sailor. As for their health, the Palmettos fared very well; only one death and eight or ten hospital cases were reported in Charleston. On the other hand, their camp was literally wrecked by a storm on December 16, requiring them to seek new quarters, this time in the horse stables and other buildings at the Charleston Race Course.[16]

On December 23, the regiment was reviewed by Adjutant General Cantey and two United States Army officers, after which Governor Johnson addressed them. The "venerable and dignified" governor implored them to remember that South Carolina looked

14. Sumter *Banner*, December 16, 1846; Gregorie, *History of Sumter County*, 154–56.
15. Charleston *Courier*, December 3, 21, 1846; Greenville *Mountaineer*, December 25, 1846; Anderson *Gazette*, December 18, 1846.
16. Pendleton *Messenger*, December 25, 1846, citing Charleston *Evening News*; H. Judge Moore, in Greenville *Mountaineer*, January 1, 1847; "W," in *ibid.*, January 8, 1847; E. G. Randolph to Mary McCreight, January 15, 1847, in E. G. Randolph Papers, SCL. Moore of Greenville had joined the Fairfield Company. He wrote regularly to the *Mountaineer*.

to them "to sustain her honor in the field." He also reminded the
volunteers that they would be associated with troops from all sections of the nation, for whom he hoped they would cultivate a
"sincere brotherly regard." They should try to rival them only in
the "prompt discharge" of their duties and be ever ready to aid a
fellow soldier in peril. As a parting thought, the governor said,
"Go—and the God of battles be with you." [17]

The next day the regiment, accompanied by two Charleston
militia companies, marched to the city hall, where Mayor T. L.
Hutchinson presented a standard prepared by the city council.
Colonel Butler responded in a speech "replete with patriotism
and feeling." He assured the council that Sergeant James Cantey,
the standard-bearer, would "vigilantly and valiantly guard and
protect the sacred charge." Also in honor of the volunteers, William Gilmore Simms composed and published just prior to their
departure a "War Song of the Palmetto Regiment."

> Now, wave the green Palmetto,
>   And cheer the glorious sign,
> That tells of many a victory,
>   Your father won and mine;
>
> . . . .
>
> Now wave the green Palmetto,
>   And when the fight is worst,
> We'll bear it on, through strife and storm,
>   'Mong charging lines, the first;—
> We'll think of ancient valor,
>   When fields at home were won,
> When Marion made the foeman skulk,
>   And Sumter made him run!—
> We'll think of friends and brothers,
>   Whose hearts with triumph burn,—
> And gentle maids, that look with tears,
>   To welcome our return. [18]

17. Charleston *Courier*, December 24, 1846; Pendleton *Messenger*, January 8, 1847,
   quoting Charleston *Evening News*.
18. Charleston *Courier*, December 25, 1846; W. Gilmore Simms, *Lays of the Palmetto:
   A Tribute to the South Carolina Regiment, in the War with Mexico* (Charleston,
   1848), 11–12.

Two or three days before Christmas, the regiment received orders to proceed immediately to Point Isabel, Texas, by way of Montgomery and Mobile. On the morning of the twenty-sixth, Major Gladden led the first five companies out of Charleston. The other five followed the next day. Moving by rail, the regiment's first stop was at Camp Johnson, a hastily improvised cantonment in a cornfield near Hamburg, terminus of the South Carolina Railroad. On the thirty-first, Governor Johnson again reviewed the troops and addressed them "in his usual felicitous style," said a reporter.[19]

At Camp Johnson the troops suffered from a lack of tents, knapsacks, and other necessary equipment, which for some unexplained reason the United States quartermaster had been unable to supply. Governor Johnson was able partially to remedy the deficiency from state stores. The regiment also lacked proper medical services, and in the cold, rainy December weather numerous volunteers were stricken with bad colds and pneumonia. Some thirty to forty were soon laid up in hotels, private homes, and the hospital in nearby Augusta. One correspondent blamed the illness on too much whiskey. But whatever the cause, many sick Palmettos had to remain behind when the regiment departed.[20]

While the Palmettos drilled and fought off illness and boredom, Colonel Butler and his staff busied themselves arranging for transportation and supplies for the trip to Mobile, part of which had to be on foot. Butler was also being pressed by the commissioner of Indian affairs for a final account of his expenses in Oklahoma, a matter Butler had not satisfactorily cleared up the previous summer while in Washington. Too, there were last-minute pleas by politicians for staff positions in the regiment, and But-

19. Marching orders were sent by R. Jones, U.S. Adj. Gen., to Colonel Butler, December 18, 1846, "Documents of the Palmetto Regiment," (Manuscript in South Carolina Department of Archives and History, Columbia), 9; Butler to Adley H. Gladden, December 25, 1846, *ibid.*, 19; Edgefield *Advertiser*, January 6, 1847; Greenville *Mountaineer*, January 8, 1847.
20. "W," in Greenville *Mountaineer*, January 8, 1847; [?] to [?], January 5, 1847; P. M. Butler to R. Jones, December 30, 1846; Jones to R. J. R. Bee, April 26, 1847, all in "Documents of the Palmetto Regiment," 22, 30, 69.

ler himself was still trying to secure his promotion to brigadier general.[21]

On New Year's Day one battalion of the South Carolina Regiment marched out of Camp Johnson, crossed the river, and passed through Augusta to entrain for Atlanta. The other battalion followed the next day. The Augusta *Constitutionalist* gave the following account of the Palmettos' entry into the town.

They were received by a salute of cannon at the Bridge, and escorted by the Augusta Artillery Guards, through our densely thronged streets, to the enlivening strains of music, amidst the huzzas of our population, who thus essayed to cheer them on their way. Many a white 'kerchief was waived by fair hands from window and balcony, and many a sweet voice bade God speed to the gallant volunteers. Often above the din and the dust that shrouded the advancing column, rose bright and clear in the moonlighted air, rocket after rocket which, in bursting, shed halos of gleaming light upon the banners of the different companies—gifts from the hands of beauty to animate the brave in the hour of battle. That they will wave triumphant in every field, and return unsullied to the land of the Palmetto, is our confident hope.[22]

According to two witnesses, the trip from Augusta to Atlanta was a harrowing experience. Many of the soldiers traveled with bad colds and fever and needed medical attention. In addition, they had no food except some stale bread for forty-eight hours. One volunteer was killed when he fell from a car and was crushed beneath the wheels. Another, seriously ill when he boarded the train, died before reaching Atlanta. His was the fifth death in the regiment.[23]

In Atlanta the weather was cold and the men wretched. A sympathetic stationmaster permitted them to sleep in empty railway coaches, but there was an insufficient number to accommodate the entire regiment. As a consequence, some were forced to en-

21. P. M. Butler to John C. Calhoun, January 14, 1847, in Calhoun Papers, CU; Butler to William Medill, commissioner of Indian affairs, January 4, 1847, in P. M. Butler Papers, SCL. See also "Documents of the Palmetto Regiment," 3–6.
22. Quoted in Charleston *Courier*, January 4, 1847.
23. Randolph to McCreight, January 15, 1847, in Randolph Papers; "Saluda," in Edgefield *Advertiser*, January 13, 1847.

dure the weather and "being badly equipped farred very badly," wrote Lieutenant John B. Moragne of the Abbeville Company. To add to their woes the officers experienced difficulty hiring wagons to transport camp equipage and commissary stores on the march to Montgomery.[24]

Because of much sickness and several deaths, it was fortunate for the regiment that Colonel Butler had received permission to bring all companies up to maximum strength of eighty privates each. A few recruits were picked up en route to Mobile. Secretary of War Marcy likewise authorized acceptance of the Newberry Company and a second Edgefield Company, the "Butler Guards" under Captain Oliver Towles. The Newberry Company, commanded by Captain James Williams, immediately headed for Mobile, leaving Hamburg on January 25.[25]

It was a different story with the Butler Guards. Their attempted organization in December had fallen short some twelve or fifteen men. In January another effort was made to recruit the minimum requisite number, but again without success. Butler's wife was angry. She wrote her husband: "The general impression is that the *men* were anxious to go but that Capt. Tollis' [Towles] *friends* were busy with cold water. Tom Bacon would glad have taken Tollis' place had he given way in time. . . . What I most hate is their taking your name & then making a failure." Thus, the Butler Guards's contribution to the war consisted only of escorting the Newberry Company through Edgefield.[26]

If the Palmettos thought their trip to Atlanta was particularly trying, it was fortunate for their morale that they could not envision what was in store for them upon leaving the railhead at Griffin, some forty miles south of Atlanta. With Lieutenant Colonel Dickinson in charge, one battalion took up its march immedi-

24. John B. Moragne to Mary E. Davis [sister], January 4, 1847, in Mary Moragne Papers, SCL; W. C. Moragne to P. M. Butler, January 5, 1847, in "Documents of the Palmetto Regiment," 28–29.

25. P. M. Butler to R. Jones, December 23, 1846; W. L. Marcy to Butler, December 28, 1846, in "Documents of the Palmetto Regiment," 16, 21; Edgefield *Advertiser*, January 13, 1847; Anderson *Gazette*, February 5, 1847.

26. Edgefield *Advertiser*, December 9, 16, 1846, January 20, 1847; Mrs. M. J. [Julia] Butler to P. M. Butler, January, 1847, in Butler Papers.

ately; the other proceeded the next day. The volunteers slogged along in miserable weather. There was cold rain for two days, followed by one or two days of pleasant weather and then a severe sleet storm, which knocked down and froze most of their tents. The thermometer dropped to nineteen degrees. It was almost impossible for the bedraggled men to keep warm, until they luckily found shelter at a Methodist campground. Fortunately, too, the citizens en route relieved their hardships somewhat through their generous hospitality.[27]

The officers had their troubles; tempers were frayed and Dickinson became piqued at Butler's "reprimand" for pushing his battalion too fast. It was evidently too fast and unpleasant for some. There were grumbling and several desertions, mainly by Chesterfield volunteers who had joined the Kershaw Company. The officers were short of funds, thus increasing the difficulty of procuring necessary wagons and supplies. After a week the regiment reached an Alabama railhead at Notasulga, about 110 miles from Griffin. By and large, Colonel Butler was pleased with the "soldierly deportment" of the regiment to date, but he dreaded to look ahead to "the suffering & loss of life incident to the [Mexican] climate, & the indescretion of young men."[28]

At Montgomery, advance agents of the regiment had hired two steamboats to transport the South Carolinians downriver to Mobile. Private W. M. Goodlett, a former Greenville sheriff, left a bitter account of the trip with Dickinson's battalion. The volunteers had boarded the ship at nightfall, expecting some comfort. "But lo and behold!" Goodlett exclaimed, "we were marched like so many hogs, on to the lower deck among the Boilers, Engines, &c." Guards confined them to their quarters, where they lacked room to lie down. They remained aboard for two nights, with the hold becoming increasingly filthy. Horses would have received

27. The story of the march was told by H. J. Moore and W. M. Goodlett, Greenville members of the Fairfield Company, in Greenville *Mountaineer*, January 22, February 5, 1847. Other accounts appeared in Edgefield *Advertiser*, January 27, February 10, 1847, and Charleston *Courier*, February 1, 1847.
28. P. M. Butler to John C. Calhoun, January 14, 1847, in Calhoun Papers, CU. For the officers' difficulties see "Documents of the Palmetto Regiment," 31–40.

better treatment. Goodlett concluded, "I said something in my last in favor of the officers—I now take it all back."[29]

Apparently the situation aboard the second steamer was even more intolerable to the enlisted men. Ben L. Posey, an Abbeville volunteer, later wrote that the men were in a "pitiful" condition, crowded below deck without food for two days. It was too much for some to endure; about forty mutinied. With fixed bayonets they stopped the boat and went ashore. No one would obey the officers' orders to arrest the mutineers; hence the officers yielded and hushed up the affair.[30]

Private William S. Johnson, a Columbia volunteer who kept a diary, also reported mistreatment at the hands of officers. William and Anna Maybin encouraged him to be philosophical about his conditions. Anna reminded Johnson that if he could "wethor the storm," he would have "learnt a good deal more of human nature." Her husband added: "I would to God I could avert your ills, but such is the facts[,] men at home who the world looks on as men[,] when clothed with authority abroad becomes tyrants. . . . All your friends joyn me saying God of the universe prop up and strenthen the poor soldiers who are tyranised over."[31]

Upon reaching Mobile, the regiment bivouacked near the docks in a large cotton warehouse called Camp Deas in honor of Colonel J. S. Deas, a prominent South Carolina resident of the port city. Colonel Butler, hoping to tighten discipline, ordered all personnel confined to camp, stationed guards at the camp entrance, and placed the regiment under a busy military routine from reveille until retreat. All reports indicated that the volunteers were in good spirits, although most were penniless and ill clad. Their uniforms, ordered from New York, had been delayed by shipwreck off the North Carolina coast and, in fact, never reached them. Meanwhile, before hurrying to New Orleans on business, Colonel Butler assembled the troops and notified them of receipt of

29. Goodlett, in Greenville *Mountainer*, February 5, 1847.
30. Gregorie, *History of Sumter Country*, 156–57, 160, citing Sumter *Watchman*, November, 1857–January, 1858, which carried Posey's narrative.
31. Anna and William Maybin to W. S. Johnson, January 24, 1847, in W. S. Johnson Papers, SCL. They had received Johnson's letter of January 18.

sealed orders about their destination, which he suspected to be Vera Cruz; whereupon, a shout erupted from the assembled Palmettos.[32]

Some of the ill feeling generated between officers and enlisted men en route to Mobile continued to be felt at Camp Deas. During Butler's absence in New Orleans, Dickinson failed to enforce an even-handed discipline. I. P. Detter, another Greenville private in the Fairfield Company, was court-martialed for being AWOL in town. Although the punishment was light, Detter complained that he only followed the example of officers in leaving camp.[33]

Private Goodlett encountered more serious difficulty. While serving on police patrol in Mobile on the night of January 20, he observed that the officer in charge did not "properly and impartially" enforce Colonel Butler's order against absenteeism. He filed an adverse report when the commander returned to Mobile two days later, only to fall victim immediately to an old game. Dickinson took exception to Goodlett's report and filed grave countercharges "as long as a marriage settlement with provisions for younger children," Goodlett wrote.

The startled and angry private was arrested and court-martialed at once with no opportunity to prepare an adequate defense. The next day the court pronounced him guilty and imposed a light sentence. Before Goodlett could appeal the sentence, Dickinson shrewdly interceded, and, with an appearance of magnanimity, requested Colonel Butler to remit the sentence and drop the case. Butler acceded, but meanwhile Goodlett's original charges were somehow lost in the confusion.[34]

However, there was at least one high moment at Camp Deas. A group of South Carolinians, headed by Colonel Deas, J. W.

32. Anderson *Gazette*, February 5, 1847; Sumter *Banner*, February 10, 1847; Pendleton *Messenger*, January 29, February 5, 1847; Edgefield *Advertiser*, January 27, 1847. Letters the volunteers sent back to South Carolina sometimes contained unintentional humor, as when Private E. G. Randolph asked his sister to tell "some of the Pretty Girls to send me something for instance a lock of their hair or one of their front teeth." To McCreight, January 15, 1847, in Randolph Papers.
33. I. P. Detter to P. M. Butler, January 22, 1847, in "Documents of the Palmetto Regiment," 52.
34. Goodlett, in Greenville *Mountaineer*, February 5, 1847.

Lesesne, J. E. Nott, and John C. Calhoun's son Andrew, hosted a barbecue for the Palmettos shortly before their departure. Colonel Butler, aware of the regiment's reputation for rowdiness, insisted that the affair be held in the camp, not in the town. It was a rousing party in which many Mobilians also participated.[35]

On January 27 the Palmettos began to board ship. True to Colonel Butler's anticipation, the regiment was destined for the island of Lobos, the rendezvous for General Winfield Scott's assault on Vera Cruz. Butler with part of the force went aboard the *Alhambra*; Dickinson, the *Oregon*; and Gladden, the *Ellerslie*. Butler sent his family a farewell note with an admonition to his little sons "to be good boys & obey Mother & love their Sister & think of Father."[36]

While the troops were still loading, a fierce storm broke over Mobile and delayed the expedition until the thirtieth. N. R. Eaves called it the worst storm in Mobile in twenty years, and the volunteers suffered "in the extream." One small boatload of Palmettos was wrecked while attempting to transfer the men to an ocean-going vessel. All were rescued but had to be placed aboard the *Alhambra* rather than their original vessel.[37]

Upon leaving Mobile the three ships were soon separated by foul weather. The *Ellerslie* and the *Oregon* arrived at Lobos about a week later without incident, except for a fire scare on the latter, momentarily frightening because of much ammunition aboard. The *Alhambra*, on the other hand, straggled into the Lobos harbor on February 12. Eaves, often given to overstatement, described the trip as "the most perilous voige ever experienced[;] we encountered three Nothern storms . . . we suffered everything that mortals could suffer except a ship reck." Another correspondent complained that the soldiers were so crowded below deck that they lacked room for proper sanitation and rest. During the storms

35. Edgefield *Advertiser*, February 3, 10, 1847.
36. J. Monroe to P. M. Butler, January 16, 1847, in "Documents of the Palmetto Regiment," 47; Butler to Behethland Butler [daughter], January 27, 1847, in Butler Papers.
37. Eaves to C. D. Melton, January 27, 1847, in Eaves Papers.

many were badly bruised by shifting cargo, and several horses were killed when dashed against the bulkheads.[38]

Despite the discomforts of the voyage, the Palmettos arrived at the beautiful tropical island of Lobos in fairly good health, with the exception of an outbreak of mumps in the Sumter Company. It spread rapidly to other companies, and within two weeks there were about two hundred cases, mainly among rural volunteers who had never been exposed to diseases common to urban inhabitants. Nonetheless, Major Gladden reported that no one seemed to suffer severely from the disease. The most difficult problem was procuring potable water. Wells sunk on the island produced only brackish water, and much of that transported from the United States had been fouled by unclean casks. In that situation diarrhea soon made its unwelcome presence felt. To offset these discomforts the men enjoyed abundant tropical fruit and bathing in the surf. On February 25 they were happily joined by their Newberry comrades, just in time to participate in General Scott's expedition to Vera Cruz.[39]

38. Eaves to Melton, February 14, 1847, *ibid*; "Saluda," in Edgefield *Advertiser*, February 10, March 24, 1847; J. F. Marshall, in Abbeville *Banner*, March 17, 1847.
39. Greenville *Mountaineer*, March 12, 1847, citing Columbia *Banner*; Edgefield *Advertiser*, March 17, 24, 1847; Charleston *Courier*, March 19, 1847; H. Judge Moore, *Scott's Campaign in Mexico: From the Rendezvous on the Island of Lobos to the Taking of the City, Including an Account of the Siege of Puebla, with Sketches of the Country, and Manners and Customs of the Inhabitants.* (Charleston, 1849), 2. Having lost his notes, Moore depended much on Goodlett's notes.

CHAPTER 4 *The Most Mischievous Man in the Senate*

WHILE COLONEL BUTLER was assembling the Palmetto regiment at its Charleston rendezvous, Congress convened and heard President Polk's explanation of American policy toward Mexico. In part he said: "The war has not been waged with a view to conquest; but having been commenced by Mexico, it has been carried into the enemy's country, and will be vigorously prosecuted there, with a view to obtain an honorable peace, and thereby secure ample indemnity for the expenses of the war, as well as to our much injured citizens, who hold large pecuniary demands against Mexico." The president did not know what to expect from General Santa Anna, but he again requested Congress to provide money for negotiations, and he hinted at securing New Mexico and California.[1]

Although Senator Calhoun privately pronounced Polk's message "a poor excuse for the Mexican war," his view was not widely held in the South Carolina press. The *Winyah Observer* regarded the message as "an unanswerable argumentative document." The *South Carolinian* and the Greenville *Mountaineer* applauded the message, and legislator Benjamin F. Perry remarked that Polk's message had received "universal favor" in the state capital. Even the Anderson *Gazette*, often a hostile critic of the president's war policy, contended that his explanation "conclusively proves that we are innocent of prosecuting an unjust or aggressive warfare."[2]

1. *Congressional Globe*, 29th Cong., 2nd Sess., 8–9.
2. J. C. Calhoun to T. G. Clemson, December 9, 1846, in Calhoun Papers, CU; George-

Notwithstanding the president's efforts, an "honorable peace" was not in the offing. Before the end of December, reports reached South Carolina that the Mexican Congress was expected to refuse peace overtures. In such an event, the Edgefield *Advertiser* advised America's next overture to be made through the "rough and ready diplomacy" of General Taylor within the walls of Mexico City. The Sumter *Banner* voiced the same sentiment. During January further news from Mexico revealed that Santa Anna had tightened his control on the government. He had induced the Mexican Congress on December 6 to elect him president. As a consequence, the Charleston *Evening News* was certain that no political party in Mexico dared propose peace so long as American troops occupied Mexican soil, a view also held by the *Mercury* and the Pendleton *Messenger*.[3]

Whereas most of the Palmetto press in December and January was sympathetic with the president or at least tactfully quiet, the *Mercury*, his archantagonist in South Carolina, continued to snipe at those "furious warmakers" in the North and West who had "pushed on the war." Nonetheless, editor J. M. Clapp professed support of the administration's efforts and was strongly opposed to an army withdrawal from Mexico. Yet, he foresaw two great evils arising from the conflict: the Wilmot Proviso and the end of free trade. On January 20 Clapp divulged information that Calhoun was soon to propose a peace plan of limited conquest.[4]

For some period of time Calhoun had considered proposing a war strategy of his own. In the late fall he had received letters from various friends elsewhere in the Union who denounced the administration, deplored the evils of war, and observed a rising public opposition to the conflict. They had been encouraging Calhoun to devise a plan to end the war.[5]

town *Winyah Observer*, December 16, 30, 1846; Columbia *South Carolinian*, December 16, 1846; Perry, in Greenville *Mountaineer*, December 18, 1846.

3. Edgefield *Advertiser*, December 30, 1846; Sumter *Banner*, January 1, 1847; Georgetown *Winyah Observer*, January 20, 1847, quoting Charleston *Evening News*; Pendleton *Messenger*, January 8, 15, 1847; Charleston *Mercury*, January 7, 1847.
4. Charleston *Mercury*, January 12, 16, 20, 27, 1847.
5. See, for example, Lumpkin to J. C. Calhoun, November 26, December 17, 1846; James Chestney to Calhoun, November 23, 1846; Conner to Calhoun, January 9,

Calhoun was heartened further by the results of the December elections in South Carolina. He himself had been reelected, without opposition, to a full term in the Senate. As his junior colleague, Judge A. P. Butler, brother to Colonel Butler, was chosen to complete Senator McDuffie's unexpired term. The latter had resigned because of ill health. For governor the legislature elected Chancellor David Johnson, a former Unionist during the nullification crisis of 1832–1833, and for lieutenant governor, William Cain.[6]

Butler's election to the Senate was almost an afterthought. Early in the contest the front-runner was James H. Hammond, a former governor and a loyal Polk Democrat. His candidacy had been promoted by William Gilmore Simms at a time when it was commonly believed that Franklin H. Elmore would also become a candidate. In addition, Simms tossed his own hat into the ring for lieutenant governor. The politically ambitious man of letters was apparently anxious to strike a blow at Calhoun, but his plans went awry. At the last moment Elmore declined to run, preferring instead to continue as president of the state bank to protect his much-involved financial interests. Thus, Judge Butler, a last-hour candidate and dark horse, emerged victorious. Hammond had been handicapped by opposition from Colonel Wade Hampton's Columbia friends and by Butler's close ties with the legal profession. As for Simms, he suffered a bitter blow in losing his contest with Cain by a single vote.[7]

Butler informed Calhoun that he could foresee "no real difference" between the two and promised to cooperate cordially in

---

1847; Fisher to Calhoun, December 2, 1846, in Calhoun Papers, CU.

6. Charleston *Courier*, December 7, 10, 1846.

7. J. Mauldin Lesesne, *The Bank of the State of South Carolina: A General and Political History* (Columbia, S.C., 1970), 68; W. G. Simms to J. H. Hammond, November 24, December 11, 1846, in Mary C. Simms Oliphant, Alfred Taylor Odell, and T. C. Duncan Eaves (eds.), *The Letters of William Gilmore Simms* (5 vols., Columbia, S.C., 1952–1956), II, 216, 234–35; Jon L. Wakelyn, *The Politics of a Literary Man: William Gilmore Simms* (Westport, Conn., 1973), 103–104. According to gossip, Hammond, while governor, had seduced one of Hampton's daughters. The evidence, though strong, is not conclusive. Robert C. Tucker, "James Henry Hammond, South Carolinian" (Ph.D. dissertation, University of North Carolina, 1958), 424–27, 455.

the Senate.[8] Both he and Johnson became loyal henchmen of the senior senator and were soon seeking his advice on political matters. Not only were the December elections highly favorable to Calhoun, but his erstwhile lieutenant, Francis W. Pickens, soon renewed his efforts to placate the senator. Their relations had been strained since the Edgefield rally the previous June, notwithstanding Pickens' attempt in August to allay his kinsman's suspicions. Now, seeing his political fortunes at a low ebb, Pickens realized that it was imperative to regain Calhoun's favor. He may well have helped to frustrate Hammond's bid for the Senate. In any event, on December 13 he sent Calhoun a lengthy explanation of his role in the Edgefield meeting. He vigorously affirmed his loyalty to Calhoun and denied any intention of embarrassing the senator. He asserted, somewhat undiplomatically, "I have *been by you* when you *needed friends*, and when to *stand by you* was no gain to any man." In view of his continued strong support of Polk and his private criticism of Calhoun, Pickens' explanation was at best misleading.[9]

It is difficult to fathom Calhoun's true thinking in December, 1846. His friends once again were promoting his candidacy for president, however secretly, and his private correspondence, despite public disavowals, indicates his approval of their actions. But how could the war effect his candidacy? What of his relations with President Polk? His friend James Hamilton, Jr., wrote him of a meeting he had with Polk in late September. The president, Hamilton said, though regretting Calhoun's opposition to the war bill, had "not the slightest feeling of unkindness." Instead, Polk "cherished for your character the most unbounded respect, and for your talents the highest admiration." Hamilton was convinced of the president's sincerity and therefore urged Calhoun not to break with the administration but to "give them a liberal and cordial support, where you can." If relations remained cordial, Hamilton believed Calhoun's chances were good for the

8. A. P. Butler to J. C. Calhoun, December 5, 1846, in Calhoun Papers, CU.
9. Pickens to J. C. Calhoun, December 13, 1846, in Calhoun Papers, CU; Edmunds, "Francis W. Pickens," 138–40; Pickens to Polk, November 30, 1846, in Polk Papers.

support of a majority of the cabinet against Silas Wright, being touted as a presidential candidate by northern antislavery forces. He closed with an admonition: "The conduct of the War you must mainly leave to your friends." [10]

A few days after Congress convened, Calhoun privately explained his views about the war. He fully expected a long conflict, because the administration could not agree on a peace treaty without a large cession of land, and Santa Anna could not agree to a large cession without risking being overthrown. And should the war be prolonged, there was danger of European intervention. But the most formidable difficulty, Calhoun correctly foresaw, dealt with slavery. Whatever cession the United States might receive, if the treaty "should be silent on the subject of slavery in the ceded territory, the North will oppose it, & if it should prohibit slavery the South would, and in either event, there would not be a constitutional majority."

Calhoun declared that he had returned to Congress prepared "to incur any responsibility and to make any sacrifice" to bring the war to an early end, but he could see no possible way to do so. Then, again reproaching his senatorial colleagues and the administration, he reiterated that had he been supported in the last session "by a single senator of any weight or influence . . . & had a single day been allowed for deliberation, the war would have been averted!" Furthermore, had his solicitude for peace with England not been greater than his desire for peace with Mexico, he would have prevented the war "by moving a resolution to arrest the march of Taylor to the Rio Grande." [11]

On December 19 President Polk adroitly invited Calhoun to the White House in an effort to win his support. In a "frank & pleasant" conversation he revealed his difficulties with Generals

10. Polk's diary confirms the drift of Hamilton's remarks, except those referring to probable cabinet support of Calhoun's candidacy. Quaife, *Diary of James K. Polk*, II, 160–61. Calhoun wrote his daughter, "The prospect is, that the party will be defeated at the next election for President, unless, as my friends think, they should rally on me." To Mrs. T. G. Clemson, November 21, 1846, and Hamilton to Calhoun, October 12, 1846, both in Calhoun Papers, CU.

11. J. C. Calhoun to Lumpkin, December 13, 1846, in Calhoun Papers, DU; Calhoun to James E. Calhoun, December 13, 1846, in Calhoun Papers, CU.

Scott and Taylor, "neither of whom had any sympathies with the Government." When Polk proposed Senator Thomas Hart Benton of Missouri as lieutenant general in command, Calhoun was "decidedly opposed." Polk did not detail Calhoun's reasons, but Calhoun feared that a victorious general would become the next president, and he considered Benton a hostile rival.

The president next proposed requesting $2 million from Congress for negotiations. Calhoun approved that amount, and more if needed. Polk then asked for Calhoun's views on boundaries. The senator viewed Upper California as important to the United States and agreed with Polk's suggestion of annexing New Mexico. As for Lower California, Calhoun "cared but little" for it.

The president, obviously pleased with the meeting, observed Calhoun to be in "a good humour." Nevertheless, Calhoun solemnly warned against any treaty with a restriction on slavery. "I told him," Polk wrote, "if such a Treaty was made Slavery would probably never exist in these Provinces. To this he readily assented, and said he did not desire to extend Slavery; but that if the slavery restriction was put into a Treaty, it would involve a principle, and . . . he would vote against it." [12]

More and more Calhoun was given to pessimism regarding the war and its consequences. There was no end in sight; the Whig party would be victorious in the next election; the national debt would soar; and the tariff would be raised. But increasingly his chief concern was the Wilmot Proviso, for he became convinced that both northern Whigs and Democrats, in "a bold & dangerous plot," were determined to exclude the South from the benefit of any Mexican cession. The proviso would be used, he warned, "as an instrument to destroy us." To his daughter Anna he added: "When the time comes to act, I shall do what duty requires be the consequences what they may. I desire above all things to save the whole [Union]; but if that cannot be, to save the portion where

12. Quaife, *Diary of James K. Polk*, II, 282–84; Polk to J. C. Calhoun, December 19, 1846, in Calhoun Papers, CU. Calhoun's view of the victorious general was expressed to Duff Green, April 17, 1847, in Jameson, *Correspondence of John C. Calhoun*, 727–28.

Providence has cast my lot, at all events." Calhoun's neighbor, Congressman R. F. Simpson, shared his alarm but promised that when the issue was joined, southern congressmen were "resolved to do their duty."

As Chaplain Morrison says, "The Proviso represented to the South a denial of the very southern equality upon which Calhoun and the other southern politicians insisted so vehemently in their constitutional arguments." And there was reason for Calhoun and other southerners to worry. Although President Polk and most northern Democrats wished to avoid agitation over slavery, certainly until a peace treaty with Mexico was concluded, the issue would not go away. Silas Wright, presidential hopeful of the antislavery Barnburner faction of the New York Democratic party, had suffered defeat for governor in the November elections, when many Hunker Democrats failed to support him. The Barnburners hoped the antislavery issue would resurrect Wright's political fortunes and help place him in the White House. To further their plans Congressman Preston King, a New York Barnburner, reintroduced the Wilmot Proviso in the House on January 4, 1847.[13]

On Christmas Eve Polk invited Calhoun to a dinner party at the White House and asked him to remain after the other guests had departed. Once again Polk sought Calhoun's support for a lieutenant general to command the army; once again Calhoun refused. He also objected to an expedition against Mexico City because he feared it would encounter "almost insuperable difficulties" and prolong the war indefinitely. Instead, Calhoun suggested a cordon of military posts to hold sufficient territory to indemnify the United States.[14] Thus Calhoun proposed his defensive policy to the president as he was later to do in Congress.

13. J. C. Calhoun to Mrs. T. G. Clemson, December 27, 1846; to T. G. Clemson, December 30, 1846, in Calhoun Papers, CU; Calhoun to David Johnson, January 13, 1847, in Calhoun Papers, SCL; Calhoun to Conner, January 14, 1847, in Conner Papers; R. F. Simpson to G. F. Townes, December 31, 1846, in Townes Family Papers; Philip M. Hamer, *The Secession Movement in South Carolina, 1847–1852* (Allentown, Pa., 1918), 1–3; Chaplain W. Morrison, *Democratic Politics and Sectionalism: The Wilmot Proviso Controversy* (Chapel Hill, N.C., 1967), 25–26, 31–34, 66.

14. Quaife, *Diary of James K. Polk*, II, 292–93; J. C. Calhoun to T. G. Clemson, January 30, 1847, in Calhoun Papers, CU.

Calhoun also revealed his defensive plan to several friends, including Governor Johnson. Once the military posts were established, America should offer to settle its differences "justly & liberally." Should Mexico refuse, America should do no more than hold what territory it controlled. Such a position could be maintained by regular forces, at little additional expense. In Calhoun's opinion, the adoption of such a policy "would save millions, & thousands of valuable lives; and save us from many & great disasters." [15]

While Calhoun privately discussed his defensive policy and awaited a favorable moment to announce it, he envisioned his own political fortunes on the rise. At the end of January he ecstatically remarked to his son-in-law: "My friends think I never stood higher, or stronger than I now do. Time has justified the wisdom of my course, in reference to the Mexican war; and the caucus machinery, which has ever been opposed to me, is evidently giving away." [16]

For the president, however, January proved to be a bleak month. At a cabinet meeting on the second, Secretary of State James Buchanan objected to the "bad policy" of sending an army against Mexico City. He preferred a defensive policy of holding California and New Mexico, combined with military aid to prospective rebels in northern Mexico. Polk discovered that all other cabinet members seemed inclined to agree. In addition, whereas he felt General Taylor "wholly incompetent" for his command, the Senate shot down his proposal for a lieutenant general. Calhoun was elated. To top it all, Congress wrangled the entire month mainly about slavery and failed to pass Polk's Ten-Regiment Bill, much needed to strengthen the army. [17]

For much of this difficulty the president blamed Calhoun and his small coterie of friends in the Senate. On February 8, when it

15. J. C. Calhoun to David Johnson, January 13, 1847, in Calhoun Papers, SCL; Calhoun to Conner, January 14, 1847, in Conner Papers; Lumpkin to Calhoun, January 6, 1847, in Calhoun Papers, CU.
16. J. C. Calhoun to T. G. Clemson, January 30, 1847, in Calhoun Papers, CU.
17. Quaife, *Diary of James K. Polk*, II, 304–59; J. C. Calhoun to James E. Calhoun, January 16, 1847, in Calhoun Papers, DU. The chief argument about the Ten-Regiment Bill was whether the regiments would consist of volunteers or regular army personnel. See *Congressional Globe*, 29th Cong., 2nd Sess., 157, 276–77.

appeared likely that the Ten-Regiment Bill would be defeated in the Senate, Polk recorded his bitter feelings toward Calhoun, who had opposed the bill as it then stood. He attributed Calhoun's obstruction to presidential aspirations and disappointment at not being retained in the cabinet. Polk added, "I now consider him the most mischievous man in the Senate to my administration." Nevertheless, the president was greatly relieved two days later when the Ten-Regiment Bill passed the Senate. The following day he signed the bill into law.[18]

The news that Calhoun would soon speak out on the Mexican War was divulged by the *Mercury* on January 20 and soon taken up by other papers. The gist of his defensive policy was generally known, and several papers published editorials of approval. The Charleston *Evening News* remarked that the nation "appears to look to him as the expounder of its true policy with regard to Mexico." [19] Calhoun's most telling boost, however, came from an erstwhile Whig antagonist, General Waddy Thompson, Jr..

In a lengthy article on February 5 in the *National Intelligencer*, the Whigs's Washington journal, Thompson gave the most scathing criticism of Polk's war policy ever pronounced by a South Carolinian. As recently as December, he recalled, the president had denied that conquest of Mexican territory was an American object. Now, he learned, Senator Ambrose Sevier, chairman of the Foreign Relations Committee, had declared that America would never make peace without the cession of New Mexico and California. Much alarmed at that prospect, Thompson argued that the United States had neither the right to seize those territories nor the right to force Mexico to sell them. He rhetorically asked,

18. Quaife, *Diary of James K. Polk*, II, 371–72. A conference committee report on the Ten-Regiment Bill was defeated 22–18, with Calhoun, A. P. Butler, and David Yulee in the majority. There was a dispute over the president's constitutional authority to appoint "inferior officers" during a congressional recess and over just what constituted "inferior officers." Calhoun's strict construction caused him to oppose the report. When the bill was passed on February 10, there was no roll call. *Congressional Globe*, 29th Cong., 2nd Sess., 349, 377.

19. Charleston *Mercury*, January 20, 1847; Georgetown *Winyah Observer*, February 10, 1847, quoting Charleston *Evening News*; Columbia *South Carolinian*, January 20, 1847; Pendleton *Messenger*, January 29, 1847; Anderson *Gazette*, February 5, 1847.

"What will the world say of this now openly confessed war of conquest?"

Thompson regarded the war "not only inexpedient, but unjust." The talk about Mexican spoliation of American citizens' property was an afterthought and a poor excuse for war. He doubted that public opinion in America supported the war, and he knew Mexican opinion universally considered America's part as "flagrantly and criminally unjust." Looking ahead, the former minister to Mexico cautioned that in time America would probably need a strong and friendly Mexico as an ally against some powerful European nation.

Thompson also predicted a long conflict unless the United States reduced Mexico to defenselessness by "a vigorous prosecution" of the war. Such an approach would encounter grave difficulties. To supply and provision an army in an assault on the Mexican capital and to garrison its approaches would cost $100 million. He reminded readers that the small-scale Seminole War had cost $42 million. Moreover, American forces would have to remain in Mexico for at least a year to produce the desired effect. Meanwhile, casualties from disease and Santa Anna's attacks might soar to twenty thousand. Such anticipated results gave him grave concern both for the widows and orphans in America, as well as for "the horrible consequences" to the Mexicans.

Sooner or later, Thompson warned, America would have to cease operations in Mexico. The administration could never do so more gracefully than at the present. The United States had control of the disputed territory between the Nueces and Rio Grande and should not further press "a gallant enemy." Finally, he proposed a public declaration of what territory the administration intended to hold. In this, America should be "generous and forbearing" and pay for that territory to which it had "no better title than the right of conquest." And, as if in anticipation of Calhoun's forthcoming speech, Thompson suggested establishing defensive border posts beyond which the United States should cease operations. In time, he believed, Mexico would be inclined to peace.[20]

20. Reprinted in Greenville *Mountaineer*, March 12, 1847.

Although the Charleston correspondent of the *South Carolinian* said that Thompson's article had attracted "considerable attention among many of our people who have great confidence in the judgment and peculiar competence of the writer," most of the state's press for the moment did not comment about the article.[21] The fact of the matter was that Thompson's pronouncement was overshadowed by Calhoun's hour-long speech in the Senate on the Three Million Bill on February 9. The president had requested $3 million for negotiations with Mexico. Undoubtedly, Calhoun had read Thompson's article, and the two men may have collaborated, for there was a striking resemblance of views. Calhoun also knew that he had been excommunicated by the administration because of his opposition to the Ten-Regiment Bill.

Speaking without notes, Calhoun explained to the Senate that he preferred a boundary along the Rio Grande to the 32nd parallel and on to the Gulf of California. He contended that a string of forts could easily defend the border. His proposed boundary was on a line that Polk himself had suggested the previous December. Beyond that the senator and the president disagreed.

Calhoun objected to Polk's efforts to conquer a peace because of costs, unfavorable climate, high casualties to be involved, and uncertain results. The national debt would soar, free trade would end for a generation, and the United States would have the problem of an alien people on its hands. He noted, as had Thompson, the high cost and difficulty involved in defeating "a paltry band of Indians" in Florida. Calhoun did not wish to humble or weaken Mexico. In fact, it was his "deep conviction" that prosperity and the maintenance of free institutions in both countries depended on America's pursuing "a just and liberal course" toward Mexico. His proposal offered an escape from a war "deeply to be deplored."[22]

Writing a few days later, Calhoun said his speech had made "a deep impression," the best proof of which was the strong attack

21. Columbia *South Carolinian*, February 17, 1847.
22. *Congressional Globe*, 29th Cong., 2nd Sess., Appendix, 323–27; Edgefield *Advertiser*, March 3, 1847. See also Wiltse, *Calhoun: Sectionalist*, 297–300.

made upon him by the Washington *Union*, the administration organ. He foresaw disaster for the party and the nation should the war continue. The *Courier*'s Washington correspondent hailed Calhoun's speech as "perhaps, one of his greatest triumphs." It had excited great public interest by "the practicability and plausibility of his views." By contrast, the correspondent called Senator Lewis Cass's reply "able and ingenious, but not satisfactory." The *Mercury* likewise lauded Calhoun's speech as "one of the most masterly" ever delivered in the Senate. Calhoun had presented a middle course between the Whig policy of withdrawal and the Democratic policy of conquest.[23]

Elsewhere in the state, Calhoun drew praise from the *Winyah Observer*, the Charleston *Evening News*, and the Pendleton *Messenger*. The first observed, "It appears that we have already quiet possession of two thirds of Mexico, and with no use for that." On the other hand, the Greenville *Mountaineer*, while respectful, did not think the present "exactly a suitable time" to implement Calhoun's defensive plan.[24]

From private sources the senator received many letters of commendation and advice, but James Gadsden cautioned that while the war was "decidedly" unpopular, "great efforts" had been made to inflame the public against Mexico. There were too many "who mistake what honor means and who are desirous to inflict chastisement . . . as well as secure ample indemnity." Hence, he doubted that Calhoun's proposed boundary, though "no doubt correct in principle," would satisfy the public. As an alternative, Gadsden suggested annexing the entire lower Rio Grande valley.[25]

Calhoun also had his revenge against Thomas Ritchie, the Virginia editor of the Washington *Union*. On February 9, only a few

23. J. C. Calhoun to T. G. Clemson, February 17, 1847, in Calhoun Papers, CU; Charleston *Courier*, February 13, 15, 1847; Charleston *Mercury*, February 16, 1847.

24. Georgetown *Winyah Observer*, February 17, 1847; Pendleton *Messenger*, February 12, citing Charleston *Evening News*, and February 19, 1847; Greenville *Mountaineer*, February 19, 1847.

25. Gadsden to J. C. Calhoun, February 13, 1847; G. F. Lindsay to Calhoun, February 23, 1847; P. S. Buckingham to Calhoun, February 21, 1847; Thomas Fitman to Calhoun, February 24, 1847; Lumpkin to Calhoun, March 11, 1847; J. Gregg to Calhoun, February 17, 1847, all in Calhoun Papers, CU.

hours after Calhoun's speech, the *Union* carried a contributed article by "Vindicator," entitled "Another Mexican Victory." While referring to the Ten-Regiment Bill, but calling no names, the article was clearly a challenge to Calhoun. The next day Senator David L. Yulee, a Calhoun lieutenant from Florida, moved successfully to exclude the editors of the *Union* from the floor of the Senate. The irate president recorded in his diary, February 13, "The foul deed was perpetrated by the votes of the undivided Federal [Whig] Senators, and Senators Calhoun & Butler of S. C. & Yulee and [James D.] Westcott of Florida." Calhoun's little group became known as the "balance of power" party.[26]

As indicated, of chief importance to Calhoun was the support of the *Mercury*. It frequently tilted with the *Union* and other Calhoun opponents. On February 1, editor J. M. Clapp was replaced by Colonel John E. Carew as "proprietor and conductor." In announcing editorial policy, Carew, a businessman and legislator, promised his influence for a vigorous prosecution of the war—in other words, support of the president's policy. But whatever the new editor's intentions, he changed his tune shortly after Calhoun's February 9 speech. William Gilmore Simms attributed Carew's support of Calhoun to financial need. Also, the dreaded Wilmot Proviso was looming on the horizon once more, and no Palmetto journal could disagree with Calhoun's position on that vital matter.[27]

During January and February events in Congress shaped up badly for the proslavery forces. In the debate on a bill to establish territorial government in Oregon without slavery, southerners,

---

26. *Congressional Globe*, 29th Cong., 2nd Sess., 366; Quaife, *Diary of James K. Polk*, II, 376. The Ritchie incident is discussed in Wiltse, *Calhoun: Sectionalist*, 299–301, and Joseph G. Rayback, *Free Soil: The Election of 1848* (Lexington, Ky., 1970), 31–32.

27. Charleston *Mercury*, February 1, 15, 1847; Charleston *Courier*, February 2, 1847. Simms wrote J. H. Hammond: "The truth is Carew is or will be soon a needy man. I am satisfied that some of his editorials already proceed from Elmore's hand." Later he added: "We know the cost of such a paper as his & in his hands it can never be made to pay expenses. He must go to the Banks and be enslaved & bought up," March 29, April 4, 1847, in Oliphant, Odell, and Eaves (eds.), *Letters of William Gilmore Simms*, II, 291–92, 298–99.

led by Armistead Burt, attempted unsuccessfully to commit the House to the principle of the Missouri Compromise. Then on February 15 the House, 115 to 106, amended the Three Million Bill by adding the Wilmot Proviso.[28] Debate on that explosive issue soon spilled over into the Senate.

On the eighteenth A. P. Butler addressed the upper house. He spoke kindly of the president and avoided censuring the administration for going to war. But he had no desire to humiliate Mexico, and, with the Wilmot Proviso uttermost in his mind, Butler repeated, "I do not want any territory." He feared a bitter wrangle if America acquired Mexican land below 36°30′. In his peroration he vowed, "I would quit this war, with all its calamities and losses rather than incur the dreadful consequences predicted, so far as regards our institutions hereafter." The *Mercury* more succinctly stated that a western cession was "of little moment to the Southern States compared with maintenance of their just rights in the Union." [29]

The next day, February 19, during the Senate debate on the Three Million Bill, Calhoun seized the opportunity to attack the Wilmot Proviso. He offered four resolutions defending slaveholders' rights and promised to speak on the issue later. His longtime antagonist Benton objected to using the Senate's time with "such a string of abstractions." Nevertheless, the Senate ordered the printing of the resolutions. Later in the day Senator Sam Houston (Texas), defending the administration's war policy, inveighed against Calhoun's defensive line as too costly to maintain. It would require 10,000 troops and a battalion of cavalry. Besides, it would not bring Mexico to terms. In Houston's opinion the United States could and should conquer Mexico.

As the Senate chamber quieted down, Calhoun rose to defend

28. Burt's amendment to the Oregon measure was defeated 113 to 82. The bill passed 133 to 35, with the five members of the South Carolina delegation present voting nay. *Congressional Globe*, 29th Cong., 2nd Sess., 187, 198, 424–25.

29. *Ibid.*, 447–50; Charleston *Mercury*, February 15, 1847. Governor David Johnson later praised Butler's support of Calhoun on the Mexican War as having given "universal satisfaction." To P. M. Butler, July 9, 1847, in "Documents of the Palmetto Regiment," 113.

himself. After repeating some of his earlier arguments, he then
focused his attention on Houston's claim of 10,000 men to defend the border. How many had Texas used? Houston was forced
to admit that the common citizens had to be their own defenders.
Benton, Cass, and others scurried about to aid their Texas colleague. After consultation, Houston revealed that Texas had had
about 2,500 men, to which Calhoun replied that he proposed a
force of only 4,000. Looking calmly about the chamber, he vehemently declared: "I know the ground I stand upon. I have indicated the course of the administration. It must be followed." A
northern Whig journal called Calhoun's performance a "memo-
rable declaration! Never was anything more electric." [30]

On February 24 Senator Calhoun came under another attack
from administration forces. In a prolonged assault Benton accused
Calhoun of responsibility for the war by the manner in which he
brought Texas into the Union. Moreover, if Calhoun had known
Taylor's march to the Rio Grande would provoke hostilities, it
was his "solemn duty" to warn the president. In a "withering reply" the South Carolinian gladly accepted credit for Texas annexation. After reiterating how the war might have been averted, he
inferred one thing from Benton's "unprovoked attack," and that
was the unpopularity of the war. There could be no mistake. However, little was decided by those acrimonious exchanges near the
end of the session, except possibly to deepen the gulf between
Calhoun and the administration. In the end the southerners did
not fare too badly, for they persuaded the Senate to delete the
Wilmot Proviso from the Three Million Bill, and the House, on
March 3, accepted the Senate's amended version. [31]

The congressional debates over the Wilmot Proviso had stirred
the entire South Carolina press, which wholeheartedly lauded
Calhoun for his resolutions of February 19—never debated or
voted on. From Charleston, Calhoun's friend F. H. Elmore wrote:

30. *Congressional Globe*, 29th Cong., 2nd Sess., 455, 459–60; Abbeville *Banner*, May
17, 1847, quoting Boston *Courier*.
31. Greenville *Mountaineer*, March 5, 1847; *Congressional Globe*, 29th Cong., 2nd
Sess., 494–501, 555–56, 573. The South Carolina congressional delegation unanimously accepted the amended Three Million Bill.

"Your resolutions & speeches upon them have the undivided approval I think of the people [.] I do not think I have ever seen you sustain yourself with more power." [32] This was heartening news for the elderly political veteran. When Congress adjourned March 4, Calhoun departed that same evening for Charleston to issue a call for southern unity.

Suffering from a severe cold when he arrived in Charleston on the sixth, Calhoun rested over the weekend, and a rally planned for Monday was postponed one day to allow him further time to recuperate. On the appointed evening he was escorted to New Theatre, where he was greeted with almost deafening cheers from an overflowing assembly. Hundreds of spectators were turned away. The prominent political and civic leaders of the city were present, and a Committee of Twenty-five presented resolutions, with a lengthy report, condemning the Wilmot Proviso. The gathered assembly unanimously approved the resolutions and also thanked Senators Calhoun and Butler and Congressman I. E. Holmes for their services in Congress.

The chief purpose of the meeting was to offer a forum for Calhoun to deliver a major address. He began by surveying the danger the Wilmot Proviso posed for the South and its institutions. Under constant prodding of an abolitionist minority, both political parties in the free states were seeking to deny the South its equal rights in the public domain. Thus, without specifically saying so, Calhoun clearly showed that any Mexican cession was fraught with danger.

Calhoun repeated, as so often in the past, that his object was to preserve the Union—if it could be done without surrendering the slave states' equality. He therefore proposed southern unity without distinction of party, and he further proposed the abolition of national party conventions to nominate presidential candidates because they were dominated by the numerically superior

32. Elmore to J. C. Calhoun, February 26, 1847; Allston to Calhoun, February 25, 1847, in Calhoun Papers, CU; Abbeville *Banner*, February 24, March 3, 1847; Georgetown *Winyah Observer*, March 10, 1847; Greenville *Mountaineer*, March 5, 1847.

North. Prolonged applause from the audience followed the conclusion of his speech, which was widely publicized in the press.
Mitchell King, a prominent Charleston merchant, exclaimed,
"May God in mercy grant that the voice of the Prophet may not
have been raised in vain."[33]

Whereas Calhoun received overwhelming support in South
Carolina for his Charleston bid for southern unity, elsewhere in
the South the reception was mixed. There was initial support from
many Whigs and Democrats, but a large number of Democrats
loyal to the administration viewed Calhoun's proposal as a selfish
attempt to gain the presidency at the expense of splintering the
party. The president himself was of that opinion. On April 6 he
recorded: "I remarked to Mr. Mason that Mr. Calhoun had become perfectly desperate in his aspirations to the Presidency, and
had seized upon this sectional question as the only means of sustaining himself in his present fallen condition. . . . He is wholly
selfish, and I am satisfied has no patriotism."[34]

James H. Hammond held much the same view. Writing to
Simms, he regarded Calhoun's appeal for southern unity as tam-
pering with the vital interests of the South for the "vile purpose"
of throwing the presidential election into the House of Representatives, where he hoped to be one of the three highest candidates.
Calhoun must have been "demented" to play that sort of game.
He had "not only prostrated his judgment, but sapped his patriotism." Hammond believed Calhoun hated Polk and wished to
prove himself right about the war. He added, "But if I mistake
not Calhoun has cut his throat this time & has made poor [A.P.]
Butler cut his in spite of all his affected independence." Simms
agreed. He viewed Calhoun's action as a calculated move to draw
Whig support to his candidacy.[35]

33. Charleston *Courier*, March 10, 1847; Columbia *South Carolinian*, March 17, 1847;
    Edgefield *Advertiser*, March 17, 1847; Greenville *Mountaineer*, April 2, 1847;
    Wiltse, *Calhoun: Sectionalist*, 308–311; Mitchell King to J. C. Calhoun, March 23,
    1847, in Calhoun Papers, CU. Holmes also addressed the meeting to rousing cheers.
34. John H. Schroeder, *Mr. Polk's War: American Opposition and Dissent, 1846–1848*
    (Madison, 1973), 132; Quaife, *Diary of James K. Polk*, II, 458–59.
35. J. H. Hammond to Simms, February 23, March 24, April 1, 19, 1847; Simms to
    Hammond, March 2, 1847, in Hammond Papers, LC. However, Hammond's strong

That Calhoun still desired to be president, that some of his friends were promoting his candidacy, that his political fortunes seemed to be rising in late 1846 have already been noted. Not the least of his difficulties was the Wilmot Proviso. His Virginia friend, R. K. Crallé, feared that Silas Wright's clique was pushing that hated instrument for the principal purpose of placing Calhoun "in direct opposition to the Administration and the War," thus cutting him off from the Democratic party. And in Simms's opinion some of Calhoun's "pretended friends" were plotting his defeat to put him "on the shelf forever."[36]

Nevertheless, Calhoun's campaign for president appeared to be making headway until February, 1847. His opposition to the Ten-Regiment Bill and his speech of the ninth angered administration supporters. Then, he and his "balance of power" clique teamed with the Whigs to censure *Union* editor Ritchie. Some charged that the attack on Ritchie, an influential Virginia Democratic boss, was part of Calhoun's presidential maneuvers. Whatever the purpose, the censure backfired. Virginians arose to the defense of their editor, and, as Hammond correctly noted, "destroyed utterly" Calhoun's prospects in that state.[37]

Many regarded the attack on Ritchie as a slap at Polk. Calhoun was consequently read out of the party. Yet, the senator publicly denied being a presidential candidate. To his colleagues in the Senate he hotly declared, "I appeal to every friend . . . if my whole course of conduct has not been this: that I would not ac-

feelings against Calhoun were not publicly known. After Calhoun's death the Charleston City Council persuaded Hammond to deliver a eulogy. "Hammond's Eulogy Upon Calhoun," *Southern Quarterly Review*, IV (July, 1851), 107–17.

36. A. T. Hayne to Burt, October 20, 1846, in Burt Papers; Holmes to J. C. Calhoun, October 2, 1846; Hamilton to Calhoun, October 12, 1846; R. K. Crallé to Calhoun, January 19, 1847; Calhoun to Mrs. T. G. Clemson, November 21, 1846, all in Calhoun Papers, CU; Simms to J. H. Hammond, December 25, 1846, in Oliphant, Odell, and Eaves (eds.), *Letters of William Gilmore Simms*, II, 245–46. For details of Calhoun's candidacy see Joseph G. Rayback, "The Presidential Ambitions of John C. Calhoun, 1844–1848," *Journal of Southern History*, XIV (August, 1948), 331–56.
37. Rayback, "Presidential Ambitions of John C. Calhoun," 338–39; Rayback, *Free Soil*, 31–32; J. H. Hammond to Simms, April 1, 1847, in Hammond Papers, LC.

cept the Presidency, unless it comes from the voice of the American people, and then only from a sense of duty, and taken as an obligation." Clearly he had not closed the door.[38]

It was after the reaction to Ritchie's censure became public that Calhoun introduced his proslavery resolutions in the Senate and made his bid at Charleston for southern unity. But neither his plan for southern unity nor hopes for Whig support, if he entertained such, bore fruit. In fact, his call for southern unity was doomed at the start without Ritchie and the Virginia Democrats. Calhoun often overrated his strength. Beverly Tucker, another Virginian, charged him with being "the most unskillful leader of a party that ever wielded a truncheon." He could always find "the most unpopular side of every question," said Tucker. Yet, Calhoun's adversary, William Gilmore Simms, conceded that he was "a very remarkable man, and, in certain respects, quite a tactician," a leader well above Pickens, Elmore, the Rhetts, and others.[39]

James H. Hammond privately admitted that Calhoun's view on the war "may not be far from right." He, too, had opposed the war from the beginning but now believed retreat to the Rio Grande would be fatal to the nation. American withdrawal should be done only "in a blaze of glory." He was therefore jubilant when news of Taylor's victory at Buena Vista reached Charleston on March 28, for now the "unfortunate *silly*" Calhoun had been frustrated in his war plans. "Alas how are the mighty fallen," gloated Hammond. A few other South Carolina political leaders agreed with Hammond but generally remained silent. The Richmond *Whig* aptly remarked that "however violently Mr. Calhoun may be assailed elsewhere, it cannot be doubted that he will be sustained with almost unanimity by the people of South Carolina."[40]

38. Charleston *Mercury*, February 17, 1847; Wiltse, *Calhoun: Sectionalist*, 302.
39. Tucker, quoted in Rayback, "Presidential Ambitions of John C. Calhoun," 340; Simms to J. H. Hammond, December 25, 1846, in Oliphant, Odell, and Eaves (eds.), *Letters of William Gilmore Simms*, II, 245–46; Morrison, *Democratic Politics*, 47.
40. J. H. Hammond to Simms, February 23, March 24, April 1, 1847; to M. C. M.

What caused Calhoun to choose the course he pursued is questionable. It seems clear that as late as December, 1846, President Polk was anxious for his support and held no malice toward him for his position on the war bill. Nor did the president press him to support his bill calling for a lieutenant general to command the army. Moreover, both men were generally agreed on the annexation of California and New Mexico. As for Calhoun's constitutional objection to the Ten-Regiment Bill, that was hardly worth a break, and the bill passed the Senate anyway. The major differences between Calhoun and Polk centered on offensive operations to be conducted against Mexico and, apparently, political jealousy.

Logically, Calhoun's presidential ambitions would have been better served if he had followed Hamilton's advice and given the administration "a liberal and cordial support" whenever possible. His son-in-law also might have benefited. Speaking French fluently, Thomas G. Clemson enjoyed the life of a diplomat in Brussels. He was quite anxious for a more prestigious and better-paying post and spoke to his father-in-law on several occasions about his chances to become minister to Prussia or Spain. In February, 1846, Calhoun wrote: "I can give you no reason to expect such good luck. I do not think Mr. Polk much disposed to favour my friends, though I do not think him hostile." Understanding the spoils system well, Calhoun failed to follow a policy that might have given Clemson a chance for promotion. Why then did he not give Polk more substantial support? At the outbreak of the war and for many months after, he was reluctant to criticize the administration publicly in the manner of his February 9 speech. Perhaps Polk was right; perhaps Calhoun hoped to reach the White House by way of united southern support on the slavery issue. Perhaps Hamilton was right when he said, "I know how

---

Hammond, March 12, 1847, in Hammond Papers, LC; Columbia *South Carolinian*, March 24, 1847, quoting Richmond *Whig*. Others who disagreed with Calhoun's war policy included former Senator W. C. Preston, and Congressmen Black and Sims. See Georgetown *Winyah Observer*, April 7, 1847; Green to J. C. Calhoun, March 6, 1847; Charles Webb to Calhoun, March 29, 1847, in Calhoun Papers, CU.

hard you find it to modify principle by the sway and influence of circumstances." [41]

Senator Benton's criticism went further and was more caustic. He quoted a letter—probably authentic—from Calhoun to an Alabama legislator in which the South Carolinian declared that the Wilmot Proviso "may be made the occasion of successfully asserting our equality and rights by enabling us to *force* the issue on the North." Calhoun further explained: "I would regard any compromise or adjustment of the proviso, or even its defeat, without meeting the danger in its whole length and breadth, as very unfortunate for us. It would lull us to sleep again without removing the danger." He was particularly disturbed by a recent Pennsylvania law which, in his opinion, violated the constitutional provisions regarding fugitive slaves, and he proposed, if necessary, southern economic retaliation. His critic Benton attributed the Pennsylvania law partly to Calhoun's agitation, and he believed Calhoun's ultimate goal was disunion.[42]

Calhoun obviously was looking past the Wilmot Proviso, for he had privately admitted that there was little likelihood that slavery would move beyond the Rio Grande. Nor was there likelihood that the slavery issue would be quieted, since it now appeared certain that there would be a Mexican cession of territory and that the abolitionists would keep pressure on Congress for the Wilmot Proviso. This was the dilemma. Senator Butler saw it when he cried out, "I do not want any territory," but he would not refuse to accept some of the Pacific. In the debate on Oregon, Armistead Burt told the House he was "heated with no lust" for territory, but "a point of honor cannot be satisfied unless Mexico makes some reparation." And Richland legislator W. F. DeSaussure regarded the acquisition of territory "a curse" because the North would insist on the Wilmot Proviso, yet he too desired a treaty that would "not compromise national honor." [43]

41. T. G. Clemson to J. C. Calhoun, November 28, 1845, January 30, 1846; Calhoun to Clemson, February 25, August 19, 1846; Hamilton to Calhoun, June 21, 1846, in Calhoun Papers, CU.
42. Benton *Thirty Years' View*, II, 698–700; Wiltse, *Calhoun: Sectionalist*, 532.
43. *Congressional Globe*, 29th Cong., 2nd Sess., 196, 447–50; DeSaussure to J. H. Hammond, March 13, 1847, in Hammond Papers, LC.

Calhoun faced the same dilemma. He clearly saw that public opinion would demand reparations from Mexico in the form of territory. He was conscious of the South's minority position, and in his own mind had genuine reason to fear the influence of the abolitionists in the northern wings of both political parties. Thus, his attempt to unite the South against the antislavery agitation "may have been an honest effort," according to Joseph Rayback.[44]

Calhoun had other real fears about the consequences of the war. Perhaps, then, he deserted the administration, not because of presidential aspirations, but despite them. His break was ironical, for Silas Wright, a leading presidential hopeful of the Wilmot Proviso proponents, died unexpectly in August. But for Calhoun there was no turning back. While he rested at his Fort Hill home, Duff Green in Washington kept him informed of the attacks upon him by the *Union*. According to Green, party leaders, by intimidation, hoped to discourage further desertions. Calhoun now had no alternative "but submission or resistance." Meanwhile, the war continued.[45]

44. Rayback, "Presidential Ambitions of John C. Calhoun," 353–54.
45. Green to J. C. Calhoun, March 17, 1847, in Calhoun Papers, CU; *DAB*, X, 565–67.

CHAPTER 5 *Pray for the Return*
of the Poor Volunteers

ON MARCH 9, 1847, the same day as Calhoun's call for southern unity, General Winfield Scott launched his attack on Vera Cruz. His army, organized into three divisions, two of regulars and one of volunteers, had sailed from Lobos a week earlier. The vanguard arrived at Vera Cruz on March 4, but landings were delayed until the area could be thoroughly reconnoitered. Following staff consultations, Scott decided to assault Collado Beach, two or three miles south of Vera Cruz. Surprisingly, there was no Mexican opposition, and more than 8,600 Americans scrambled ashore without incident. The Palmetto regiment was part of Brigadier General John A. Quitman's brigade in Major General Robert Patterson's volunteer division. The two divisions of regulars were commanded by Brigadier Generals William J. Worth and David E. Twiggs.[1]

The South Carolina volunteers had seemed happy enough to leave Lobos, where comforts had been minimal, provisions poor, water hardly potable, training monotonous, and disease on the increase, especially mumps and diarrhea. On top of these discomforts, the troops had yet to receive their uniforms or see "the colour of Uncle Sam's money." The news of the invasion raised their morale, and many sanguine volunteers agreed with Captain J. Foster Marshall that the treaty of peace with Mexico was "to

1. Gettys, "To Conquer a Peace," 245; Bauer, *Mexican War*, 240–44.

be conquered, *sealed with our blood*." More than nine hundred Palmettos were ready and eager for the invasion.[2]

Upon boarding ship at Lobos, the South Carolina volunteers received only dry bread for dinner. Private William S. Johnson, of Columbia, said everyone was soon in "a bad humour, except the officers who feast in the Cabbin." The volunteers' quarters, he recorded, were "second choice to a pig Sty." Thus, they spent a cramped and uncomfortable five days aboard ship before being ordered to disembark. Unfortunate for the restless men, a storm threatened, forcing a postponement of the assault. Goodlett wrote, "So we turned in on the planks, with knapsacks as pillows, and rested, or rather roasted, until morning, for somehow or other it was twice as hot as usuall." The delay continued for two days, while the men became as nervous as "a fiery steed, with rider mounted, champing the restraining bit."[3]

When the delayed landing finally got under way, General Quitman's brigade, which also included regiments from Alabama and Georgia, was in the second wave to hit the beach. They bivouacked the first night without baggage and remained in reserve while other forces moved inland over the sand dunes in an effort to invest Vera Cruz as quickly as possible. When Mexican artillery and cavalry began to harass Scott's advance units, Quitman's brigade was ordered inland on the eleventh to furnish relief. Part of the brigade, including three Palmetto companies, skirmished with and drove off a reported one thousand Mexicans. Although one South Carolina volunteer called it a "fierce engagement" in which enemy artillery gave "some uneasiness," casualties were light.

2. Marshall, in Abbeville *Banner*, March 17, 1847; M. H. Wilson, in *ibid.*, March 24, 1847; Edgefield *Advertiser*, March 31, 1847; Pendleton *Messenger*, April 9, 1847. It was reported that the Palmetto regiment was at it greatest strength in March, 1847, having 966 men on its muster roll. R. G. M. Dunovant, *The Palmetto Regiment, South Carolina Volunteers, 1846–1848. The Battles in the Valley of Mexico, 1847* [Part I], (Columbia, S.C.: 1895), 20. Accuracy of the number may be questioned. A detailed report, company by company, of Palmetto casualties to March 1, 1847, listed 14 deaths, 41 desertions, 11 discharges, 40 ill left behind, and 37 mustered in. Columbia *South Carolinian*, June 22, 1847.
3. John Hammond Moore (ed.), "Private Johnson Fights the Mexicans, 1847–1848," *South Carolina Historical Magazine*, XLVII (October, 1966), 205; Goodlett, in Greenville *Moutaineer*, April 23, 1847; Bauer, *Mexican War*, 242.

Among the Palmettos Lieutenant Colonel Dickinson and three others were slightly wounded. Colonel Butler was pleased that the Palmettos behaved with a coolness "not to be expected among volunteers." Within another two days American troops had pushed their line from sea to sea, completely sealing off Vera Cruz.[4]

During the siege of the doomed city the Americans encountered more difficulty from the weather, annoying insects, and a lack of transport than from the usually ineffectual Mexican artillery. A fierce norther blew in on March 12, cutting off cummunication with the American fleet. Having no tents or blankets, the Palmettos endured the miserable rain and sand as best they could. Food was also in short supply for several days, forcing the men on half rations. In a few instances they were able to round up stray Mexican cattle.

By the sixteenth the food situation had become so critical that Adjutant Cantey rushed word to the commissary to "send *quick* for we are starving." Nevertheless, when supplies arrived, the Palmettos found the commissary fat salt pork and hard biscuit almost inedible. In addition, the water was brackish and disagreeable. When the norther blew itself out, the soldiers were once more at the mercy of the scorching sun. Worst of all were the sand fleas and flies, and there was no relief from their torment. They seemed worse at night when the weary troops were trying to rest —that is, those who had not been detailed to the beach to bring up supplies. One volunteer described the sandy area around Vera Cruz "the most dreary spot" he had ever seen.[5]

With an improvement in the weather on March 17, General Scott landed his artillery, strengthened his siege lines, and on the twenty-second called upon General Juan Morales, the Mexican commander, to surrender Vera Cruz and its massive Fort San Juan

4. John A. Quitman to Eliza Quitman, April 10, 1847, in Quitman Family Papers, SHC; Edgefield *Advertiser*, April 21 (Butler's report), May 5, 1847. Goodlett judged the Mexicans to have "none of our energy; if they had, it would be the greatest country in the world." Greenville *Mountaineer*, April 23, 1847.
5. John A. Quitman to Eliza Quitman, April 10, 1847, in Quitman Family Papers; Charleston *Courier*, April 22, 1847; J. W. Cantey to N. R. Eaves, March 16, 1847, in Eaves Papers; Greenville *Mountaineer*, May 7, 1847; Abbeville *Banner*, April 14, 1847; Bauer, *Mexican War*, 245–48.

de Ulúa. At Morales' refusal Scott ordered a bombardment from land and sea. Another norther struck, drove thirty American ships aground, played havoc with the siege lines, and cut off ammunition from the land-based artillery. On the twenty-fifth the navy resumed landing ammunition. By then the Mexicans were ready to quit. The surrender took place on March 27.[6]

Some years later General Quitman termed the capture of Vera Cruz "one of the most brilliant achievements of Gen. Scott's remarkable campaign." In Colonel Butler's opinion the city surrendered as quickly as it did because of starvation and the effect of the bombardment on the property of private interests. As for the Mexicans, Butler had little regard for "those poor d——ls," who generally cared no more for one government than another. At the surrender of their city they moved out with as much unconcern as "a gang of negroes, going from one cotton field to another." He happily reported that Dickinson was again fit for duty and that with his own "general bad health" he had found Major Gladden's "great efficiency" indispensable.[7]

Immediately after capturing Vera Cruz General Scott turned his attention to the pressing need for beef cattle for provisions and additional horses and mules for transport. To secure these he decided to send an expedition to Alvarado, the center of a ranching area some fifty miles south of Vera Cruz. General Quitman's brigade was selected for an overland march and instructed to coordinate with Commodore Matthew C. Perry's fleet.

On March 31 Quitman's force of 2,200 men, consisting of the Alabama, Georgia, and South Carolina volunteer regiments, and a squadron of cavalry, departed for Alvarado with little expectation of Mexican resistance.[8] Nor did anyone anticipate what a painful and grueling march was in store for the volunteers, each

6. Bauer, *Mexican War*, 249–53.
7. P. M. Butler to David Johnson, [April] 10, 1847, in Columbia *South Carolinian*, May 12, 1847; J. F. H. Claiborne, *Life and Correspondence of John A. Quitman: Major-General, U.S.A., and Governor of the State of Mississippi* (2 vols., New York, 1860), II, 370.
8. John A. Quitman to Eliza Quitman, March 30, 1847, in Quitman Family Papers. W. M. Goodlett was apprehensive that the Palmettos might be used only for garrison duty at Vera Cruz or Alvarado. Greenville *Mountaineer*, April 23, 1847.

of whom carried his own provisions, gear, and forty rounds of ammunition. Few pack animals were available.

Leaving Vera Cruz about midafternoon the Americans were in jovial spirits as they moved southward along the sunlit sandy beach. When darkness fell, they continued by moonlight to the Madellin River, about eight miles from Vera Cruz. They rested well the first night, replenished their canteens with slightly brackish water, and crossed the Madellin the next morning on a makeshift pontoon bridge that Perry's men had hastily constructed. So far so good.

During the second day's march the brigade left the beach after some seven or eight miles and headed inland across a treeless, waterless prairie. The heat became almost unbearable; their canteens were soon empty; but as they had reached no waterhole by sundown, their officers ordered them onward in the darkness. Private H. Judge Moore later wrote, "After night I passed scores of soldiers lying by the road-side, completely exhausted from thirst and fatigue . . . notwithstanding the danger of falling into the hands of prowling bands of guerrillas." Many of the weary volunteers did not straggle into camp until early morning.

About 9 P.M. the thirsty column reached a pond of warm, muddy water, the first they had seen since leaving the beach. Discipline vanished as men and animals together rushed with "most splendid confusion" into the pond. Before half the men could quench their thirst and fill their canteens so much mud had been churned up that even the thirsty horses refused to drink.

During the third day's march the volunteers again exhausted their water supply, poor though it was, and many now suffered from swollen, blistered, and bleeding feet. Discipline was difficult to maintain. On one occasion the sweating and cursing men broke ranks to pursue the mirage of a lake. About midafternoon the brigade reached a pond, much like the one of the previous evening. Quitman tried to encourage his men by telling them he had lived on worse water for several weeks at a time. His story was unconvincing, and many of the volunteers vomited after their first drink. Moore also noticed a dead alligator in the pond.

The column reached the beach again before nightfall and camped in a palmetto grove. As there was no fresh water, the soldiers dug numerous shallow wells, only to have salt water seep in. The brigade had also exhausted its rations and could procure nothing from the commissary before reaching Alvarado. Several private parties, against strict orders, crept into the prairie and slaughtered and roasted wild cattle. The officers obviously had little control over the weary, thirsty, hungry, and footsore troops.

The next morning, their fourth day, the volunteers filled their canteens with salty water that had risen in their little wells overnight. Moore remarked, "It was hard to tell which was its predominating quality, to quench or excite thirst." The march without food or good water, sometimes on the beach, sometimes inland in burning sand, brought the brigade to Alvarado at midafternoon on April 2. The sick and exhausted volunteers—diarrhea and probably amoebic dysentery had set in—entered the town and took up quarters in deserted buildings near the plaza. They encountered no Mexican resistance because the navy had seized the town two days earlier.[9]

Colonel Butler also experienced a painful trip, especially since twenty days of exposure and bad water at Vera Cruz had given him a "cold intermittent fever & the worse Rheumatism—I ever felt, finally—neuralgia." By the time he reached Alvarado he was completely prostrated. He undressed, took some medicine, and went to bed in a filthy room, where he was set upon by fleas, flies, and mosquitoes "too numerous for comfort." His only cheering note in that low, hot, filthy town was a visit by Commodore Perry, who kindly sent him a bottle of wine and a plate of soup.

Butler was also concerned about the well being of the South Carolina volunteers in such a debilitating and unhealthful climate. The fatiguing march had put their patriotism to the test. They had had no comforts, tents, provisions, or transportation.

9. The most detailed account of the march is in H. Judge Moore, *Scott's Campaign*, 44–49. See also Goodlett, in Greenville *Mountaineer*, May 7, 1847; Claiborne, *Life and Correspondence of John A. Quitman*, I, 297–98; P. M. Butler to Bethethland Butler, April 4, 1847, in Butler Papers.

The small vessel with tents and supplies had been wrecked. Theirs was "an odious & bad" service. About 150 Palmettos were suffering from illness and sore feet, 60 of whom were unable to march back to Vera Cruz.[10]

General Quitman's brigade remained in Alvarado for two days. Contrary to Quitman's report of limited success, the mission was, in Butler's words, "a wild goose chase." Most of the inhabitants had fled before Quitman's arrival, and no livestock was procured, though town officials, thankful for the protection of their property, promised to round up five hundred horses for the American commissary. The Mexican citizens who remained during Quitman's occupation were hospitable, and the shopkeepers were quite happy to get American money. On April 4 the brigade began its march back to Vera Cruz; those too ill to do so returned by boat. Among the latter was W. M. Goodlett, who believed it was the only time in his life that he had "rejoiced at such disposition of Providence." He would be content if only the regiment moved to some place with good water.[11]

The failure at Alvarado was due, at least in part, to Lieutenant Charles G. Hunter of the steamer *Scourge*. Ordered to keep watch on Alvarado, Hunter on the evening of March 30 thoughtlessly fired a few rounds at the Mexican fort guarding the mouth of the river. Forewarned, the defenders destroyed their military stores and gunboats and evacuated the town. To complicate matters further, Hunter steamed into the river, seized Alvarado, and followed the retreating garrison several miles farther upstream. Thus, Perry lost an opportunity to seize enemy ships, and Quitman lost a chance for military glory and a supply of livestock. There was a rumor that Quitman and Perry had arranged to arrive at Alvarado simultaneously and "have all the credit to themselves." The thoughtless lieutenant spoiled their plans. Perry was so outraged

---

10. P. M. Butler to Behethland Butler, April 4, 1847, in Butler Papers.
11. P. M. Butler to Behethland Butler, April 4, May 2, 1847, in Butler Papers; Claiborne, *Life and Correspondence of John A. Quitman*, I, 297–98; Goodlett, in Greenville *Mountaineer*, May 7, 1847; H. Judge Moore, *Scott's Campaign*, 49–53.

that he reprimanded Hunter and dismissed him from the squadron. Back in South Carolina Hunter was regarded as a hero. The editor of the *South Carolinian* proclaimed that "this brave officer" should be awarded a medal instead of a reprimand. Others agreed.[12]

On the return to Vera Cruz the weary brigade, by forced marches, arrived at its destination on April 6, too ill and exhausted to move forward for several days. "Saluda" (Lt. Joseph Abney), writing to the *Advertiser*, was of the opinion that Mexican guerrillas could have killed hundreds of American stragglers on the return march had they tried to do so. Even Quitman privately admitted that the "fatiguing march" had forced his exhausted brigade to remain at Vera Cruz when the rest of the army moved out toward Jalapa.[13]

Actually the march to Alvarado and back was a disaster, especially for the Palmetto regiment. The Georgia and Alabama regiments, somewhat acclimated while with General Taylor, suffered fewer casualties than did the unseasoned Carolinians. The Palmetto regiment never really recovered from the trip. When Quitman began his delayed march toward Jalapa, more than a hundred Palmettos remained behind in the hospital.

One Alabama critic contended that the high casualty rate among the Palmettos was due to an excess of fruit and liquor and a lack of cleanliness. A defender retorted that the grueling trip without good water, prolonged by an ignorant and treacherous guide, was sufficient to have killed half the regiment. The same writer then castigated General Scott for neglecting to transport the brigade to Alvarado by water. While the men plodded overland, a surplus of shipping under government pay lay idle in the

12. Bauer, *Mexican War*, 260; Claiborne, *Life and Correspondence of John A. Quitman*, II, 324; H. Judge Moore, *Scott's Campaign*, 52; Goodlett, in Greenville *Mountaineer*, May 7, 1847; Pendleton *Messenger*, April 30, May 28, June 4, 1847. The rumor was repeated by Lt. A. M. Manigault to Henry Manigault, April 9, 1847, in "A Letter from Vera Cruz in 1847," *Southwestern Historical Quarterly*, XVIII (October, 1914), 216–17.
13. Moore, *Scott's Campaign*, 53; "Saluda," in Edgefield *Advertiser*, May 5, 1847; John A. Quitman to Eliza Quitman, April 7, 1847, in Quitman Family Papers.

Vera Cruz harbor. As a consequence, hundreds of the "best blood" of South Carolina had been "cut off in the bloom of their youth." [14]

Thereafter there was much concern for the health of the South Carolina Regiment. The company officers, said Butler, "are uncommonly attentive, and evince great grief at the loss of a comrade. Most conspicuous, was the case this morning [April 9] in the burial of young [Henry S.] Dickson. This young man, with two others about the same age, were the universal admiration of the whole Regiment." Dickson's last letter home, written in a melancholy refrain, had concluded with the words, "Pray for the return of the poor volunteers."

Butler had developed a deep feeling that the rookie volunteers were inappropriate for duty in Mexico. Admittedly, they were less careful about diet and cleanliness than they should have been, but they lacked proper facilities for cooking, and their only water was brackish and invariably caused diarrhea. He feared that many more would die. He regarded them as no more than auxiliaries who should be replaced with regulars. [15]

Lieutenant John B. Moragne affirmed Colonel Butler's assessment of the regiment's poor health. "No day passes without the solemn sound of the death march in the camp," he sadly wrote. The officers' quarters were pleasant and he enjoyed Vera Cruz but was ancious to leave before the *vomito*—yellow fever—struck. Governor Johnson and Senator Calhoun also agreed that the volunteers were unsuited for military duty in Mexico. Calhoun expressed "deep feelings of regret" that they had been called from their homes, an exigency he had tried to prevent. [16]

Colonel Butler defended the medics as giving "all possible at-

14. Pendleton *Messenger*, September 3, 1847, quoting Montgomery *Advertiser*; "Marlborough," in Edgefield *Advertiser*, February 23, 1848. General M'Laurin to Claiborne, July 16, 1860, affirmed the report that on returning from Alvarado the South Carolinians suffered much higher casualties than other troops. Claiborne, *Life and Correspondence of John A. Quitman*, II, 324. No one else mentioned an ignorant and treacherous guide.

15. P. M. Butler to Behethland Butler, April 4, 1847, in Butler Papers; Butler to David Johnson, April 9, 1847, in Columbia *South Carolinian*, May 12, 1847; J. Dickson to John A. Dickson, May 1, [1847], in Dickson Family Papers, SHC.

16. John B. Moragne to Mary E. Davis, April 12, 1847, in Moragne Papers; J. C. Calhoun to David Johnson, January 13, [1847], in Calhoun Papers, SCL.

tention" to the ill Palmettos, but others felt differently, and Adjutant Cantey admitted that the regiment "suffered a great deal from the want of medical attention." The most severe indictment came from Lt. A. M. Manigault. He wrote: "Our medical staff is a most inferior one, not fit for the service, they are unaccustomed to hard work, do not like to soil their hands, but prefer being either in Vera Cruz, or at some other business more agreeable. . . . I really think that some have died thro neglect." Manigault mentioned the case of young Dickson and the surgeon's explanation that he was unaware of his illness until twelve hours before he died.

Part of the difficulty was due to a lack of doctors. Drs. James Davis and Elbert Bland, original appointees, had been delayed in joining the regiment. Dr. F. A. Ross, hired in Mobile, had departed on April 9 for the United States. And after his arrival in Mexico Dr. Davis himself had become so ill he could hardly practice. Cantey appealed to General Quitman for more medics. Meanwhile, the volunteers suffered.[17]

On April 16 General Quitman's brigade began its march toward Jalapa. Lacking sufficient transport for supplies, Quitman ordered each soldier's knapsack loaded with seven days' rations and forty rounds of ammunition. For several days, according to their commander, the brigade toiled through sands infested with "venomous insects," drank "hot and acrid water," endured "sultry oppressive air," and suffered torment at night from fleas, sand flies, and ants. Their hair and beards became matted and their clothes filled with sand.

Four days out from Vera Cruz the troops began to ascend the tableland, and the climate improved greatly. Much to their regret, they were too late to participate in the "glorious victory" of Cerro Gordo on April 17 and 18. When the brigade reached the battlefield on the twenty-second, some two hundred Mexican dead lay scattered about. To W. M. Goodlett "the smell, for miles, was

17. P. M. Butler, in Columbia *South Carolinian*, May 12, 1847; Goodlett, in Greenville *Mountaineer*, May 21, 1847; Adjutant [James Cantey] to [Governor Johnson?], March 20, 1847; to John A. Quitman, April 26, 1847, in "Documents of the Palmetto Regiment," 61–62, 67; Manigault, "Letter from Vera Cruz," 216–17.

very offensive" and continued so all the way to Jalapa. Goodlett observed wounded of both armies dying daily. In a lighter vein he proudly noted the capture of Santa Anna's carriage, his artificial cork leg, and a large sum of money. Shortly, the Anderson *Gazette* humorously called attention to the auction of a "Santa Anna" clock—"warranted to run without stopping." [18]

The American victory at Cerro Gordo and General Worth's capture of Jalapa two days later did not increase Colonel Butler's optimism for an early end of the "profitless" war. While at Alvarado he had expressed the opinion that Mexicans had no national pride and were not worth fighting. He considered them "ignorant in mind[,] imbecile in body & treacherous in character—not equal as a mass to our slaves." But he believed they would accept an American proclaimed peace plan.

A month later at Jalapa Butler feared the Cerro Gordo defeat had "roused the whole nation to bitterness & desperation" and dimmed the prospect for peace. The Abbeville *Banner* likewise entertained the view that the war would be protracted, although the Mexicans "might as well attempt to resist the progress of the sweeping whirlwind as to stay the advance of our troops." Lieutenant L. F. Robertson, of the Charleston Company, expected war "to the knife" and no peace until the American army reached Mexico City. Editor F. W. Symmes of the Pendleton *Messenger* and Lieutenant John B. Moragne forecast an indefinite struggle, if Santa Anna resorted to guerrilla warfare. But General Quitman doubted much further organized resistance, because the Mexicans were "so much panic struck" by Cerro Gordo. [19]

18. Claiborne, *Life and Correspondence of John A. Quitman*, I, 299; John A. Quitman to Louise Quitman, April 23, 1847, in Quitman Family Papers; Goodlett, in Greenville *Mountaineer*, May 21, 1847. W. S. Johnson confirmed Goodlett's nauseating picture of battlefield casualties, which created "a horrible stench." John Hammond Moore (ed.), "Private Johnson Fights the Mexicans," 213. See also "L.F.R." [Lt. Robertson], in Charleston *Courier*, May 21, 1847; Anderson *Gazette*, May 27, 1847.
19. P. M. Butler to Behethland Butler, April 4, May 2, 1847, in Butler Papers; Abbeville *Banner*, April 21, 1847; "LFR," in Charleston *Courier*, May 19, 1847; Pendleton *Messenger*, April 30, 1847; John A. Quitman to Eliza Quitman, May 2, 1847, in Quitman Family Papers; Moragne to Davis, May 3, 1847, in Moragne Papers.

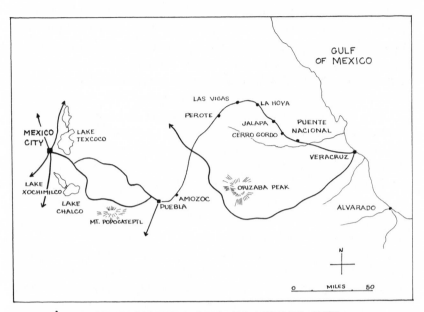

SCOTT'S ROUTE FROM VERA CRUZ TO MEXICO CITY

The Palmettos were highly pleased to reach Jalapa, "the Heaven of Mexico," a small city of about ten thousand people, with a high elevation and a daytime temperature of 65° to 70°. The streets were clean and neat, the Mexicans hospitable, and the women prettier than those in Vera Cruz. There were many fountains of mountain water; ice was available; and the scenery, with snow-capped Orizaba in the distance, was breathtaking. Every sort of tropical fruit was in plentiful supply and flowers were luxuriant. Almost overwhelmed by the climate and splendor, Captain William Blanding of the Charleston Company commented, "Our officers and men are so delighted, they talk of taking up their abode here instead of returning home." [20]

The euphoria at Jalapa soon evaporated, for the high disease

20. Blanding, in Charleston *Courier*, May 18, 1847; H. Judge Moore, in Greenville *Mountaineer*, June 11, 1847; Manigault, "Letter from Vera Cruz," 216.

rate continued despite the change in climate. The rainy season had begun, and the Palmettos were unprepared for cold, wet nights. They lacked tents and many were without blankets, having left them behind in Vera Cruz or thrown them away on the march. Many had also disposed of their heavy clothing and purchased summer outfits from sutlers in Vera Cruz, much against "earnest entreaties" of the officers. Now colds, pneumonia, and measles joined diarrhea and dysentery in rendering another 150 unfit for service between April 23 and May 7, the date the regiment departed for Puebla. Butler himself still suffered from rheumatism.[21]

Meanwhile, many of the ill Palmetto volunteers left behind in the hospital at Vera Cruz were faring poorly. Surgeon Charles T. Darby sent Butler an alarming report that he had "never seen men so emaciated by any disease." He recommended their transfer to the bracing atmosphere of Jalapa. The ill were not transferred, but in time several recuperated sufficiently to rejoin their regiment. A few were discharged and sent home. Others died. In mourning the deaths of two Abbeville volunteers, Lieutenant Moragne remarked, "I have regretted their deaths very much, and much more as I was compelled to leave them behind in the hands of strangers."[22]

While the main body of General Scott's army rested at Jalapa awaiting supplies from Vera Cruz, General Worth's division pushed on to Fort San Carlos de Perote, thirty-three miles away. Perote fell to him without opposition, and there he rescued a number of American prisoners, including six Palmettos, captured when a gale wrecked their vessel off the coast on the night of disembarkation. Two of the Palmettos, Worth reported, had slipped away from their captors the night before the American army arrived at Perote and had reached safety "in a most deplorable con-

21. "Marlborough," in Edgefield *Advertiser*, February 23, 1848; H. Judge Moore, *Scott's Campaign*, 69–70; P. M. Butler to Behethland Butler, May 2, 1847, in Butler Papers.
22. Charles T. Darby to P. M. Butler, May 7, 1847, in "Documents of the Palmetto Regiment," 75; J. B. Moragne to Mary E. Davis, May 3, 1847, in Moragne Papers. Five Abbeville volunteers, for example, were discharged because of ill health. Greenville *Mountaineer*, May 14, 1847.

dition, half-starved and almost naked" and "entirely crippled."[23]

Before resuming his march General Scott decided to send home those twelve-month volunteers who would not reenlist for the duration. As their term of service neared completion, Scott apprehended increasing disciplinary problems. Finding only 10 percent of the 12-month recruits willing to reenlist, he separated seven volunteer regiments, including those from Alabama and Georgia in General Quitman's brigade. These veterans of service along the Rio Grande and northern Mexico were "almost in ecstacies of joy" at leaving, observed Private Moore, though many shed tears at parting with their South Carolina comrades.[24]

Major General Patterson, division commander over Quitman's brigade, also left for the United States with the volunteers because of wounds received at Cerro Gordo. In his stead Quitman was promoted to major general and, in preparation for the move against Puebla, given command of four volunteer regiments: two from Pennsylvania, one from New York, and the Palmettos.[25]

On May 7 General Scott's reduced army, with Worth's division in the vanguard, began its march toward Puebla. Quitman's brigade followed some miles behind. Scott decided to live off the countryside as nearly as possible, and he pushed the troops hard. Goodlett complained of a "killing" 18- to 20-mile march the first day. He regarded the grueling pace as evidence of "a want of judgment and feeling" by the commanding officer. Nevertheless, the army continued its 20-mile-a-day advances, regardless of toll. Horses collapsed and died; straggling became endemic despite the increasing danger of prowling Mexican guerrillas.

Moore saw several stragglers who had been robbed, stripped, and murdered. Their mutilated bodies, with throats cut, served as a stern warning of "what kind of enemy we had to deal with." On one occasion Moore himself dropped exhausted by the roadside

23. Worth, in Edgefield *Advertiser*, June 2, 1847; Charleston *Courier*, May 19, 1847; Bauer, *Mexican War*, 268. The two escapees were Richard Watson, Abbeville, and William Z. Bailey, Barnwell.
24. Bauer, *Mexican War*, 268; H. Judge Moore, *Scott's Campaign*, 69–70.
25. Claiborne, *Life and Correspondence of John A. Quitman*, I, 300–308; Quitman to Eliza Quitman, May 6, 1847, in Quitman Family Papers.

and feared for his life. Luckily, a commissary captain gave him a ride in a wagon—an act of kindness not to be expected from some officers. The difficulty of the long marches was compounded by a scarcity of rations. With Mexican troops foraging ahead, the Americans often were unable to procure any food "for love or money." [26]

During the march from Jalapa to Puebla there was no regular Mexican resistance until Worth's division reached Amozoc, about ten miles from Puebla. At that time, May 14, Santa Anna decided to attack Quitman's small brigade, marching well to the rear and escorting a large wagon train. Quitman had only about 1,000 troops because his two Pennsylvania regiments had remained on garrison duty at Jalapa, and many of the Palmettos were in hospitals. Santa Anna thus had reason to believe he could overwhelm Quitman with 3,000 cavalry he sent to the attack. Upon hearing distant artillery fire, Quitman's worn-out volunteers moved with new life. Most of the sick struggled from wagons to join the thin battle line made ready for the attack. Excitement ran high but the Mexicans kept their distance. Worth, anticipating an assault on Quitman, had held up at Amozoc instead of pushing on to Puebla. A few rounds from his artillery warned Santa Anna that he would have to deal with over 4,000 aroused Americans. The Mexican leader discreetly withdrew and retreated toward Mexico City.[27]

At 3 A.M. on the fifteenth Quitman's brigade, having united with Worth, resumed its march. The Palmettos, drenched from a rainstorm, cold, sleepy, and without rations for breakfast, were in a foul humor. Colonel Butler eased their discomfort somewhat by doling out a gill of brandy to each man. Luckily, too, about an hour outside Amozoc the column met a Mexican mule team laden with bread, which Butler either purchased or confiscated to feed his hungry regiment. Later that day American troops entered Puebla without incident. Quitman glowingly wrote his wife, "I

26. Goodlett, in Greenville *Mountaineer*, July 2, 1847; H. Judge Moore, *Scott's Campaign*, 73, 88–89, 95.
27. Goodlett, in Greenville *Mountaineer*, July 2, 1847; Claiborne, *Life and Correspondence of John A. Quitman*, I, 300–308; Bauer, *Mexican War*, 270–71; L. F. Robertson, in Charleston *Courier*, July 2, 1847.

begin to think we shall enter Mexico [City] without another battle." Within a few days Scott brought up the rest of his force and settled down in Puebla to await reinforcements before advancing farther.[28]

While en route to Puebla, Colonel Butler learned of a newspaper attack upon his and the other officers' conduct. Earlier there had been some enlisted men's complaints of mistreatment since the regiment left Charleston. Private Goodlett, the former Greenville sheriff, contended that he was the victim of an officers' conspiracy while in Mobile. After the regiment sailed for Lobos, reports of mistreatment continued to filter back to Palmetto newspapers. "Alpha," in the Sumter *Banner*, complained that en route to Lobos the officers rode in style and ate at the captain's table, while the enlisted men, many ill with mumps, were crowded below deck. "Dan," in the *Mercury*, wrote, "God help the sick soldier!—for verily his trust in those whose duty it is to minister to his wants, is the poorest that can be imagined."[29]

At Vera Cruz, Goodlett, the outspoken critic of the officers, drew up a lengthy list of complaints against the "tinsel-coated gentry" who reveled late at night in the city. The enlisted men were generally restricted to camp, and "notwithstanding some of the privates are gentlemen when at home," Goodlett remarked, "they are hardly looked upon as human beings here." The officers' servants enjoyed more privileges, and it was always at night that "the poor d——d private" was detailed to the beach to bring up rations.

After their rough march to Alvarado the privates had been confined to quarters while the commissary and numerous officers made their way to a coffee house to eat and drink, this without having issued any rations to the privates. In addition, the officers assigned two hungry sentinels to keep enlisted men out of the coffee house. Long after dark the commissary, finally driven "by the

28. H. Judge Moore, *Scott's Campaign*, 94–96; Goodlett, in Greenville *Mountaineer*, July 2, 1847; John A. Quitman to Eliza Quitman, May 21, 1847, in Quitman Family Papers; Bauer, *Mexican War*, 271–72.
29. Sumter *Banner*, March 24, 1847; "Dan," in Charleston *Mercury*, April 1, 1847.

frequent calls of the suffering men," issued meat and bread for the night. In closing, Goodlett commented, "I could say much more in relation to the dereliction of officers, but to do the subject justice, would occupy too much time." There were exceptions though "not very numerous."

However, on the march to Jalapa Goodlett revised his judgment. He now wished to announce that the officers had paid "every possible attention" to the men and seemed inclined to do their duty "as becomes South Carolinians." Private W. S. Johnson did not revise his judgment, and when promotions were handed out at Puebla, there was much grumbling among the men that the "only road to preferment" was a volunteer's aristocratic position back home. Johnson bitterly observed, "There are Some commissioned Officers in the Regt. who after Serving more than eight months in the Army would disgrace a squad of malitia at home."[30]

Much of the volunteers' dissatisfaction stemmed more from weariness, disease, and the conditions under which they marched and lived, than from officers' misconduct. The officers also found duty in Mexico distasteful. Shortly after the Alvarado fiasco Butler admitted, "The universal voice of the Army, Navy, and Volunteers is for terminating this contest; and peace would be to them most welcome news." General Quitman, in a moment of despondency, privately confessed, "I almost wish I was wounded so that I might again see home." The war weariness was succinctly summed up by Private B. L. Posey at Puebla: "All the volunteers are anxious that the war should be brought to a close on any terms, in plain English they are tired of the service."[31]

The newspaper attack seemed to be more serious than the occasional complaint of a volunteer. It was led by the Hamburg *Republican*, which accused the officers, "with one or two exceptions," of the "gravest neglect" of duty, and the "most total inefficiency in every department of their duty." The editor insinuated

30. Goodlett, in Greenville *Mountaineer*, May 7, 21, 1847; John Hammond Moore (ed.), "Private Johnson Fights the Mexicans," 219.
31. P. M. Butler, in Columbia *South Carolinian*, May 12, 1847; John A. Quitman to Eliza Quitman, April 29, 1847, in Quitman Family Papers; B. L. Posey, in Abbeville *Banner*, June 30, 1847.

that the state's gift of twenty thousand dollars to the regiment had been misappropriated or squandered. "Saluda" (Lt. Abney), in the Edgefield *Advertiser*, defended the officers. True, the troops had suffered privations and temporary inconveniences, but not from any fault of Butler or Dickinson. Moreover, Butler's foresight had enabled them to arrive at Lobos in time to join the expedition against Vera Cruz. Otherwise, the regiment probably would have spent the summer in garrison along the Rio Grande. As for the twenty thousand dollars, "Saluda" had discussed the matter with Major Eaves, the paymaster, who produced vouchers to account satisfactorily for expenditures.[32]

The open charges stung Colonel Butler and the other Palmetto officers. A select committee of three examined the regiment's acounts and reported them to be "perfectly correct." They explained that money was spent to care for the ill volunteers left behind, for musicians and instruments, for camp equipage and utensils. These articles had not been received from the government till near the end of January. The eleven company commanders signed the report, dated April 30, 1847, and it soon appeared in South Carolina newspapers.[33]

Not content with his officers' defense, the irate Butler sent his own explanation to the *Mercury*. He accounted for their expenses to date, related how their uniforms had been delayed by shipwreck, and pronounced their rations plentiful. Butler reminded his readers of the rough sea voyage and "most trying marches in a climate notoriously the worst in the world." He deplored the illness in the regiment and regretted that the sick had not received the nursing and attention they might expect at home. He thought it fair that a strict accountability should be demanded when the regiment returned, but while undergoing great hardships in Mexico, he felt it unjust to have "fires in our rear" from friends at home. Privately, Butler could not account for "these insidious at-

32. "Saluda," writing from Lobos and quoting a copy of the *Republican*, in Edgefield *Advertiser*, March 24, 1847. The Charleston *Mercury*, April 12, 1847, having received several letters of complaint about the twenty thousand dollars, also asked for clarification.

33. Greenville *Mountaineer*, June 25, 1847; Edgefield *Advertiser*, June 30, 1847.

tacks." His officers were indignant, but he thought the criticism was intended principally for himself.[34]

Feeling further defense necessary, Colonel Butler wrote on June 3 directly to the Hamburg *Republican*. He said he subscribed to four South Carolina newspapers, without indicating which, but had received only three numbers since leaving the state. Unfortunately, in each issue he had read something derogatory to the regiment. "One would infer," he continued, "that the State was in a bad humor for having furnished a quota of men, or that the means she so handsomely voted them, were given with regret." The drift of the *Republican*'s comments and those of its "kindred spirits" indicated three main charges: (1) the regiment might have been "bettered" in its chief officers, (2) the nonofficer ranks had been "shamefully neglected," and (3) public funds appropriated for the regiment's benefit had been "grossly abused."

Butler pleaded "guilty" to the first charge, saying only that he had not solicited the position. To the second charge he pleaded "not guilty." After repeating earlier explanations about climate, inadequate supplies, et cetera, he declared, "I can say before God that I have spared no pains or labor in attention to its [the regiment's] wants." Furthermore, he was convinced that every officer under his command had given the volunteers "all the humane attention" within his power. As for the third charge, it was "slanderous." The indignant Butler closed his letter by upbraiding the editor for his strictures. Several Palmetto editors rushed to Butler's rescue and the criticism was soon quieted. Nonetheless, the state continued to worry about the high mortality rate among the volunteers.[35]

34. P. M. Butler, in Charleston *Mercury*, May 29, 1847; Butler to Behethland Butler, May 2, 1847, in Butler Papers.
35. Edgefield *Advertiser*, June 30, 1847, quoting Hamburg *Republican*, and July 14, 1847, quoting Spartanburg *Spartan*. At least one officer was derelict in his duty. Captain Francis Sumter, of the Sumter Company, was an admitted alcoholic. After almost being cashiered he pledged not to drink as a condition to his remaining in the regiment. Sumter to P. M. Butler, April 9, 1847, in "Documents of the Palmetto Regiment," 66.

CHAPTER **6** *Everybody Is Tired of This War*

WHEN GENERAL SCOTT'S army stormed ashore at Vera Cruz on March 9, the South Carolina press, as others, followed its progress with keen interest. Always thirsty for intelligence from the battlefronts, the Palmetto papers relied heavily on the Mobile and New Orleans journals, especially the New Orleans *Picayune* with George W. Kendall's reports. Ordinarily, news dispatches from the Gulf Coast reached Charleston in five to seven days. To speed up service, William S. King, editor of the Charleston *Courier*, in cooperation with Moses Y. Beach of the New York *Sun*, organized a pony express along part of the route north of Mobile. This effort cut one or two days from the mail delivery time.[1]

The first war news to reach Charleston via the *Courier*'s "exclusive express" arrived on March 27, 1847. Coincidentally, it was not about Scott's activities at Vera Cruz; it was an announcement of General Taylor's significant defensive victory over General Santa Anna at Buena Vista on February 22 and 23. The *Courier* rushed out reams of extras the next day, Sunday, and word of Taylor's triumph quickly spread through the city. A large excited crowd, hungry for details, gathered at the *Courier*'s office, and a newsman obligingly read the dispatches aloud. In its Monday is-

1. William L. King, *Newspaper Press of Charleston*, 134–36. The news of the surrender of Vera Cruz was published in Mobile on April 4, and the published report reached Charleston on April 7. Charleston *Courier*, April 8, 1847.

sue the *Courier* praised the "indomitable volunteers," who were the mainstay of Taylor's small force. While mourning the heavy American losses—about seven hundred men—the editor exclaimed, "It was their fate to fall, but they fill no coward's grave, and they fell not unrevenged."[2]

On April 7 "glorious news" arrived in Charleston and Columbia of the surrender of Vera Cruz. Spontaneous celebrations erupted wherever the news reached. In Columbia the downtown area was lit up with torches, lanterns, and rockets. Main Street resembled "a miniature Broadway." Bands played, cannon fired, and Carolina students in torchlight procession gave three loud cheers at every street intersection. Hotels shone like "gem set palaces of Alladin." To climax the revelry the state arsenal fired a thirty-gun victory salute.[3]

Colonel B. T. Watts, private secretary to Governor Johnson, forwarded the welcome news to the governor, then vacationing at up-country Limestone Springs. Watts suggested that Johnson issue a proclamation setting aside a day of thanksgiving for South Carolinians to celebrate "and give vent to that fulness and intense feeling that is cherished by all hearts." The governor duly accepted Watts's suggestion and by proclamation appointed May 6 as a day of "Thanksgiving and Prayer to Almighty God." Before the appointed day arrived, news reached Charleston of General Scott's victory at Cerro Gordo on April 18.[4]

May 6 was a day of jubilation throughout South Carolina. Everywhere ceremonies were begun with artillery salutes at sunrise. In Greenville, besides the initial salute and later church services, the ceremonies were conducted after dark. At a given signal, lights blazed forth from nearly every building in the town. At the public square a large procession was formed with torches, banners, and transparencies of many designs and mottoes. Led

2. Charleston *Courier*, March 29, 1847; Georgetown *Winyah Observer*, March 31, 1847. Taylor lost about 14 percent of his 4,594 men. Bauer, *Mexican War*, 217.
3. Charleston *Courier*, April 8, 1847; Columbia *South Carolinian*, April 14, 1847.
4. B. T. Watts to David Johnson, April 8, 1847; Johnson to Watts, April 11, 1847, in Watts Papers; Greenville *Mountaineer*, April 30, 1847; Charleston *Courier*, May 5, 1847.

by the Greenville brass band, the procession marched around the town and returned to the courthouse to hear a stirring speech by Major Benjamin F. Perry.

Perry, a veteran editor and politician, recounted the American victories in Mexico. He then lamented the lives lost. "But they have met a glorious death on the field of victory," he exclaimed, "and history will immortalize their gallantry and valor. Such a death is worth an eternity of living in insignificance!" He even professed to believe that the war was of "unspeakable advantage" to the Mexicans, because America, through its army, gave them an opportunity to become emancipated from "their ignorance and lethargy." Perhaps they would become infused with "something of Anglo-Saxon spirit, energy and comfort." He also observed that Europe now recognized America's ability to fight and defend its national honor as well as to work. The local editor called the celebration "one of the most brilliant evenings ever witnessed . . . [by] the largest assembly of people ever seen in the streets of Greenville after sunset." [5]

The next day news of Cerro Gordo reached Greenville. Local citizens quickly organized another rally. Shortly after 8 P.M. the band came forth, and its martial airs attracted another large crowd. The banners and transparencies of the sixth were paraded again, along with one especially prepared to honor Cerro Gordo. It was six feet square, well lighted, and borne by four men. Each cornor was surmounted with flags, and painted on its sides were (1) CERRO GORDO, (2) a picture of Santa Anna escaping on his mule with the motto The Leg I Left Behind Me, (3) 18TH APRIL 1847, and (4) a large wooden leg marked TROPHY. After the parade the procession gathered again at the courthouse to hear impromptu speeches by several prominent citizens. [6]

The Charleston press reported May 6 to be "the most joyous thanksgiving" that was ever celebrated in the city. Its ceremonies lasted all day, with military parades, cannon firing at different in-

5. Greenville *Mountaineer*, May 14, 1847.
6. The speakers were C. J. Elford, Colonel G. F. Townes, Colonel Tandy Walker, Major R. H. Speers, and a Dr. Crook. The meeting broke up at 10 P.M. *Ibid.*

tervals, flags and banners flying, and huge throngs in the streets. That evening a well-attended concert was given, followed by rockets and a soaring balloon. Everywhere that ceremonies were held there was a mixture of euphoria, chauvinism, and national pride, though not always on a grandiose scale. A correspondent, reporting the Pickens celebration, proudly remarked that the assembly, with no sign of whiskey, dispersed at an early hour in good order.[7]

Meanwhile, in Puebla, Worth's division and Quitman's brigade settled down to nervous garrison duty. There was apprehension that the populace of eighty thousand might rise up and, in cooperation with guerrillas, fall upon the small American force. H. Judge Moore reported that atrocities were committed almost nightly upon American troops who wandered too far from their quarters. Discipline was tightened; guard duty was increased; and no one was permitted out alone without side arms.[8]

The feared uprising did not occur, and Quitman attributed the calm to the conciliatory good conduct of the American troops—a view disputed by Private Goodlett. He wrote that the New York Regiment in Quitman's brigade was composed generally of a "rough set of customers" who robbed and committed "all sorts of deviltry" upon the Mexicans. According to another account, several New Yorkers were court-martialed for their "gross behavior." By contrast the Palmettos had commanded "the universal respect" of all by their sterling behavior. Whatever the truth of the matter, the tense situation was eased after two weeks by the arrival of Scott with the remainder of the army.[9]

The Palmettos who were in good health enjoyed the delightful climate of Puebla, the beautiful scenery, "the prettiest ladies in the world," the plentiful supply of fresh fruit, and ice cream frozen in snow brought down from the mountains. There were also card games, billiards, bull fights, and an American circus to amuse the troops. One amazed Palmetto volunteer exclaimed, "What can't

7. Charleston *Mercury*, May 8, 1847; Pendleton *Messenger*, May 28, 1847. See also Anderson *Gazette*, May 14, 1847.
8. H. Judge Moore, *Scott's Campaign*, 97–98, 117.
9. John A. Quitman to Eliza Quitman, May 21, 1847, in Quitman Family Papers; Goodlett, in Greenville *Mountaineer*, July 2, 1847; Pendleton *Messenger*, July 16, 1847, citing Raleigh *Register*.

the Yankees do—to think of seeing an American circus in Puebla, Mexico!" On Sundays fashionable Mexicans drove in the park, while American officers, from General Scott down to the lowest lieutenant, pranced about on horseback.[10]

Whereas those who were healthy enjoyed the delights of Puebla, a discordant note ran through the regiment because of the continued high rate of disease. Shortly after arrival, Quitman mentioned that the whole army, including himself, had suffered "a little" from diarrhea, but he had been cured by prudent dieting. Many Palmettos were not so fortunate. It is now difficult to determine the exact number affected, as reports were sometimes fragmentary, sometimes conflicting. A surgeon's report of May 26 stated that 140 South Carolina volunteers were in the hospital at Jalapa. Two days later 50 recuperated Palmettos arrived by wagon train in Puebla. On June 3 Colonel Butler reported that over 150 were still at Jalapa or Vera Cruz and that there was a "large" sick report at Puebla, though he was optimistic for the recovery of all but two "dangerous" cases.[11]

Late in July a George W. Kendall dispatch to the *Picayune* stated that the Palmetto regiment had suffered more than any other. He placed the South Carolina dead at 140, the sick left behind at 200, and the number in the Puebla hospital at 160. Without furnishing details, Kendall said that the Palmettos' companion regiment from New York had suffered comparatively little. Scattered reports of illness in various Palmetto companies seemed to confirm Kendall's dismal dispatch. The situation became sufficiently critical for Butler to disband the Lancaster Company and to assign its surviving personnel to other companies in the regiment.[12]

10. Goodlett, in Greenville *Mountaineer*, July 2, 1847; Sumter *Banner*, July 14, 1847; John A. Quitman to Eliza Quitman, June 3, 1847, in Quitman Family Papers; J. M. Perrin, in Columbia *South Carolinian*, November 26, 1847.
11. John A. Quitman to Eliza Quitman, May 21, 1847, in Quitman Family Papers; P. M. Butler, in Edgefield *Advertiser*, July 21, 1847; Dr. McLaren, in Abbeville *Banner*, June 16, 1847.
12. Greenville *Mountaineer*, August 20, 1847, quoting Kendall, in New Orleans *Picayune*; "Documents of the Palmetto Regiment," 107–108, 199. See also "J," in Abbeville *Banner*, June 30, 1847; Georgetown *Winyah Observer*, November 24, 1847; Edgefield *Advertiser*, July 7, 1847.

The South Carolina journals published some sober accounts of suffering and dead among the Palmettos. Joseph Abney, describing the deaths in early June of William Cobb and Nathan DeLoach, of the Edgefield Company, observed that Cobb had died of "a nervous fever, arising from great debility and much exposure." Despite Cobb's state of "utter exhaustion," when Santa Anna threatened the brigade at Amozoc, "he formed into the ranks of war, with an unfaltering resolution worthy of a true hero." As for DeLoach, "skeleton as he was," he too shouldered his musket at Amozoc and joined the battleline.[13]

In reporting ten recent deaths, J. M. Perrin, of the Abbeville Company, sorrowfully wrote, "Your heart would sicken at a detailed account of the misery, the wretchedness of the sick in camp." It was "thrice awful" for the "poor fellows" to die unattended and uncared for in a strange land. Even in death they often were disturbed, for at night Mexican grave robbers would disinter their bodies and steal their coffins and funeral sheets to resell to the American army.

An account after the war by an unidentified volunteer—probably Perrin—furnished a severe indictment of inattention and improper care received by the ill volunteers. At Jalapa they were only partially shielded from the weather by tents and were left in the care of an ignorant physician whose panacea was opium, which he measured in varying quantities to the sick each morning, regardless of the nature of the disease. At Perote the sick were laid close together without blankets on the cold stone floor of the castle. They received no attention at night. At Puebla 140 of the regiment died within three months from lack of proper treatment, often including a lack of nourishing food. The resentful volunteer declaimed, "We expected to forego many of the comforts of civilized life, and cheerfully endured unavoidable privations; but to resign ourselves to petty tyrants to be treated as mere cattle and renounce all the rights and immunities of a citizen, was never dreamt of in our philosophy."[14]

13. "JA" [Joseph Abney], in Edgefield *Advertiser*, June 30, 1847.
14. Perrin, in Columbia *South Carolinian*, November 26, 1847; "Recollections of a

Besides climate and improper care, other reasons given for the high disease rate of the Palmettos included "rotten lime water" drunk on the march, alcohol, and intemperance in eating fruits and other luxury items, especially those purchased in Mexican markets. Assistant surgeon C. J. Clark warned Butler of the danger of eating Mexican food and fruit, and he scored the Palmettos for their lack of cleanliness. Some were sent to the hospital with no clean clothing.

Clark was particularly irritated with deadbeats on sick call. These men, he informed Butler, would collect their medicine and disappear into the streets to eat and drink every sort of thing. As a partial remedy Clark began to require each soldier to swallow his medicine before leaving the dispensary. Within two days the number reporting on sick call dropped from 157 to 124. As a further precaution he recommended that a noncommissioned officer march the sick to and from the dispensary each morning. Clark also suggested a detail from each company to wash the clothing of the ill volunteers. In closing, he gratuitously remarked that the Palmettos were ill clad for Puebla's cool, rainy season. Butler knew that and worked constantly to procure extra clothing supplies from spare army stores. In fact, the volunteers, despite their griping, appreciated their commander's efforts and occasionally lauded the work of other officers.[15]

If the Palmettos indulged their appetites in Puebla, they could hardly be censured. They had finished a grueling series of marches, had missed every opportunity for military glory, and, after many

---

Campaign," in Abbeville *Banner*, July 15, 1848. The article sounded much like others by Perrin, who frequently wrote to the *Banner* while in Mexico. See also H. Judge Moore, *Scott's Campaign*, 118–19.
15. C. J. Clark to P. M. Butler, May 21, 23, 1847, in "Documents of the Palmetto Regiment," 87, 89; Abbeville *Banner*, June 30, 1847; "Marlborough," in Edgefield *Advertiser*, February 23, 1848; Anderson *Gazette*, September 2, 1847; Claiborne, *Life and Correspondence of John A. Quitman*, II, 375. Prior Feliz de Segovia, of the Convent St. Domingo, complained of the filthiness and destructiveness of Palmettos stationed in the convent. He feared the outbreak of an epidemic. To Butler, July 18, 1847, in "Documents of the Palmetto Regiment," 122–23. Captains J. Foster Marshall and Joseph Kennedy and Dr. A. N. McLaren were singled out for their attention to and concern for the volunteers.

months, had finally received their first pay. Moreover, they received additional inducement to buy food in the city because of the poor-quality rations the army issued. In mid-July Butler, after complaints from the officers, informed Quitman that the "poor and slimy" meat ration was the cause of much sickness, and he advised that no more be issued. The commissary had contracted for good beef, Butler had learned, but the Mexicans were delivering worn-down work cattle.

General Quitman called for an investigation and promised his "active cooperation to remove the evil complained of. The men must have good meat regularly served them." But as the general wrote, Private Johnson recorded in his diary, "Our rations of beef for to day was so abominable that it was condemned and we get no more till night and 'tis more than probable it will be very little better." He said there was a common complaint against the commissary for "a Systematic Course of plundering the Regt. of all he could in way [of] rations." He foresaw no improvement. Nevertheless, we may assume that there was some satisfactory settlement of the unpleasant matter, for no further complaints were recorded.[16]

The health problems the South Carolina Regiment encountered were common, in varying degrees, to other units in the army. By late spring, 1847, casualties had risen so sharply that the War Department stepped up recruiting. Governor Johnson was requested to recruit a company of infantry and one of cavalry for two regiments of regulars authorized by Congress. It was "dull business," the governor confessed, and for that reason he had refused to publicize a part of Butler's April 1 letter describing the hardships of the service.[17]

To aid the governor in his "dull business" General Scott assigned Captain Joseph Kennedy of Fairfield, Lieutenant J. B. Kershaw of Kershaw, and Captain Preston Brooks of Edgefield to re-

16. P. M. Butler to John A. Quitman, June 15, 21, 1847; Quitman to Butler, July 4, 1847, in "Documents of the Palmetto Regiment," 97–99, 109–110; John Hammond Moore (ed.), "Private Johnson Fights the Mexicans," 217.
17. David Johnson to P. M. Butler, May 15, 1847, in "Documents of the Palmetto Regiment," 77–78.

cruiting duty back in South Carolina. Their goal was to sign up three hundred volunteers for the Palmetto regiment by November 1. The three officers were given leaves from Mexico because of ill health. In Brooks's case he had aggravated an old back injury—probably a ruptured disc—on the march to Alvarado. Afterwards he contracted typhoid fever at Vera Cruz. The gravely ill officer insisted on accompanying the regiment to Jalapa, though forced to ride in a wagon. En route Dr. Davis candidly warned that he would die if he remained in Mexico. Brooks arrived in Edgefield on May 25.[18]

Brooks began recruiting in his hometown by speaking at militia musters and by advertising in the local paper, whose editor hoped "the spirit of patriotism" would induce many to fill the depleted ranks. In August, Brooks appeared in Anderson, where he emphasized the $12 bounty and $42 clothing allowance for each recruit, plus 160 acres or $100 in treasury notes to be paid at the end of the war. He played down the yellow fever at Vera Cruz. One day's march would carry a person out of the danger zone. The Palmettos were now in the healthy climate of Puebla, away from the dread disease.

In September, Brooks appeared in Greenville before Colonel Thomas P. Butler's militia regiment. With high hopes from a regiment that had eagerly supplied a company in June, 1846, Brooks delivered a "bold, manly and eloquent appeal" to the militiamen "to redeem their duty" and "prove the revolutionary blood." A correspondent, especially impressed with Brooks's address, regretfully noted that the success of his appeal was "not commensurate with its merit." The disappointed Brooks received only "a meagre promise or two, a glorious nibble or so."[19]

Information about recruiting in South Carolina, though sketchy, is sufficient to show that it was a difficult task. Captain John S. Sitgreaves of York District, in charge of recruiting a company of

18. Edgefield *Advertiser*, June 2, July 7, 1847; statement of James Davis, October 7, 1847 (copy), in Brooks Papers.
19. Edgefield *Advertiser*, July 14, 1847; Anderson *Gazette*, August 26, 1847; Charleston *Courier*, September 22, 1847.

cavalry for the regulars, reported on June 12 that he had completed
his roster. Yet, a month later he could count only 63. James L.
Petigru, whose son Daniel was a first lieutenant in Sitgreaves'
dragoons, commented that none of the new companies had been
filled. And so it went. Records do not reveal how many new volunteers were recruited in South Carolina. However, in October
about 275 officers and men left Charleston for Mexico. There
was no mention of Sitgreaves' company, nor did the news account indicate where the men had been recruited. A few recruits
were picked up from American civilians in Mexico, but Preston
Brooks later called them "all a set of vagabonds—generally team-
sters who had been turned off for drunkenness and had not the
means of getting home." It appears that few replacements joined
the regiment directly from South Carolina.[20]

Throughout the spring and early summer of 1847, as Scott's
army worked its way inland and settled down at Puebla, Senator
Calhoun, from his Fort Hill home near Pendleton, privately kept
up his criticism of the Polk administration. Its scheme for power,
he said, was "war for the West, spoils for the North, & free trade
for the South." He repeated, as he had so often, that the war could
have been avoided easily had Polk so desired. But what of the free
trade with which the South was to be "soothed & satisfied"? The
heavy expense of war had settled that question. Indeed, everything for which the Democratic party apparently had been con-
tending for the past dozen years had been lost, Calhoun feared,
"by the corrupt & dreadful line of policy" that Polk had pursued.
With much determination the senator declared: "I have taken my
course. Nothing can drive me from it."[21]

---

20. Carson, *Petigru*, 258; Edgefield *Advertiser*, October 27, 1847; Georgetown *Win-
    yah Observer*, June 9, 1847; Charleston *Courier*, June 17, 1847; Preston Brooks to
    Governor W. Seabrook, February 11, 1849, in "Documents of the Palmetto Regi-
    ment," 235. In one instance an editor castigated a recruiting sergeant for trying to
    lure school boys into the service without parental consent. It turned out that the
    boys had deceived the recruiter. Anderson *Gazette*, June 10, 1847; Abbeville *Ban-
    ner*, June 23, 1847. In April, 1848, Kennedy arrived with forty to fifty recruits.
    Edgefield *Advertiser*, April 19, 1848; Moore, in Greenville *Mountaineer*, May 26,
    1848.
21. J. C. Calhoun to Wilson Lumpkin, April 6, 1847, in Barrow Papers, SHC.

At the same time Calhoun's son Patrick, the debonair army captain who moved freely among Washington and New York society, reported that the Polk administration appeared to have reached its "lowest ebb." Gossip in New York was that Taylor's victories would elevate him to the presidency in the next election. The elder Calhoun soon entertained the same view. "Indeed," he explained to his son-in-law, "it would seem to be an established principle with us, that the party in power, which makes war, will be turned out of power by it;—if successful, by the successful General; and if not, by the opposition." If the administration had had the sagacity to understand that principle, General Taylor would never have been ordered to the Rio Grande. Perhaps it would be well to elect Taylor. It might be the only way to stop the war mania, and it would serve as a lesson to future administrations.[22]

Calhouns' antagonists, Simms and Hammond, were not particularly concerned that the war might elevate Taylor to the White House. They hoped it would kill off Calhoun's presidential ambitions. American victories at Vera Cruz and Buena Vista, Simms remarked, "were quite as fatal to Mr. Calhoun as to the Mexicans." The success of American arms, in Hammond's opinion, proved Calhoun's shortsightedness.[23]

However slender Calhoun's chances for the presidency had become, he still had strong support for his war views from Joel R. Poinsett, Waddy Thompson, and Governor Johnson. As a matter of fact, Thompson and Johnson went much further than Calhoun in their censure of Polk's war policy. If Polk's object was to annex land beyond the Rio Grande, Johnson declared, "I repudiate it from the bottom of my heart." America already had more

22. P. Calhoun to J. C. Calhoun, April 5, 1847; J. C. Calhoun to T. G. Clemson, May 6, 1847, in Calhoun Papers, CU. Calhoun wrote an almost identical letter to Conner, May 14, 1847, in Conner Papers. Clemson agreed with his father-in-law that the war was "most disastrous" and feared that Scott's army would meet the same fate as Napoleon's in Russia. To J. C. Calhoun, March 28, 1847, in Calhoun Papers, CU.
23. Simms to J. H. Hammond [April, 1847], in Oliphant, Odell, and Eaves (eds.), *Letters of William Gilmore Simms*, II, 297; Hammond to Simms, April 19, 1847, in Hammond Papers, LC.

territory than it could use for the next fifty years, and to rob Mexico "would be a blot upon our escutcheon which a flood would not wash out."

Whereas Johnson spoke privately, Thompson launched a vigorous public attack on the administration's war policy. "Everybody is tired of this war," he wrote, "and anxious for peace . . . but actual peace, with or without a treaty." No view of national interest required further attacks upon "a feeble, vanquished but gallant enemy." Thompson objected to the Vera Cruz operation. Instead, he proposed that the United States occupy only the territory it planned to keep, which, in his judgment, should be restricted to territory east of the Rio Grande. In fact, he seriously doubted that America had a valid claim to land west of the Nueces. Nevertheless, he proposed a string of army posts along the Rio Grande—a modified version of Calhoun's policy. These posts, along with a naval blockade, would probably bring the Mexicans to terms. But to those southern imperialists who wished to despoil Mexico he emphatically warned that slavery would never exist beyond the Rio Grande, whether restricted or not by Congress.[24]

The *Mercury*, as usual, gave Calhoun aid and comfort and reminded its readers that Poinsett and General Taylor generally agreed with the senator's defensive-line policy. Other reports encouraged Calhoun to hew to the line. Robert Barnwell Rhett and Robert Toombs, a Georgia Whig congressman, foresaw a commanding position for Calhoun in the next session of Congress. They believed the Polk administration had lost popular support and was doomed to defeat in 1848. However, Calhoun's friend James Hamilton, Jr., having recently traveled in Georgia, cautioned him that the Democratic press was in "full cry" against him.[25]

Calhoun seemed little concerned about opposition papers in

24. David Johnson to P. M. Butler, May 15, 1847, in "Documents of the Palmetto Regiment," 77–78; Waddy Thompson, in Greenville *Mountaineer*, May 7, 1847.
25. Charleston *Mercury*, April 20, 1847; Hamilton to J. C. Calhoun, April 24, 1847; R. B. Rhett to Calhoun, May 20, 1847; Lumpkin to Calhoun, April 13, 1847; Robert Toombs to Calhoun, April 30, 1847, all in Calhoun Papers, CU.

other states. What worried him were reports in late May of an "All Mexico" movement supported by some members of the administration. On June 10 Calhoun wrote his daughter Anna that if America conquered and held Mexico in subjection, the military would control America for at least a generation. A few days later he added, "The farther we advance, the more appearent [*sic*] the folly and wantonness of the war; and the more fully will the wisdom and patriotism of my course be vindicated." Later in June his friend Rhett, writing from Washington, eased his anxiety somewhat by revealing that Polk was opposed to the All Mexico movement, though still desirous of conquering a peace. Rhett was essentially correct; while some congressmen were increasing their demands because of Mexican intransigence, the administration in early summer, 1847, still held to its original plan of absorbing only Upper California and New Mexico.[26]

As noted earlier, during the spring the South Carolina press was jubilant over American victories. When Waddy Thompson castigated the administration in his open letter, the Greenville *Mountaineer* replied, "The 'blunders' of the Administration, of which Gen. Thompson says it is so often guilty, have certainly achieved the most successful and brilliant results in Mexico, and we trust will soon 'conquer a peace,' when these 'blunders' are finally carried out." In this and other journals it was widely hoped that the American victories would bring the stubborn Mexicans to their senses.[27]

Regardless of American hopes, by June the Mexicans still had not come to terms. An uneasiness settled upon South Carolinians. There was a Kendall report that Santa Anna dared not make a treaty. Rumors abounded that he had resigned and Mexico

26. Fisher to J. C. Calhoun, May 25, 1847; N. Towson to Calhoun, May 27, 1847; Calhoun to Mrs. T. G. Clemson, June 10, 1847; Calhoun to T. G. Clemson, June 15, 1847; Rhett to Calhoun, June 21, 1847, all in Calhoun Papers, CU; John D. P. Fuller, *The Movement for the Acquisition of All Mexico, 1846–1848* (Baltimore, 1936), 56–57. To Clemson, Calhoun wrote that except for Benton's "ravings" he believed all assaults on himself had ended.
27. Greenville *Mountaineer*, May 7, 1847; Edgefield *Advertiser*, April 21, 1847; Georgetown *Winyah Observer*, April 21, 1847; Charleston *Courier*, May 5, 1847; Pendleton *Messenger*, May 14, 1847.

was falling into anarchy. The *Winyah Observer* plaintively asked, "When will distracted Mexico come to terms of an honorable peace?" The Abbeville *Banner* rejoined, "Shall our brave soldiers be compelled to remain in garrison for years, wasting away, and increase the debt of the Government, to an enormous amount?" Even Hammond had become perplexed. "It is a curious problem," he wrote, "how & when this war is to end. I own I cannot solve it."

The *Mercury* had an answer: retire behind a defensive line. Its editor happily noted that the Washington *Union*, the administration's mouthpiece, now seemed inclined to support a similar defensive posture. With the dreaded Wilmot Proviso in mind, the *Mercury* called for an end of the war before "a struggle for spoils substitutes a more serious war at home." [28]

July 4 came and went with the usual outpouring of patriotism. There were the usual toasts to the bravery of the South Carolina volunteers and Generals Scott and Taylor; Calhoun was still regarded as "a wise and fearless statesman." Others were toasted, including the president, Senator Butler, Governor Johnson, the ladies, and even, in jest, Santa Anna. [29]

Patriotic speeches and warm toasts notwithstanding, in midsummer there appeared to be no improvement in America's military position. During July General Scott and his diplomat companion, Nicholas Trist, tried to bribe Santa Anna to come to terms, but the cagey Mexican leader believed that public opinion required him to make at least a token defense of Mexico City. For

28. Abbeville *Banner*, June 16, 1847; Georgetown *Winyah Observer*, June 2, 1847; Charleston *Mercury*, May 1, June 19, 1847; Pendleton *Messenger*, June 18, 1847; Columbia *South Carolinian*, June 1, 1847; J. H. Hammond to Dr. John Hammond, May 13, 1847, in Hammond Papers, LC. As recently as May 12 the *Winyah Observer* had called for annexing all of Mexico. The problem of bringing Mexico to terms was succinctly expressed by an unidentified Palmetto officer, writing from Jalapa on May 1. "We are involved with a stubborn and foolhardy people, who do not know when they are conquered, and would not acknowledge it if they did." In Charleston *Mercury*, May 29, 1847.

29. Most ceremonies were held on Saturday, July 3. Pendleton *Messenger*, July 16, 1847; Greenville *Mountaineer*, July 16, 1847; Abbeville *Banner*, July 28, 1847; Anderson *Gazette*, July 8, 1847; Edgefield *Advertiser*, July 7, 1847; Charleston *Courier*, July 16, 1847; Georgetown *Winyah Observer*, July 28, 1847.

this latest diplomatic failure the Edgefield *Advertiser* angrily blamed the administration. It should have sent reinforcements promptly to Taylor and Scott. As matters then stood, three months had been wasted. The editor proclaimed a truism: "No power on earth ever negotiated with success unless military force were displayed on a scale commensurate to its pretensions."[30]

Surveying the military situation, the Abbeville *Banner* characterized Santa Anna to be "one of the most extraordinary men of the age." He apparently had eliminated his opponents and secured almost dictatorial powers. He was reported to be fortifying Mexico City, and peace was not at hand. Captain Kennedy, recently returned from Puebla to recruit, likewise agreed that there was no prospect of an early peace. Mexican guerrillas were organizing and attacking American wagon trains "with harassing rapidity." The Anderson *Gazette* worried about the safety of Scott's small army deep in Mexico and shortly lampooned Polk's "to conquer a peace" policy:

Hallo! Jim! You great six footer you. What are you beating that poor old nigger for?

Why, Lord bless your soul massa, I is trying to conquer a peace! You see dis old nigger keep a fuss all de time 'bout me taken' his tater-patch. I ax de ole fool, if he didn't know 'twas my destiny, an' if he ever hear 'bout de Angler Saxums, as how dey was bound to take ebery thing dey could. But he jis go on sayin' it was his'n. Den I jis takes half patch from him, and told him help unself if he could. Den I gives um jesse a few times, an' he kicks back, an' now I is tarmined to conquer a peace, as Massa Polk says, an' take de hull patch from him for his sas.[31]

While Scott awaited reinforcements at Puebla, Calhoun expressed his usual forebodings about the war. He correctly doubted that peace was imminent and predicted in late July that the con-

30. Bauer, *Mexican War*, 285–86; Edgefield *Advertiser*, August 4, 1847; Pendleton *Messenger*, August 20, 1847; Oakah L. Jones, Jr., *Santa Anna* (New York, 1968), 114–17.
31. Abbeville *Banner*, July 14, 1847; Edgefield *Advertiser*, July 7, 1847, quoting Kennedy, in Columbia *South Carolinian*; Anderson *Gazette*, July 28, 1847. Complaints of frustration were common in the press. See also Georgetown *Winyah Observer*, July 21, 1847; Pendleton *Messenger*, August 20, 1847.

flict might last for twenty years. He repeated his belief that the election of General Taylor might be a beneficial warning to the nation that making war would ensure defeat of the party in power, but he would not support a caucus candidate.

In August he wrote Anna in Brussels, expressing satisfaction with the "deep impression" American victories had made in Europe. On the other hand, he awaited the next session of Congress with concern for the future of the South. "We shall, before it [Congress] terminates," he warned, "begin to realize the train of events, to which the Mexican war was destined to lead. I shall be prepared to speak the truth fully & boldly, and to do my duty regardless of responsibility." His chief fear was the Wilmot Proviso, and he reported in September that the "states rights party" had subscribed a large amount to establish an independent press in Washington, which he hoped would be in operation when Congress convened—it never was.[32]

With military operations at a near standstill, Calhoun's close friends, in both North and South, continued to encourage his leadership. They feared that the annexation of Mexican territory, coupled with the Wilmot Proviso, would be the undoing of the South. There were the usual expressions of no confidence in the Polk administration and doubts that the Whigs would actively try to stop the war. If peace had not come before Congress convened, they agreed that Calhoun, from his commanding position in the Senate, should take the lead in terminating the war. Both political parties, according to Pierre Soulé, the fiery Louisiana congressman, "would be compelled to look to you [Calhoun] as a counsellor and guide."[33]

Thus, by late summer, 1847, it was fairly obvious that the op-

32. Benjamin F. Perry Diary, August 1, 1847, in SHC; J. C. Calhoun to T. G. Clemson, July 8, September 8, 1847; to Mrs. T. G. Clemson, August 13, 1847, in Calhoun Papers, CU; Calhoun to J. W. Lesesne, July 19, 1847, in J. W. Lesesne Papers, SHC.
33. Lesesne to J. C. Calhoun, August 21, 24 (quoting Soulé), 1847; Rhett to Calhoun, September 8, 1847; Lumpkin to Calhoun, August 27, 1847; Byrdsall to Calhoun, July 19, 1847, all in Calhoun Papers, CU. In early summer the Georgia Whig party convention endorsed resolutions of thanks to Calhoun for his "independent and patriotic course" toward the war. Pendleton *Messenger*, July 16, 1847.

timism caused by American successes at Vera Cruz, Cerro Gordo, and Buena Vista had largely vanished. The hopes for an early peace were dim; there was constant worry about the poor, ill-fated Palmettos. During these months Calhoun bided his time. Though he looked to the next session of Congress with great uneasiness, many friends assured him he would be in a strong position to influence war policy.

CHAPTER 7 *We Have Done All We Can Do by Fighting*

DURING THE late summer of 1847, while South Carolinians chafed at Scott's inaction and Mexican refusal to come to terms, war talk subsided somewhat. In its stead many gave primary consideration to various railroad schemes then being energetically pushed in the state. For instance, the Edgefield *Advertiser* published numerous letters and news items of public meetings promoting a railroad for the town, whereas its war correspondent "Saluda" was silent. But one of the dreaded consequences of the war, the Wilmot Proviso, remained foremost in the public eye. Hardly a day passed without the *Mercury* referring to the proviso, and from August 9 to 14 John Carew ran a series of scorching editorials about the hated abolitionist ploy, crowding most other news from the editorial page.[1]

In the interim, after fruitless negotiations with Santa Anna, Scott began to reorganize his army at Puebla in preparation for an assault on the Mexican capital. The reorganized force of some ten thousand men, with reinforcements, consisted of a cavalry unit under Colonel William S. Harney, three regular infantry divisions under Generals William J. Worth, David Twiggs, and Gideon Pillow, and a volunteer infantry division under John A. Quitman,

1. Edgefield *Advertiser*, July–August, 1847, *passim*; Charleston *Mercury*, July–August, 1847, *passim*. See also Anderson *Gazette*, August 12, 1847, quoting Camden *Journal*; Greenville *Mountaineer*, August 13, 1847; Pendleton *Messenger*, August 20, 1847; Georgetown *Winyah Observer*, September 1, 1847. See also Morrison, *Democratic Politics*, 68–70.

now a major general. The 1st Brigade of Quitman's volunteers was commanded by Brigadier General James Shields and composed of the South Carolina and New York regiments and six companies of the 1st Pennsylvania Regiment. The tall and handsome Shields, a former jurist from Illinois, had been almost fatally wounded at Cerro Gordo. He was now back on duty with an enhanced reputation as a fearless fighter.[2]

On August 7 Scott began his march toward Mexico City. Twiggs's division led the way, followed at one-day intervals by Worth, Quitman, and Pillow. Colonel Thomas Childs remained at Puebla with a small garrison to guard supplies and the ill. Adjutant Cantey later stated that only three hundred Palmettos were well enough to shoulder muskets when Shields's brigade moved out of Puebla. Another fifty or more were too ill to ride in the wagons and were left behind in Colonel Childs's care. Santa Anna offered no resistance to Scott's advancing column, which reached the vicinity of the Mexican capital on August 15. The first significant battle occurred at Contreras four days later.[3]

General Quitman had been ordered to remain on guard with his division at San Agustín, while Pillow and Twiggs pushed on toward Contreras, about three miles to the west. Contrary to Santa Anna's orders, headstrong General Gabriel Valencia had taken up a position near the town, from which he believed he could inflict a damaging blow to the Americans and gain personal glory. Scott, also in San Agustín, had expected no battle that day, but upon hearing heavy gunfire about midafternoon, he investigated and ordered Quitman to send two regiments to reinforce Pillow and Twiggs.

Quitman later related that Colonel Butler arose from his sickbed, appeared in full uniform, and expressed "the most anxious desire" for the Palmettos to be sent into battle. When Quitman

2. Justin H. Smith, *The War with Mexico* (2 vols., New York, 1919), II, 77–78; Bauer, *Mexican War*, 75; Order #9, July 9, 1847, in "Documents of the Palmetto Regiment," 200; *DAB*, XVII, 106–107.
3. Bauer, *Mexican War*, 273–74, 290–93; Cantey, in Camden *Journal*, January 12, 1848. Cantey said one hundred were left behind. H. Judge Moore placed the number at fifty. Greenville *Mountaineer*, December 24, 1847.

objected because of his illness, Butler replied that he "should ever be an unhappy man" if for that reason his regiment was overlooked. At length Quitman yielded and ordered Shields's brigade into action. The Palmettos were scattered, some drawing rations, others wandering around town. The long roll quickly mustered them, and they were on their way in minutes. As they filed by General Scott, he tipped his hat and exclaimed, "Hurrah for the South Carolinians, they'll give it to 'em." [4]

According to Cantey the night march to Contreras was "one of the most severe and trying . . . that men ever encountered." Led by the ill but indomitable Butler, the Palmettos, with the rest of the brigade, marched in stormy darkness over hills, through lava beds (the *pedregal*), and across deep chasms. Because of the rough terrain many officers lost their horses. About 1 A.M. the brigade reached its assigned position.

During the night Twiggs and Pillow outmaneuvered Valencia, who mistakenly thought he had the Americans on the run. At daybreak on the nineteenth the Americans struck from two sides, and within minutes Valencia's men broke and ran, their leader among the foremost. In their pell-mell retreat the Mexicans ran through a gauntlet of heavy fire from Shields's men. As a result, Valencia's force disintegrated. About 700 Mexicans died, and over 800 were taken prisoners. One Palmetto claimed that Butler himself led the charge of two Palmetto companies against the Mexican line of retreat and captured 200 to 300 of the enemy, including General Nicolas Mendoza. [5]

Santa Anna, incensed over Valencia's insubordination, had failed to aid him in the crisis and thus ensured his defeat. The Mexican leader preferred to contest the American advance at Churubusco, about four miles south of Mexico City. For his part, General Scott immediately followed up his victory at Contreras by attacking the Mexican defenses at Churubusco later the same day. The main American forces struck simultaneously from the

4. Bauer, *Mexican War*, 291–94; Claiborne, *Life and Correspondence of John A. Quitman*, II, 377; "Marlborough," in Edgefield *Advertiser*, March 8, 1848.
5. Bauer, *Mexican War*, 294–95; H. Judge Moore, *Scott's Campaign*, 132–35; Cantey, in Camden *Journal*, January 12, 1848; Jonathan Davis, in Greenville *Mountaineer*, February 4, 1848.

south and west, while Shields's brigade, circling from the west, moved behind Churubusco and played a disputed role in the notable victory. The price was dear; about one-third of the brigade fell before Mexican fire.[6]

The news of Contreras and Churubusco reached Charleston by way of the *Courier's* exclusive express on September 12. Immediately, the newspaper office and the street outside were again thronged with excited citizens anxious for information about the battles. For some days thereafter, additional details continued to arrive, including letters from General Shields and several Palmetto participants.

When Shields moved his brigade behind Churubusco in an effort to cut the causeway to Mexico City, his troops ran into heavy gunfire from some 4,000 Mexican infantrymen entrenched on the causeway and in the village of Hacienda de los Portales. First, the New York Regiment and then the Palmettos retreated in some confusion to the shelter of a hacienda. Apparently, there had been a mix-up in orders. At that moment Shields regrouped and, finding himself unable to outflank the enemy because of swampy ground and ranging cavalry, decided on a frontal assault. He personally led the attack against a deadly fire "as terrible perhaps as any which soldiers ever faced." Specifically, Shields reported that of 600 men in his brigade who saw action 240 were killed or wounded. Among the dead was the "noble and gallant" Colonel Pierce Butler.[7]

Butler's role in the Mexican War was attended with ill fortune. He was prostrated from arthritis and diarrhea during most of the campaign. His regiment had also suffered much from illness, and he and his regiment had missed every chance for military glory. The Montgomery *Flag* editorialized that when their main opportunity finally arrived before Churubusco, Butler arose, "pale, exhausted, and almost fainting," remounted his horse and moved to the front, "for he was determined while he lived, no man would

6. Jones, *Santa Anna*, 115–16; Bauer, *Mexican War*, 294–301.
7. Charleston *Courier*, September 13, 1847; Shields to Gov. Johnson, August [24?], 1847, in Greenville *Mountaineer*, September 24, 1847. For a detailed account see Gettys, "To Conquer a Peace," 296–307.

take his place." In the action that followed, Butler's horse was shot beneath him. Moments later the colonel himself was painfully wounded in the knee and forced to yield command to Lieutenant Colonel Dickinson.

After receiving first aid for his wound, Butler hobbled on foot back to the front. He had hardly arrived when a musket ball to his head killed him instantly. One story of his death told how he had just placed his hand on the head of a young volunteer, who, indifferent to danger, calmly loaded and fired at the enemy. The fatal bullet struck Butler as he remarked, "My good soldier and my friend, while we have such spirit as you exhibit, we can never be defeated."[8]

Butler was stricken at a moment when the outcome of the battle seemed in doubt. Seeing the Carolinian fall, Shields dashed along the lines calling out, "Palmettoes! Your Colonel has fallen! Avenge his death." The volunteers bounded forward "muttering curses of vengeance" upon the enemy, who panicked and fled. Speaking to a Palmetto reunion years later, Quitman glowingly contended that in the whole history of war "there had never been a more striking example of indifference to death" than shown by the Palmettos at Churubusco. However, Shields, attacking with 600 men against 4,000 entrenched Mexicans, should not have expected success. As a matter of fact, forward units of Worth's division were advancing along the causeway when Shields launched his assault. Professor Gettys concluded, "The sacrifices of the Palmettoes proved that South Carolinians could stand and fight, but contributed little to the American victory at Churubusco."[9]

The Palmetto losses on August 19 and 20 were heavier than those of any other American regiment. Kendall of the *Picayune* listed 137 killed or wounded of a field strength of 331. This was almost 14 percent of Scott's total loss of 998 men. Among the wounded was Dickinson, though his injuries were not thought to be serious. During his confinement, command of the regiment

8. Greenville *Mountaineer*, September 24, 1847, quoting Montgomery *Flag*, and February 4, 1848, quoting Mexico City *Yankee Doodle*.
9. H. Judge Moore, *Scott's Campaign*, 144–45; Claiborne, *Life and Correspondence of John A. Quitman*, I, 343–44; Gettys, "To Conquer a Peace," 306.

rested with Major Gladden. Somewhat later "Marlborough" described in vivid detail the carnage at Churubusco—the groans and last words of the dying, the frantic work of the surgeons, the joviality of the slightly wounded.

Of the dying Lieutenant Robert Williams of Barnwell, "Marlborough" wrote: "A greenish substance mingled with clotted blood oozes from his mouth and nostrils. . . . Long heavy gaspings and the most unearthly sounds proceed from his senseless form. These terrible sighs make the heart quake. . . . They are the last hollow groans of a soul struggling to free itself from the shackles of mortality." Two days after the battle the wounded Palmettos were moved to a hospital at San Agustín—a painful wagon trip, according to W. S. Johnson, one of the wounded.[10]

South Carolinians gloried in the news of victories at Contreras and Churubusco, and appropriate ceremonies were held in towns, at courthouses, and at militia musters. But there was mourning for the heavy casualties of their already stricken regiment. It seemed doomed to misfortune. It was recalled that when Colonel Butler had received the flag at the Charleston City Hall, a wing of the eagle fell from the staff, thereby presaging disaster for the Palmettos. South Carolinians had especially heavy hearts for the loss of the popular Butler. His superiors and the press praised him unstintingly. He was "gallant, noble and accomplished," "the pride of Carolina's chivalry," and so on. The Columbia *South Carolinian* devoted almost an entire issue to the dead hero. The editor published a lengthy eulogy, reprinted a report of an officer who witnessed his death and a glowing tribute from the New Orleans *Delta*, carried two notices of a public meeting to honor him, and published resolutions of grief and sympathy endorsed by four private organizations.[11]

10. Greenville *Mountaineer*, September 24, 1847, quoting New Orleans *Picayune*; "Marlborough," in Edgefield *Advertiser*, March 29, 1848; John Hammond Moore (ed.), "Private Johnson Fights the Mexicans," 222; Bauer, *Mexican War*, 301. Marshall's Abbeville Company was guarding prisoners and did not participate at Churubusco. Charleston *Mercury*, September 22, 1847.
11. Georgetown *Winyah Observer*, September 15, 22, 1847; Columbia *South Carolinian*, September 14, 21, 1847; Greenville *Mountaineer*, September 14, October 1, 1847; Edgefield *Advertiser*, September 15, 29, 1847; Anderson *Gazette*, September 23, 1847.

The *Courier*'s editorial seemed to voice the South Carolina consensus: "No more will the shrill trumpet cause him to bound from his soldier bed to lead his bold and fearless warriors on to victory. We mourn his loss, but we have the melancholy consolation that he died on the field of glory, and his glory will be embalmed in the heart of every true patriot." General Worth wrote Senator Butler, the colonel's brother, that "he fell when it was God's will, precisely as he would have desired to die." The senator's consolation was that his brother's "honorable sacrifice" had prevented his "meeting another in single combat." This was reference to Colonel Butler's impending duel with Colonel Mason—a source of "painful anxiety" to his friends.[12]

In writing Senator Butler, Worth enclosed what was probably his brother's last letter. It was written before Contreras, when Butler was worried lest his regiment miss the action. He informed Worth that Dickinson desired a place "near the flashing of the guns" and hoped Worth would oblige. The request proved to be unnecessary, and four days later the wounded Dickinson filed his own battle report, in which he praised the conduct of the Palmetto officers for effectively leading raw and inexperienced troops.

On August 31 Shields wrote Dickinson's wife about the nature of her husband's wound. A musket ball had passed through his foot and, though in pain, he had no broken bones. The surgeons now pronounced him fast recovering and out of danger. Yet, Dickinson died unexpectedly on September 12 from what news accounts said were complications of his battle wound, but Cantey attributed his death to a "low typhoid fever."[13]

Cantey was probably correct, for other reports listed his wound as not serious. Had gangrene set in, the surgeons certainly would have amputated. There were the usual panegyrics about Dickin-

12. Charleston *Courier*, September 13, 1847; W. J. Worth to A. P. Butler, August 26, 1847, in Greenville *Mountaineer*, September 24, 1847; Butler to Hamilton, October 2, 1847, in Charleston *Mercury*, October 8, 1847.
13. P. M. Butler to Worth, August 19, 1847; J. P. Dickinson to Shields, August 23, 1847, in Greenville *Mountaineer*, September 24, 1847; Cantey, in Camden *Journal*, January 12, 1848. For some reason Shields did not post the letter to Mrs. Dickinson. In Columbia, on December 19, he endorsed the original and added a note of consolation to Mrs. Dickinson. Charleston *Courier*, February 4, 1848.

son's bravery, gallantry, and patriotism. "He was in truth the soul of honor and chivalry," exclaimed one. "Marlborough," though praising his chivalry, energy, and bravery, judged him deficient as a leader. He was too emotional, too hotheaded, too strict in his discipline, and men did not wish to serve under him.[14]

General Scott hoped the defeats the Mexicans suffered on August 19 and 20 would induce their leaders to negotiate in order to spare their capital from an American take-over. On the twenty-third he consented to a short armistice. The *Winyah Observer* deemed Scott's decision "sound judgment" and commented that the American commander did not wish to crush the "national pride" of a sister republic. Quitman too believed peace was at hand. "Mexico is now so crippled," he wrote his wife, "that she can make but feeble resistance. We could enter the city in a few hours without much loss." Lieutenant Moragne was also convinced that the Americans could have easily swept into Mexico City but for the armistice, which had been concluded "much to the annoyance of the army." Should Santa Anna come to terms, however, Moragne doubted that the Mexican Congress would approve.[15]

Moragne was correct, for Santa Anna's position was too insecure politically to permit serious discussions. Nicholas Trist accomplished nothing in meetings with Mexican negotiators. In view of the deadlock, Santa Anna on September 3 began to prepare for a resumption of fighting. Three days later Scott renounced the armistice. J. M. Perrin said that Scott, in trying to be generous to the Mexicans, had discovered them to be "devoid of honor and honesty," and that the American army, "indignant at the treachery," had again taken to the field.[16]

General Scott's first move was against the Molino del Rey (mill

14. Greenville *Mountaineer*, November 5, 1847, quoting Charleston *Evening News*; "Marlborough," in Edgefield *Advertiser*, May 8, 1848. "Marlborough" noted that the "best surgeons" considered amputation of his foot unnecessary.
15. Bauer, *Mexican War*, 306–307; John A. Quitman to Eliza Quitman, August 23, 1847, in Quitman Family Papers; J. B. Moragne to Mary E. Davis, September 5, 1847, in Moragne Papers; Georgetown *Winyah Observer*, September 15, 1847.
16. Bauer, *Mexican War*, 307–308; [J. M. Perrin], in Abbeville *Banner*, November 24, 1847.

of the king) buildings, about a thousand yards west of the castle of Chapultepec. He had received information that the Mexicans were casting cannon in the Molino. General Worth's division led the attack. Although the Mexican defenders drove off the first assault, Scott's deadly artillery fire and the persistence of the American infantrymen drove out the defenders. Worth's division suffered almost eight hundred casualties in a needless attack. The capture of the Molino revealed no casting of guns.

Scott still faced the problem of selecting the best route to attack Mexico City. There were three causeways, each about a thousand yards long, connecting American positions with the city's southern *garitas* (gates). Two other causeways approached the city from the west, via the castle of Chapultepec. After an engineers' survey and a conference with his generals, Scott gambled on the western approach, partly because it would entail less time and work to prepare his batteries. Scott's plan called for Quitman's division, reinforced by a small storming party from Twiggs's division, to attack Chapultepec from the south and east. Pillow's division, with aid from Worth, would advance on the castle from the west.[17]

The American assault on Chapultepec took place September 13 after a bombardment of the castle. Attacking from the south, Shields's brigade moved obliquely to the left, whereas Quitman's other brigade, under Brigadier General Persifor Smith, circled to the east. Shields's men came under intense fire from Mexican defenders protected by a 15-foot stone wall on the lower part of the hill, and the general's arm was shattered by a musket ball. He nevertheless refused to leave the field.

Quitman, also in the vanguard, told the Palmettos that the fate of the day depended on carrying the breastworks and the stone wall and that the Palmettos were the ones to do it. Cantey recalled: "If ever there was a proud and enobling moment of a South Carolinian's life, it was that in which, this fragment of a Regiment [200 men] . . . heard this address of the gallant Quit-

17. Bauer, *Mexican War*, 308–16.

man. Immediately, Maj. Gladden said, come boys, we will try it
—and every man moved forward with a firm step and unflinch-
ing determination to succeed." [18]

Holding their fire, the small South Carolina group, with New
York and Pennsylvania comrades, advanced in good order, crossed
a meadow and several ditches of water, and moved toward a partial breach in the wall, caused by earlier artillery fire. Upon reaching the wall, the Palmettos used bayonets to loosen other stones
and permit entry. But for all their bravado they were not needed.
The Mexican defenders had deserted that part of the fortifica-
tions to help sorely pressed comrades engaged in mortal conflict
with Pillow's troops, storming the castle from the west. By the
time that Gladden had assembled his men to join the battle some
two hundred yards up the hill, the victory had been won, largely
by Pillow's division. Quitman's chief contribution to victory was
Persifor Smith's attack on two Mexican batteries guarding a causeway on the eastern side of Chapultepec. In storming the batteries
with rifles and bayonets, seven Palmetto volunteers also participated, five of whom were killed or wounded. [19]

Chapultepec capitulated at 9:30 A.M., and Scott immediately
moved Worth's division and two other brigades down the causeway toward the Garita de San Cosmé at the northwest corner of
the city. He planned to make his main attack at that point. He ordered Quitman to make a feint at the Garita de Belén at the south-
west corner.

The vainglorious Quitman, having seen little personal action,
was determined to push a full-fledged attack against Belén, about
one and one-half miles distant. Gathering his scattered regiments
and what other units he could collect in the confusion, Quitman
advanced down the causeway. In the forefront were the Palmettos
and four companies of Major W. W. Loring's Rifles. Although
held up temporarily by an artillery duel, the Palmettos and Lor-

18. Claiborne, *Life and Correspondence of John A. Quitman*, I, 359–60; Cantey, in
    Camden *Journal*, January 12, 1848.
19. Bauer, *Mexican War*, 316–18; Smith, *War with Mexico*, II, 176–57, Claiborne,
    Life and Correspondence of John A. Quitman, I, 359–60; Gettys, "To Conquer a
    Peace," 311–15.

ing's companies drove the Mexicans from the *garita* shortly after 1 P.M.[20]

Quitman, "black with smoke, and stained with blood," leaped
upon a battery and called for a flag. Second Lieutenant F. W. Selleck of Abbeville, "a young and dauntless Carolinian," vaulted to
the General's side, scrambled to the top of the wall, and planted
there the bullet-ridden Palmetto banner—claimed by many, including Quitman, to be the first American flag to wave above the
Mexican capital. Selleck's bold but foolhardy deed attracted Mexican gunfire, and thus like "the famous Jasper of the Revolution,
he fell under its folds." Below, the Palmettos gave three cheers for
the Americans within the *garita*, three for General Quitman, and
three for the other units with Quitman.[21]

Having attacked and seized the *garita* contrary to Scott's orders, Quitman attempted to strengthen his position by pushing
into the city. His path was blocked by a massive stone citadel and
the Belén prison. Here Santa Anna had personally organized the
defenses with artillery and seasoned troops. A devastating Mexican fire drove the Americans from their forward positions, and
they were barely able to hold the *garita* itself against counterattacks. Major Gladden was wounded, and Captain R. G. M. Dunovant temporarily took command of the Palmettos. Meanwhile,
Worth's forces had broken through the Mexican defenses at San
Cosmé to the north, and during the night Santa Anna abandoned
the city. This was fortunate for Scott, who was running low on
men and supplies and faced a potentially hostile city of 200,000
enemy citizens.[22]

American casualties on September 13 were 130 killed, 703
wounded, and 29 missing. Of these, Quitman's division suffered
an unnecessarily heavy portion, largely because of his thirst for
glory. Nearly every member of his staff and all his artillery offi-

20. Gettys, "To Conquer a Peace," 315–18; Bauer, *Mexican War*, 318–19.
21. Claiborne, *Life and Correspondence of John A. Quitman*, I, 363–64; Charleston
    Courier, November 15, 1847. Selleck was wounded, not killed. Loring's men dis-
    puted the Palmetto claim of the first American banner to fly over Mexico City.
22. Bauer, *Mexican War*, 319–21; Gettys, "To Conquer a Peace," 318–20; John E.
    Weems, *To Conquer a Peace: The War Between the United States and Mexico* (Gar-
    den City, N.Y., 1974), 427–29.

cers were wounded. As for the dwindling Palmetto regiment, its casualties were 16 or 17 killed and from 83 to 86 wounded, 5 of whom died later.

Perrin called the Palmettos an "orphan regiment"—its first two commanders dead, the third wounded, the adjutant and acting adjutant wounded, the quartermaster and the commissary ill. There were hardly enough men for duty to protect the sick and wounded. Among others whose loss he mourned was Lieutenant Moragne, a West Pointer who had joined the Abbeville Company. Moragne had objected to the armistice after Churubusco as needlessly giving Santa Anna an opportunity to strengthen his weak defenses. A Mexican cannonball decapitated him at the height of the action within the Garita de Belén. Perrin wearily concluded: "We have done all we can do by fighting. I think there is at present a prospect of a long rest, and Heaven knows it is much needed." [23]

The Palmetto losses, apparently greater than those suffered by any other regiment, served as an illustration of the "horrors of war," commented the Richmond *Whig*. After furnishing statistics on illness and death, the editor estimated there was a Palmetto remnant of 135. What a contrast would be the return home of the present "shattered corps" with the "pride, pomp, and circumstance" that attended their departure for Mexico! The Charleston *Mercury* chided, "We might ask to what end is all this heroism, so profusely shown, so proudly accounted for?" In late October J. Foster Marshall reported 142 Palmettos fit for duty and 90 in the hospital. He exclaimed, "The hand of God has laid heavily upon us." [24]

On September 14 General Scott's victorious army made a triumphal entry into Mexico City. Unluckily for the Palmettos, they failed to participate in the grand procession due to a confusion of

23. [Perrin], in Abbeville *Banner*, November 24, 1847; Bauer, *Mexican War*, 319–21. The exact number of casualties for the Palmettos varied with different reports. One account mentioned that Sergeant William Blocker, acting commander of the Edgefield Company, was killed with four other "96 Boys" by a single cannonball. Edgefield *Advertiser*, October 27, 1847, citing Charleston *Evening News*.
24. Georgetown *Winyah Observer*, October 20, 1847, quoting Richmond *Whig*; Charleston *Mercury*, October 20, 1847; Marshall, in Abbeville *Banner*, December 8, 1847; Claiborne, *Life and Correspondence of John A. Quitman*, II, 376–77.

orders. Nevertheless, a few days later they were garrisoned in the National Palace, where they remained until December. Scott appointed Quitman governor of the city and imposed harsh conditions to wipe out sniper fire, which lasted until the seventeenth. The following day Quitman wrote of the city's capture and the dispersal of the Mexican army. Santa Anna had resigned as president, and Quitman was confident that the Mexican Congress then assembling at Querétaro would be disposed to negotiate. "I now predict a speedy peace," he said.[25]

Momentarily, many agreed with Quitman, and Scott's army settled down to routine garrison duty, awaiting developments on the diplomatic front. But for Americans in Puebla no end of hostilities was in sight. Scott had left some 500 ill and convalescent soldiers at Puebla, including about 50 or more South Carolinians, when he began his march toward Mexico City. He had delegated approximately 1,200 men under Colonel Childs to protect the ill and keep the city under control. Almost immediately Childs's troops suffered from Mexican harassment. As a foretaste of what was to come, on August 25 Mexican cavalry seized 700 animals at an American muleyard outside the city and killed 10 Americans who intervened.

Some of Childs's sick men, including the Palmettos, were convalescing at Tivoli, a beautiful garden spot on the city's outskirts. In view of stepped-up guerrilla activities Childs ordered the convalescents back to the general hospital at San José Church, near the citadel, which served as garrison headquarters. Among the Palmettos at Tivoli was H. Judge Moore. On the afternoon of their move to San José, he and an ill comrade fell behind the wagons. Upon hearing firing in the center of the city, they quickened their pace and presently, with sentries urging them to hurry, passed the bodies of several Americans who had been overtaken by quick-striking guerrillas and lanced to death.[26]

25. Gettys, "To Conquer a Peace," 322–23; Bauer, *Mexican War*, 321–22; John A. Quitman to Eliza Quitman, September 18, 1847, in Quitman Family Papers.
26. Bauer, *Mexican War*, 328–29; H. Judge Moore, *Scott's Campaign*, 212–14; Moore, in Greenville *Mountaineer*, December 24, 1847.

On the night of September 13, at the very moment Santa Anna was evacuating Mexico City, General Joaquin Rea infiltrated Puebla with about 4,000 men and began a 28-day siege of the American stronghold. Childs refused to heed Rea's demand for surrender, and his forces drove off two Mexican attacks on his fortified position. Santa Anna himself arrived on September 22 with a large force and several artillery pieces. Again the Mexicans demanded the garrison's surrender; again Childs refused. Sporadic Mexican attacks and American counterattacks continued until General Joseph Lane's brigade from Vera Cruz fought its way into Puebla on October 12.

During the siege the Mexicans cut off the Americans' food and water supply. Moore estimated that some fifteen to twenty Americans died daily in the hospital and had to be buried within the walls of their defenses. Another Palmetto volunteer asserted that he "never was so nearly starved" in all his life. He had only a flour and water gruel for food but was proud to announce that he had killed at least one enemy. A daring Mexican had boldly walked into the street and taken aim at an American sentinel, "but ere his musket fired, my rifle went off, and down fell the villainous fellow."

With the arrival of Lane's force peace was restored to Puebla. Santa Anna, who had resigned earlier as president, retired with his forces to Querétaro. Moore now reported breaking "the restraints which military aristocracy would throw around the liberties of a soldier" by visiting the city's coffee houses for mutton chops, coffee, or brandy and by strolling where he could "exchange salutation's with some dark eyed Senorita." Like many others, he found his soldier's life "not entirely void of sunny spots." 27

The American victories in and near Mexico City brought forth numerous editorials and public meetings in South Carolina commemorating the Palmetto regiment and paying honor to its fallen heroes. But, as in early summer, the euphoria over American tri-

27. Greenville *Mountaineer*, December 24, 1847. "WLH," in Abbeville *Banner*, December 8, 1847; Bauer, *Mexican War*, 329–31.

umphs soon began to fade and so did optimism for a speedy peace. The situation in Mexico appeared confused. There were conflicting reports about Santa Anna's role in the government. Was he still in charge or not? Worse still was Quitman's report in mid-October that guerrillas had disrupted American communications between Vera Cruz and Mexico City. But he was strongly opposed to evacuating the Mexican capital. Such a move would lengthen the war. He was "inclined to think" that the United States would be compelled to annex Mexico. Later in the month the Anderson *Gazette* painfully noted that Mexico was still not conquered and there were "but little hopes of a speedy termination of hostilities." [28]

28. John A. Quitman to Eliza Quitman, October 13, 1847; to H. S. Foote, October 15, 1847, in Quitman Family Papers; Pendleton *Messenger*, November 12, 19, 1847; Anderson *Gazette*, October 28, 1847.

CHAPTER **8** *Tell Him I Did My Duty*

RECRUITMENT IN South Carolina for the Mexican War was often "dull," as Governor Johnson noted, and within a few weeks of arrival in the tropical enemy land many Palmetto volunteers had become disillusioned about the service. They grumbled about the climate, disease, poor food and water, the lack of ordinary comforts, and mistreatment from their officers; and they began to resent the chauvinists who had induced them to sign up. While marking time at Puebla, Private W. S. Johnson bitterly noted that "of all the valient men who stired up the more quiet country-loving audience by loud declamation and invection [against Mexico]—of those men of wind I have not seen one of them in Mexico." [1]

On the other hand, in the early months of the regiment's active service there had been an occasional critical comment back home about misconduct among the volunteers. However, the tragic consequences of disease and battle evoked great sympathy throughout South Carolina for the shattered regiment. After news of Churubusco, meetings were held to honor the Palmettos. Fulsome praise poured forth. The words *duty, courage, chivalry, honor, bravery*, and *glory* were overworked in describing the character of the volunteers.

One of the first such gatherings took place on October 6 at the

1.   John Hammond Moore (ed.), "Private Johnson Fights the Mexicans," 219.

Charleston City Hall before a large audience. After a "few eloquent remarks" by the chairman, a committee of sixty, including nearly every prominent Charlestonian, was appointed to draft resolutions to honor the Palmettos slain near Mexico City. Six resolutions were offered and the preamble read as follows. "That a body of comparatively raw recruits . . . should, in their first battle, have had half their number stricken down in the field, and with their chief killed, and their second in command disabled, early in the action, have continued without a moment's faltering, without an instant's confusion, fighting on to the close with unbroken front, and unabated ardor, is an achievement which stands in honorable parallel with any incident in the annals of ancient or modern warfare."

The resolutions applauded the heroes, expressed sympathy to their families, declared an obligation of the nation to care for the families of the fallen, and remonstrated that "if this charge be not sacredly fulfilled, the fame of the dead will be a reproach to the living." After six speakers had aroused considerable emotion, the assembly unanimously endorsed the resolutions. The *Courier* exultantly proclaimed that Colonel Butler's name would occupy "as brilliant a page in history as that of MARION, and SUMTER, and MOULTRIE."[2]

Young Heyward Trezevant, of a prominent Columbia family, was barely eighteen when killed among the foremost at Chapultepec on September 13. In penning a note of consolation to the youth's father, the Richland Company commander, Captain De-Saussure said, "While I deeply sympathize, dear Sir, with you, in your deep affliction, let us recollect that he died gloriously, in the hour of victory, having himself faithfully discharged his duty in the combat."

Another friend of Trezevant later wrote:

A mysterious warning reached his soul that his hour was come. He told his comrades the night before the battle, that he should not survive the morrow. He was serious and reflective, and his bible was often in his

2. Charleston *Courier*, October 5, 7, 1847; Edgefield *Advertiser*, October 20, 1847, quoting Charleston *Evening News*.

hands. And, when the morrow came, calm and unfaltering, he pressed onward to his doom, and soon the last pulses of his brave young heart beat beneath the bible, as it lay, where so long it had been in life, upon his bosom. To his bravery, his lofty bearing, the Palmettoes all bear witness.[3]

Private George S. James, who left Erskine College to join the Edgefield Company, attended the dying Sergeant William B. Blocker and Corporal Llewellyn Goode, both mortally wounded by the same cannonball at Mexico City. "Both seemed conscious that death was at hand," James related, "and waited the event in Christian fortitude. Not a whisper of complaint escaped their lips." The dying Blocker asked James to give his Bible to Sergeant Whitfield Brooks and to tell his father, "I died in command of my company with my companions; tell him I did my duty." James's father, noting that Brooks had also died, added, "Should my son's life be spared, I am sure he will scrupulously observe the sacred charge committed to him."

Blocker had been placed in command of the '96 Boys after all the company's officers had fallen victims to battle injuries or disease. He was described as one who "stood aloof" from "temptations consequent to war, not forgetful of his duty to his God." A sympathetic correspondent implored, "Let not then the tears of parental tenderness long flow, for he has woven for himself a wreath of fame that time will not wither."[4]

The unfortunate Whitfield Brooks was younger brother to Preston S. Brooks, original commander of the Edgefield Company, and son of Colonel Whitfield Brooks, a prominent planter and politician. Brooks lingered for forty days after being wounded at Churubusco and was frequently visited by General Shields, who repeatedly tried to cheer up the wounded youth.

When Shields toured South Carolina in December, 1847, the elder Brooks sent him an extract from his dying son's last letter, in

3. DeSaussure to D. H. Trezevant, October 25, 1847, in Columbia *Daily Telegraph*, December 6, 1847; Charleston *Courier*, January 29, 1848.
4. George S. James to John S. James, October 24, 1847; John S. James to B. Blocker, December 4, 1847, in Abbeville *Banner*, January 5, 1848; "G," in Edgefield *Advertiser*, December 29, 1847.

which he told how the general had urged the troops to follow him
in a charge against the enemy. The young man wrote: "I jumped
from the ranks and said, I would follow him to death, if necessary. After the men returned from the charge, he [Shields] came
immediately to where I was lying, and said with tears in his eyes
—'you poor brave boy, you must not die.' I asked him if I had
discharged my duty. His reply was, 'like a man, that I was an
honor to myself, to my family, and to my country.'" In consoling
the father, Shields verified the story that his "brave and noble"
son "was one of the first who darted forward to follow me, and
he followed me to death."[5]

Throughout the state appeared similar reports of homage and
sorrow. The *South Carolinian*, happy to announce the victories
in which "the gallant sons of our State have won immortal renown," was bereaved by the deaths of "our noble and valorous
soldiers"—deaths that filled the hearts of their countrymen "with
deep regret and desponding sorrow." But the Edgefield *Advertiser* reminded the families of the fallen that they were "not without consolation," for the state would "ever cherish their memo-
ries." The Charleston *Evening News* proclaimed that no other
American regiment had established a better showing in battle
than the "devoted" Palmettos.[6]

The Pendleton *Messenger* reprinted tributes from out-of-state
papers. The Augusta *Constitutionalist*, while deploring the "un-
precedentedly severe" losses in the South Carolina Regiment,
asserted that it had "nobly sustained the martial fame of the Palmetto State." The New Orleans *Delta* contended that the Palmettos' "Spartan-like devotion and sublime courage [were] unsurpassed in history." Later, the *Delta* quoted an officer of another
regiment as saying that the Palmettos "had never learned to coun-
termarch or retreat, and in going into battle, knew no other step

5. Shields to Whitfield Brooks, December 19, 1847, in Edgefield *Advertiser*, December
   29, 1847, and also see December 22, 1847, January 26, 1848.
6. Edgefield *Advertiser*, October 27, November 3, 1847, quoting Columbia *South
   Carolinian*; Anderson *Gazette*, October 28, 1847, quoting Charleston *Evening
   News*. See also Camden *Journal*, January 12, 1848; Greenville *Mountaineer*, November 5, 1847.

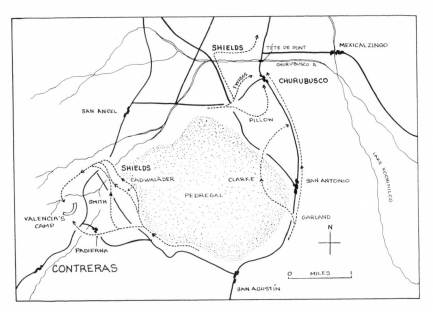

BATTLES OF CONTRERAS AND CHURUBUSCO

but the quick step." Speaking of the American fighting spirit in general, the Abbeville *Banner* warned, "It is high time the Mexicans had learned the invincibility of American arms." Like his "patriot ancestors of the Revolution," the American soldier was willing to fight in rags and without pay "to uphold the glories of his country, and this is the secret of our victories."[7]

Not only did the South Carolina press and political leaders extol the Palmettos for their duty, honor, courage, and chivalry, but, insofar as records reveal, many of the volunteers accepted their military duty with all seriousness. Colonel Elias Earle, a Greenvillian who enlisted as a private in the Fairfield Company, explained that his motto was "victory or death." Preston Brooks,

7. Pendleton *Messenger*, September 5, 1847, quoting Augusta *Constitutionalist*, and October 15, 1847, quoting New Orleans *Delta*; Camden *Journal*, January 5, 1848, quoting New Orleans *Delta*; Abbeville *Banner*, November 24, 1847.

temporarily detailed back to South Carolina because of illness, wrote from Vera Cruz in mid-October, 1847: "If I can but get in one battle, and feel that I too have spilt my blood with the brave Palmetto Boys, I shall be content. . . . Oh! how my heart grieves, when I think of the brave 96 Boys, but every blow I strike shall be *for* them and poor Butler."

Ill luck dogged Brooks. He never had an opportunity for military glory. The great battles were over before his return to Mexico. Later, in 1856, he enjoyed notoriety for beating Senator Charles Sumner into insensibility with a heavy cane. He was condemned in the North as "Bully" Brooks, and though his home state honored him, many in the South disapproved of his act. In any event, his "fame" was fleeting, for whatever it was worth. He died suddenly the following year.[8]

The idea of one's duty was expounded by First Lieutenant John B. Moragne, a young Edgefield lawyer who joined the Abbeville Company. His brother, W. C. Moragne, served as a lieutenant in the Edgefield Company. Writing to his sister shortly after leaving the state, Moragne said:

I have always had an elevated notion of our duty to our country and to mankind. I do not think my life my own entirely. Certainly we are all bound to exert ourselves to be useful and to act in that capacity in which we may prove most useful. I am satisfied that I am now labouring in a proper field.

The war whatever may be objections to it is one which we are bound to prosecute. A good citizen never looks beyond what the honor and reputation of his country calls for.

Moragne would not question his government's action. He believed America was carrying out the designs of Providence. For himself, he explained, "I may be destined to die unknown and unhonored . . . but I will do nothing which will leave a stain upon my name." He died in the assault on Mexico City.[9]

There is one recorded instance of a volunteer's exerting special

8. Elias Earle, in Greenville *Mountaineer*, December 17, 1847; Preston Brooks, in Charleston *Mercury*, November 17, 1847. For the Brooks-Sumner episode see David Donald, *Charles Sumner and the Coming of the Civil War* (New York, 1961), 285–311.
9. John B. Moragne to Mary E. Davis, January 24, 1847, in Moragne Papers.

effort to disprove cowardice. Joshua R. Beall, of Captain Marshall's Abbeville Company, learned of a rumor accusing him "of not standing up" to his post during the assault on Chapultepec. He hastily sent home an explanation of his conduct, along with affidavits from three officers who testified that he had left the battlefield on direct orders to remove the body of a dead officer to the rear.[10]

Although the Palmettos probably differed little from soldiers in other regiments in courage, patriotism, and conduct, their high battle casualties convinced many South Carolinians of their superiority. One editor attributed their "fire" in battle to their youth —average age of twenty-three—"but where did they get their steadiness?" he asked. It was explained that a majority were gentlemen's sons. "Marlborough," reminiscing about the war, likewise observed the "intelligence and high breeding" of the enlisted men. And he attributed their "superiority of general conduct" in part to the firm discipline instilled by Colonel Butler.

These judgments are questionable. Butler may have been fair and admired by his men, but he was no strict disciplinarian. No doubt most of the South Carolina volunteers were young; so were those from other states. There were, however, a few elderly soldiers in the regiment. There were Privates Doyle Sweeny and Samuel Weir of Columbia, and Captain Leroy Secrest of Lancaster, who were veterans of the War of 1812. There were, moreover, few gentleman's sons in the ranks. The roster of the Charleston privates, for instance, was almost devoid of prominent family names. And one may surmise that many privates held the same view toward the war as did John P. Cantwell, a Richland volunteer. He wrote: "I can tell you what it is: Soldiering *aint* what it is cracked up to be and the singing of Bullets, Grape, and cannister is any thing but comfortable. Glory and all that is nothing but Fudge, although I must confess that the idea of making the enemy fly is exciting in the extreme." [11]

10. Edgefield *Advertiser*, February 28, 1848, quoting Abbeville *Banner*.
11. Edgefield *Advertiser*, December 8, 1847; "Marlborough," in *ibid.*, March 1, 1848; Columbia *Daily Telegraph*, December 10, 1847; Camden *Journal*, January 19, 1848; Charleston *Courier*, June 29, 1846; John P. Cantwell to Ben Lucas, October 27, 1847, Manuscript in South Carolina Historical Society, Charleston.

Not only did the South Carolina press laud the Palmettos, but various towns, communities, and militia musters followed Charleston's lead in holding special ceremonies to honor the regiment. Typical of those meetings was a large public gathering on October 25 at the Edgefield courthouse. Colonel Pickens and Senator Butler addressed the meeting, after which resolutions were adopted mourning the "melancholy loss" of many Palmetto heroes. Finally, a subscription was begun to defray the expense of returning the bodies of dead Palmettos to their native soil. Other meetings were reported from Camden, Georgetown, Greenville, Abbeville, Hamburg, Columbia, South Carolina College, and Gillisonville in Beaufort District.

Everywhere the oratory was similar to General W. E. Martin's jingoistic declamation at Gillisonville: "The gallant Palmetto Regiment, *enlisting for the war*, has proved to the world that the blood which circulated in the veins of her Sumters, her Marions, her Moultries, and her Butlers, has not degenerated in the bosoms of their descendants. Sir, at the names of *Butler and the Palmetto Regiment*, I am made to feel that the heart and not the lips should tell the rest." [12]

In accord with the Edgefield views there was a feeling in the state that the bodies of the dead heroes should be brought home. The Camden meeting resolved that the General Assembly should defray the expense, place the remains of the dead heroes in a common grave and erect a suitable monument. In addition, they called for voluntary subscriptions for "suitable provisions" for Butler's and Dickinson's widows and for the General Assembly to aid widows and orphans of all Palmetto dead.

The Columbia meeting appointed a committee to collect contributions for Butler's widow and made elaborate plans to send subscription lists to all militia regiments in the state. Contributions of one dollar per person were suggested. The editor of the

12. Edgefield *Advertiser*, September 29, October 27, December 22, 1847; Abbeville *Banner*, October 27, November 3, 1847; Greenville *Mountaineer*, October 22, 1847; Columbia *Daily Telegraph*, November 4, 1847; Georgetown *Winyah Observer*, November 10, 1847; W. E. Martin, in Columbia *South Carolinian*, October 19, 1847.

Mountaineer offered to aid in the collection. The Georgetown resolutions supported those of Columbia and Camden and also recommended life pensions at state expense for the wounded.[13]

Apparently the freewill collection for Butler's widow was embarrassingly small, for no report of the amount was publicized. When the legislature convened in November, Governor Johnson reminded the lawmakers of the "unsurpassed renown" won by the Palmettos. He proposed that their widows and orphans be given the state's "peculiar care." The legislature responded, but with a niggardly five thousand dollars for their "immediate wants." The legislature also resolved to erect a suitable monument for the fallen and to furnish appropriate medals for each Palmetto or, if deceased, his representative. Upon learning that several returning volunteers were destitute in New Orleans, the legislature voted another five thousand dollars to defray homecoming expenses for those in dire need.[14]

The smallness of the appropriation for widows and orphans rankled "Old 96." Writing to the *Mercury*, he reminded the legislators that "the Greek valor of Butler, the Roman intrepidity of Dickinson, and the heroic and glorious band who died with them" had done more to kindle "a noble and high enthusiasm" among Carolina children, done more for the "fame and moral worth" of the state than whole generations of modern enterprisers "reposing in inglorious ease and luxurious indulgence." He called upon the General Assembly to bestir itself in behalf of the heroes and their surviving families. In the meantime, the legislators had gone home.[15]

While the General Assembly was in session, several Mexican War heroes appeared in South Carolina. The first to arrive was N. R. Eaves, veteran senator from Chester District. Although

13. Columbia *Daily Telegraph*, November 4, 1847, quoting Camden *Journal*; Georgetown *Winyah Observer*, November 10, 1847; Greenville *Mountaineer*, November 5, 1847. See also Edgefield *Advertiser*, December 15, 1847.

14. *Journal of the House of Representatives of the State of South Carolina. Being the Annual Session of 1847* (Columbia, 1847), 23–24; *Reports and Resolutions of the General Assembly of the State of South Carolina, Passed at the Annual Session of 1847* (Columbia, 1847), 392, 401–402; Greenville *Mountaineer*, December 3, 1847.

15. "Old 96," in Charleston *Mercury*, January 6, 1848.

he was a fifty-eight-year-old major in the militia, Eaves had volunteered as a private and, bearing his company's banner, had marched sore-footed with the other Chester volunteers to Columbia. Governor Johnson had commended him for giving up his comforts "to become a tenant of the tented field" but had assured him of his reward. "Old Chester will not forget her own." [16]

Although given administrative duties as the regiment's paymaster, the "Little Warrior" participated in battle action and was slightly wounded. After the capture of Mexico City he requested a six-month furlough to attend the 1847 legislative session, whereupon General Scott gave him an honorable discharge instead.

Eaves arrived in the state capital and resumed his place in the Senate December 7, well into the session. His colleagues unanimously approved Senator James Rhett's resolutions welcoming the volunteer and extending "hearty thanks for the patriotism and bravery" he had displayed in battle. Later, there was talk of pushing Eaves's candidacy for governor, but nothing came of it. Ever adventuresome, the elderly bachelor later volunteered for, and served briefly in, Confederate military service. [17]

Eaves's return was soon overshadowed by the arrival of Brigadier General Shields, commander of the brigade in which the Palmetto regiment had fought at Churubusco, Chapultepec, and Garita de Belén. Born in Ireland in 1806 and emigrating to America about twenty years later, Shields had studied law and risen high in Illinois politics before the Mexican War. He resigned from the Illinois Supreme Court to accept a commission in the volunteers. His daring charge at Churubusco was later commemorated in a painting placed in the national capitol. [18]

On December 15 General Shields crossed the Savannah River

16. David Johnson to Eaves, May 15, 1847, in Eaves Papers.
17. *Journal of the Senate of the State of South Carolina. Being the Annual Session of 1847* (Columbia, 1847), 81–82, 169–71; Greenville *Mountaineer*, March 10, 1848; Anderson *Gazette*, December 16, 1847; Emily B. Reynolds and Joan R. Faunt (comps.) *Biographical Directory of the Senate of the State of South Carolina, 1776– 1964: Compiled under the Direction of the Senatorial Research Committee*, (Columbia, 1964), 212.
18. After the war Shields served as United States senator from three states: Illinois, Minnesota, and Missouri. *DAB*, XVII, 106–107.

at Augusta to the noise of booming cannon and wild cheers from South Carolinians. He told a Hamburg welcoming committee that he felt as if he were almost a Carolinian. After the local ceremonies he was escorted to a new railway coach, named "Colonel Butler," expressly outfitted for his journey to Columbia.[19] At Branchville junction Shields was met by a committee from the capital city and two aides of Governor Johnson.

In Columbia the entire city, including the legislature, turned out en masse to greet General Shields late the same afternoon. The distinguished visitor was welcomed with a 13-gun salute and a speech by General Buchanan, a local militia officer. In reply Shields praised the Palmettos for their "most daring and intrepid bravery." It had been an honor to command these men, he said, and whenever there was a post of danger, he threw in the Palmettos. He commented on the tragic death of Colonel Butler and was certain South Carolina would care for the orphans of those who had fallen in battle and had "so gallantly, bravely, and chivalrously sustained the honor of the State."

After initial ceremonies Shields was ushered into a magnificent landau, to lead a lengthy carriage procession up Gervais Street to Governor Johnson's quarters at the United States Hotel. The Governor's Guards, the Richland Volunteer Rifle Company, and the college cadets, all arrayed in colorful uniforms, furnished a military escort as the procession moved along to band music, cheers, and flying banners. No sooner had the general disappeared into the governor's quarters than the noisy throng on the street clamored for his reappearance and another speech, to which he obliged. After dark the college students held a torchlight parade, and the city was lighted up for the occasion.

The next day, December 16, General Shields addressed the General Assembly, which in turn adopted appropriate resolutions and presented the hero a sword "as a testimonial of its high estimation of his gallant bearing in the Mexican War, and as a tribute of gratitude for his parental attention to the Palmetto Regi-

19. Anderson *Gazette*, December 23, 1847, quoting Hamburg *Journal*.

ment." Afterward, Shields attended a ceremony at South Carolina College. Reviewing the cadet corps, he remarked, "I could
have done fine work with you boys at Churubusco."

During the general's stay in Columbia a military ball and several receptions were held in his honor. The handsome officer was
lionized by huge throngs wherever he went, and ladies smothered
him with kisses. John L. Manning, a bachelor state senator from
Clarendon, commented that "the whole population of the country—all its wealth, beauty, and talent are following him in his triumphal procession." Serving on Shields's reception committee,
Manning added: "Perhaps if I keep sufficiently close to him I may
receive by mistake some of the myriad kisses intended for him,—
just the superabundance—the overflowings you know. He is quite
an adept however in that art, having practiced so much among
the Mexican senoritas." [20]

Leaving Columbia on the twentieth aboard the "Colonel Butler" and accompanied by the governor and other dignitaries,
Shields headed for Charleston. The hero stopped briefly in Orange-
burg to be welcomed by several hundred local citizens. General
D. F. Jamison delivered an oration, and the local belles presented
the general a wreath and a poem. One verse read as follows:

Our brave Palmettoes oft shall tell,
    And pride will glow as each reveals,
That he has bravely been led forth
    With honor, by the gallant Shields. [21]

Cannon boomed as Shields's train approached the Charleston
station. A special committee from the city council received the
general and the governor and ushered them to seats in a fine carriage. Shields's reception was dazzling, probably unrivaled in the
port city's history. It was a beautiful sunlit day for the gala occasion. Bands furnished music, and the parade route to city hall was

20. Details of Shields's visit were in Columbia *South Carolinian*, December 17, 1847,
and Columbia *Daily Telegraph*, December 15–20, 1847. See also Greenville *Mountaineer*, December 24, 31, 1847; J. L. Manning to D. H. Gordon, December 20,
1847, in Williams-Chesnut-Manning Papers. For Shields's visit to South Carolina
College, see Joseph A. Gamewell MS [n.d.], SCL.
21. Charleston *Mercury*, December 22, 1847.

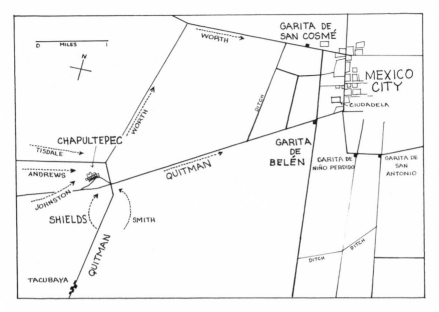

BATTLES OF CHAPULTEPEC AND MEXICO CITY

lavishly festooned with banners. Even the ships in the harbor were decorated for the day. Seven uniformed militia companies led the procession down King Street to Citadel Square and then down Meeting Street to the city hall, while literally thousands—the old, the young, whites and blacks—lined the parade route to cheer the hero. At intervals, roaring cannon almost drowned out the band music.

At city hall the mayor welcomed Shields with a brief but emotional address that "deeply affected" the visitor, who replied in kind. The hero said he knew the Palmettos well, had suffered with them, had shed blood with them, and "never did a State send better troops to the field of battle." Afterward, the Charleston ladies presented Shields a deep blue satin sling for his arm, badly wounded at Churubusco. On the sling were embroidered a gold palmetto tree and a motto, "Jasper sustains the Palmetto—the Palmetto will sustain a Shields."

Then began a series of receptions and dinners. When General Quitman arrived in Charleston two days later, he greeted his former brigade commander with the remark: "Why Shields, are you here? I thought they had killed you with kindness." It was nearer the truth than he realized, and the ceremonies were to be repeated.

Quitman reviewed troops and spoke from a balcony on Broad Street to "thousands" below. As expected, he paid glowing tribute to the Palmettos and the dead Butler. After loud applause the crowd called upon the weary Shields, standing in a balcony across the way. He politely refused, saying with a smile that he had an engagement with "them Hibernians, and you know I shall want all the strength, and all the talking, and all the power I possess." But he promised a speech later if he should "get away *alive* from them."

The lavish Hibernian affair that evening was also attended by Governor Johnson, General Quitman, and other notables. The *Mercury* listed forty-two toasts and speeches at the banquet and further stated, "A number of other toasts and sentiments were drank interspersed with speeches and songs"; but their reporter was unable to procure copies in time for publication. Chairman Henry W. Conner officially adjourned the revelry near midnight, and Shields slipped back to his hotel, almost dead from kindness.

The following evening Shields, Quitman, and Johnson were guests at a banquet and ceremony put on by the Masons, which they left at 9:30 to attend a ball given by the Washington Light Infantry. The *Courier* reported the ball to be "one of the most magnificent affairs" ever held in Charleston. Dancing was temporarily adjourned at 1 A.M. for food and refreshments. The exhausted Shields and Quitman departed late Christmas Eve by boat for Wilmington but not before a farewell military review in front of the Charleston Hotel.[22]

During the winter and early spring of 1847–1848, newspa-

22. Charleston *Mercury*, December 21–25, 1847; Charleston *Courier*, December 21–25, 1847; Greenville *Mountaineer*, December 31, 1847. Quitman, after his rising political career in Mississippi, returned to South Carolina in May, 1858, to address the Palmetto Association of Mexican War veterans. He died less than three months

pers reported on a number of ill or wounded Palmettos returning home. About forty reached Mobile on December 30 and were soon in South Carolina. They were usually honored in some manner, especially if prominent in their home districts. In January Lexington citizens held a torchlight procession and gave a barbecue for Colonel H. J. Caughman, who had volunteered as a private and returned home wounded. Barnwell held a reception and bestowed a medal on Captain N. G. Walker. Sumter duly recognized Captain Francis Sumter, who returned suffering from battle wounds and bad health. For Private W. M. Goodlett, the ex-sheriff, Greenville held a parade with music, banners, torches, transparencies, and speeches. Probably the most honored was Colonel Elias Earle; ceremonies were held for him in Greenville, Laurens, and Anderson.[23]

After General Shields's triumphal tour of South Carolina, the state paid its greatest attention to the funeral ceremonies for Butler, Dickinson, Moragne, and others whose remains were returned from Mexico. There was a move to have the bodies of all dead Palmettos brought home. From Mexico City Lieutenant Joseph Abney explained the difficulty of such action. Writing to B. R. Tillman about his slain son Thomas, brother of the future senator, Abney said that his body had been placed in a common grave with ten or twelve soldiers, all dressed alike and with no mark of distinction. Identification was now impossible. The same was not true of dead officers. Under Major Gladden's direction they had been buried separately in temporary wooden coffins constructed from theater benches. Abney had witnessed the exhuming of two bodies, which were then placed in lead coffins for shipment to South Carolina.[24]

---

later. Claiborne, *Life and Correspondence of John A. Quitman*, II, 379. During the Civil War, Shields became persona non grata in South Carolina because he fought on the Union side. The Clarisophic Society of South Carolina College struck his name from their roll as an honorary member. Daniel W. Hollis, *South Carolina College*, Vol. I of *University of South Carolina* (2 vols., Columbia, 1951), 245.

23. Greenville *Mountaineer*, January 21, 28, February 25, March 17, April 14, 1848; Charleston *Courier*, January 4, 7, 19, April 21, 1848; Sumter *Banner*, April 19, 1848; Charleston *Mercury*, April 21, 1848.
24. Abney to B. R. Tillman, December 6, 1847, in Edgefield *Advertiser*, April 5, 1848.

The first to be returned were the remains of Colonel Butler and Lieutenant Colonel Dickinson. On January 8 they arrived in Columbia from Charleston by special train with military escort. Their bodies lay in state, with a cadet guard, at the Arsenal Academy, while preparations were being made for funeral ceremonies. The chosen day was January 18. At a "gray misty hour" early on the eighteenth, firing artillery gave first notice of the ceremonies to follow. All business establishments were closed, and many visitors and almost the entire Columbia citizenry gathered at the arsenal. At 11:30 A.M. marshals organized the procession, one-half mile long, in the following order: fourteen militia companies (nine from Charleston), twelve pallbearers with Butler's casket, Butler's horse led by a family slave, Butler's family, Palmettos who had returned, an Edgefield committee of six, twelve pallbearers with Dickinson's casket, his horse led by a family slave, Dickinson's family, more Palmettos, Governor Johnson, President William C. Preston of South Carolina College and the governor's aides, the Society of Masons, the Society of Odd Fellows, the honorable judges, state senators and representatives, South Carolina College faculty and students, professors of the Arsenal Academy, intendant and wardens of Columbia, "Principal Engineers" of the railroad and assistants, citizens on foot, and citizens in carriages.

At an artillery signal the procession began its slow march down Main Street toward the state capitol. The procession was accompanied by tolling church bells, guns firing, and the "grand Dead March whose tunes, wrung from the heart of mourning music, re-echoed for the first time upon the ears of the world." The music had been composed especially for the occasion by a Mr. Mayer.

At the Statehouse, Governor Johnson briefly spoke to the audience and then introduced Colonel Preston, the principal orator of the day. A more fortunate choice could hardly have been made for the occasion. Preston had been noted as an orator of unsurpassed skill since his days in the United States Senate. For nearly an hour, he extolled "the virtues, the talents, the patriotism, the chivalric character, of the honored heroes." His oration moved almost the entire audience to tears.

After the ceremonies at the Statehouse, Butler's remains were removed to Grace Episcopal Church for services and burial, with military honors at graveside. The *Daily Telegraph* reported the entire ceremony as being "one of the most imposing ever seen," and the *Courier* said it was of the "most brilliant character." The *South Carolinian* agreed but was further grieved by the sight of "battle maimed and broken" Palmettos in the procession.[25]

Dickinson's remains were taken with military escort to Camden for burial on the twenty-second. The ceremonies there were much the same as in Columbia: a lengthy procession, martial music, two funeral odes by a choir, a funeral oration at the Dekalb monument, and a farewell military salute at graveside. The ceremonies were well attended but not as brilliant as those in Columbia. Local citizens especially regretted the absence of Governor Johnson.[26]

In the meantime, the body of Lieutenant John B. Moragne arrived in Abbeville on January 10, and preparations were made for his burial services at Willington Presbyterian Cemetery on the twentieth. The *Banner* published a poem composed by "J. McC" and dedicated to the dead hero. The first verse was as follows:

Another brilliant star has set!
John B. Moragne is no more!
His patriotic blood has wet the soil of a sullen foe.
We mourn his death—yet we are proud,
His country's flag has been his shroud.

Banner editor Charles Allen praised Moragne as one who was "distinguished for his coolness and bravery, and [who] nobly fell at his post." Continuing, the editor said, "Let us now give him a 'green grave in the land of his fathers' and ever cherish his memory in our hearts."

On the nineteenth the Abbeville Light Infantry accompanied Moragne's body to Mount Carmel. The next morning the little town bustled with what was probably the largest assembly in its

25. Greenville *Mountaineer*, January 28, 1848, quoting Columbia *Daily Telegraph*; Edgefield *Advertiser*, January 26, 1848, quoting Columbia *South Carolinian*; Charleston *Courier*, January 19, 1848. For Preston's oratorical reputation, see Lander, "Calhoun-Preston Feud," 24.
26. "Hobkirk," in Columbia *South Carolinian*, January 25, 1848.

history. Several thousand persons from the Abbeville and Edgefield districts, including many brilliantly arrayed militia officers,
gathered to participate in the ceremonies. The procession to the
Willington cemetery, four miles distant, was one-half mile in
length. Cannon boomed every ten minutes. After a funeral oration by the Reverend D. MacNeil Turner, a dirge by the Willington band, and a farewell graveside rifle volley, the young officer
was laid to rest with his Huguenot ancestors.[27]

On January 24 and 25 the bodies of Lieutenants David Adams
and Whitfield Brooks of Edgefield, James R. Clark of Fairfield,
Robert W. Williams of Barnwell, Sergeant B. F. Mattison of Abbeville, and Privates D. H. Trezevant and Jack Kennerly of Richland arrived by boat in Charleston. On the twenty-sixth, their
caskets were escorted in an elaborate military ceremony to the
railroad station to be sent to their respective districts.[28]

Each was buried with full military honors. In Whitfield Brooks's
case the chief orator, Captain James N. Lipscomb, was requested
at the last moment to include remarks about Private Joseph Gassaway, a returned Edgefield volunteer who had died the previous
day of influenza. Much to his embarrassment, Lipscomb knew
nothing of Gassaway but managed to improvise a glowing tribute. Young Brooks was well remembered for the words he spoke
when mortally wounded: "I asked him [General Shields] if I had
discharged my duty." The incident was commemorated by William Gilmore Simms in a poem entitled "Young Whitfield Brooks"
and included in his *Lays of the Palmetto*.

> "Tell me," cried the young when dying,
>   "Tell me that I do not shame,
> That dear land that gave me being
>   And my father's honor'd name."
>
> . . . .
>
> Then the gallant chieftain weeping,
>   O'er the dying youth, replied:

27. Abbeville *Banner*, January 12, 20, 26, 1848; Anderson *Gazette*, January 20, 1848;
    H. H. Townes to Mrs. Rachael Townes, January 15, 1848, in Townes Family Papers.
28. Charleston *Courier*, January 25–26, 1848; Edgefield *Advertiser*, February 9, 1848.

"By these eyes that speak my sorrow,
      I shall speak your deeds with pride.[29]

After the last of the funerals Mrs. Anna C. Maybin of Columbia informed Private W. S. Johnson, still in Mexico, that there had been "quite a stur here and considerable feeling with regard to the remains of our brave palmetos that have had the good fortune to be returned to their native land to find a resting place among their friends." She summed up her feeling by adding, "Oh how my heart sikens when I reflect on that war."[30]

29. Simms, *Lays of the Palmetto*, 30–31; Edgefield *Advertiser*, February 2, 9, 1848, especially for Adams' funeral; for Mattison's, see Anderson *Gazette*, February 17, 1848; for Clark's, see John R. Shurley Diary, February 2, 1848, SHC; for Trezevant's and Kennerly's, see Columbia *Daily Telegraph*, January 29, 1848. In March Sergeant W. B. Blocker (Edgefield) and Lieutenant Willis Cantey (Kershaw) were interred with military honors. Edgefield *Advertiser*, March 22, 1848; Camden *Journal*, March 22, 29, 1848.
30. Anna Maybin to W. S. Johnson, April 7, [1848], in Johnson Papers.

CHAPTER 9 *When and How Is This Peace To Be Conquered?*

WHILE PEACE remained elusive in the autumn of 1847, the prolongation of the war hardened American resolves to annex Mexican territory and thus satisfy American honor and indemnify the nation for its sacrifices. In all regions except New England and the Southeast, the All Mexico movement seemed to be gaining strength. The *Courier*'s Washington correspondent noted that a strong party had arisen in Congress in opposition to all appropriations for the war, unless the United States withdrew its troops to a boundary line it intended to hold. On the other hand, there was another party, perhaps stronger, that favored subjugating and annexing all of Mexico.[1]

In light of Mexican intransigence, the president himself was becoming more belligerent. On September 4 he informed his cabinet that he was no longer prepared to pay the sum for California and New Mexico that in April he had authorized Nicholas Trist to offer. Three days later he asked the cabinet to consider whether the amount of territory to be demanded from Mexico should be increased. Secretary of State James Buchanan, a presidential hopeful, suggested 31° or 31°30' instead of 32°, to which Polk assented. Two other cabinet members proposed the annexation of the state of Tamaulipas with the port of Tampico, to which the president also agreed, "if it should be found practicable to do so." But await-

1. Charleston *Courier*, October 8, 1847.

ing further military developments, the administration made no change in policy.[2]

Polk found considerable support in South Carolina for harsher peace terms. Colonel Francis W. Pickens wrote the president: "The moderation and humanity you have heretofore displayed must have satisfied the world that you now have no alternative left you. . . . [Now] public feeling loudly calls for a change in the system." Pickens proposed dividing Mexico into military districts and imposing a tax sufficient to defray the cost of occupation. An Abbeville public meeting, also noting "unexampled moderation and forbearance" in America's conduct toward Mexico, called for an all-out effort to subdue the enemy.[3]

The minimum territory that most South Carolinians wanted was California, New Mexico, and the Rio Grande. This view was expressed by editor Townes of the Greenville *Mountaineer* and by Benjamin F. Perry at Pickens Court House in early November. Perry said the war was caused by Mexican "arrogance and folly" and prolonged "in spite of all efforts of the United States to effect an honorable peace." Since the Mexicans were incapable of paying a monetary indemnity, Perry supported the administration claims for California, New Mexico, and the Rio Grande.[4]

In some cases attitudes changed. In late October the newly established Columbia *Daily Telegraph*, published by John Stubs and Edward Sill, the city intendant, called for public support of the administration "to prosecute the war vigorously," yet a month later suggested withdrawal of American troops from Mexico City. Conversely, the *Winyah Observer*, shortly before news of the capture of Mexico City, commented that the conflict was "probably the most unfortunate and disastrous war" in which America was ever engaged. Three weeks later the same editor contended that American forbearance was "too badly appreciated" by Mex-

2. Fuller, *Movement for the Acquisition of All Mexico*, 67–68; Quaife, *Diary of James K. Polk*, III, 159–65.
3. Pickens to Polk, October 31, 1847, in F. W. Pickens Papers, DU; Abbeville *Banner*, October 27, 1847.
4. Greenville *Mountaineer*, October 29, 1847; B. F. Perry, in Pendleton *Messenger*, December 17, 1847.

ico, and he therefore hoped that the United States would take over the entire country and "make Mexico do us justice." [5]

With "Manifest Destiny" gaining momentum, the Wilmot Proviso assumed increasing importance in the eyes of South Carolinians and other southerners. In August, *Mercury* editor John E. Carew repeatedly warned the South of the danger of the region's becoming surrounded by hostile people who would undermine the institution of slavery. Carew clearly explained that slavery was the South's solution to the racial problem created by a large Negro population; there could be no other. Before the end of the month Carew's harangues were bearing fruit. On August 27 the Pendleton *Messenger*, for instance, devoted its front page to Calhoun's anti-Wilmot Proviso resolutions submitted to the Senate on February 19, to a lengthy *Mercury* editorial on the subject, and to an *Evening News* editorial advocating southern unity.[6]

There soon followed the greatest flurry of anti-Wilmot Proviso activity yet to be seen in South Carolina. On September 6 a rally in Edgefield endorsed the Virginia resolutions of the previous February, which condemned the hated proviso. Within the next few weeks similar meetings were reported from Abbeville, Darlington, Laurens, Anderson, Edisto Island, Georgetown, Barnwell, Columbia, Pickens, and Greenville. Surely there were others.

All meetings were well attended, and the speakers were invariably the leading citizens of the district. Rarely was the slightest dissent reported and that primarily over the wording of resolutions. Emotions ran high and the meetings generally agreed with the sentiment of a Laurens resolution that read, "We would not submit to the principles contained in the Wilmot Proviso though the dissolution of the Union be the result." [7]

5. Columbia *Daily Telegraph*, October 30, November 25, 1847; Georgetown *Winyah Observer*, October 13, November 3, 1847.
6. Charleston *Mercury*, August 9–14, 1847; Pendleton *Messenger*, August 27, 1847; Morrison, *Democratic Politics*, 68–70.
7. Pendleton *Messenger*, October 22, 1847; Greenville *Mountaineer*, September 17, October 8, December 3, 1847; Edgefield *Advertiser*, September 8, October 20, 1847; Anderson *Gazette*, October 21 (Laurens meeting), November 11, 1847; Charleston *Mercury*, October 11, November 8, 1847; Hamer, *Secession Movement*, 5–14.

But to deny application of the Wilmot Proviso to a Mexican cession was beyond the ability of the South, a minority region. Was there then, General Waddy Thompson asked, no way to avoid the "fearful alternatives of a dissolution of our Union, or a degrading submission to dangerous usurpation, insult and outrage?" Speaking before the Greenville anti-Wilmot Proviso rally on October 4, Thompson proposed a remedy; it was to acquire no more territory. He preferred not to go beyond the Nueces and thus leave the Rio Grande valley an unsettled neutral zone, a proposal Mexican authorities had suggested to Nicholas Trist.

Thompson offered compelling reasons in support of his doctrine. First, the United States already had sufficient vacant land for a swelling population. Second, American military superiority did not give the United States the legal right to Mexican territory. Third, the domain contemplated was "no promised land." It was already owned by Mexican citizens; hence, the United States would acquire no free land but only "worthless and troublesome" people of an alien race. Fourth, the previous year 300,000 immigrants had poured into America, only 2,000 of whom had come South. The others had settled in the North and West "with imported sentiments hostile to our welfare." As a result, the nonslaveholding states had a "dangerous and constantly increasing preponderance" in the Union. Thompson would therefore "stake his life" that no part of the territory could, or would, be occupied by slaveholders, with or without the Wilmot Proviso. He emphatically declared that "he would consent to be gibbeted, or, if dead, that his bones be dug up and made manure of, if ever a slaveholding State were formed out of any portion of it." [8]

Thompson's speech created quite a sensation. Not only was it publicized in the South Carolina press, it was republished and given wide circulation by the *National Intelligencer*, a moderate Whig journal in Washington. Soon other Whigs were repeating Thompson's views in support of their "no more territory" doctrine. The Charleston *Courier*, usually sympathetic to Polk, sent

8. Greenville *Mountaineer*, October 15, 1847; Charleston *Courier*, October 9, 1847; Fuller, *Movement for the Acquisition of All Mexico*, 92.

a reporter to interview the former minister to Mexico. After restating Thompson's opposition to the war "as unjust in origin, unwise in policy and conduct, and fraught with issues perilous to the South and to the Union," the reporter commented that "passing events seemed to be setting the seal of prophecy" on his views.[9]

Thompson's views on the war were strenuously opposed by Colonel G. F. Townes, also a speaker at the Greenville meeting and editor of the local newspaper. In a lengthy editorial, Townes called the Whig policy of no territory and no indemnity a desperate move to hold both northern and southern Whigs together at the expense of the South. To propose to give back all the territory to Mexico was a vain delusion. In the history of the world, Townes said, no nation had been provoked to war, conquered vast territory at the expense of millions of dollars and much of the "best blood" of the land, and then "ingloriously" given back the conquered territory to the defeated enemy.

Townes brushed aside as "a great mistake" Thompson's view that slavery would not go beyond the Rio Grande. He denied that the former diplomat knew any more about that region than anyone else and said there had been good reports about it from Palmetto volunteers. Moreover, the editor called attention to recent political conventions in New York and Pennsylvania that had condemned the Wilmot Proviso. Townes's objection to returning all the conquered territory to Mexico was supported generally in the state. Even the Charleston *Mercury* was not in favor of "no territory" as an answer to the Wilmot Proviso.[10]

Undaunted by adverse criticism, Thompson later in October pleaded with Calhoun to use his influence to stop "this most disastrous war." Repeating his view that the United States had no right to any Mexican territory and that slavery would never go beyond the Rio Grande, Thompson said that in his opinion peo-

9. Washington *National Intelligencer*, October 21, 1847; Charleston *Courier*, October 15, 1847; Merk, *Manifest Destiny*, 169, 173.
10. Greenville *Mountaineer*, October 15, 1847; Charleston *Mercury*, September 28, 1847.

ple everywhere, except in the warlike West, were "sick of carnage
& slaughter and fruitless victories—and are daily becoming more
so." Now that the American army was in Mexico City "our troubles are just commencing." He noted that Joel R. Poinsett, another South Carolina diplomat who had served in Mexico, agreed
with his views. A few days later he wrote again, expressing dread
of ten or twelve new free states in the West.[11]

Calhoun agreed with Thompson as to the cause and disastrous
consequences of the war, but he reminded the former diplomat
that large majorities of both parties by their recorded votes stood
committed to the war. Worse still, they had committed large por-
tions of both parties outside Congress to the war "as just and unavoidable." Calhoun was particularly critical of the Whigs, whose
vote for war had rendered them impotent as an opposition party.
This, along with America's brilliant victories, made it impossible
"to terminate the war in the manner you propose." [12]

Calhoun had reason to be cautious. Although friends such
as Wilson Lumpkin, former governor of Georgia, and John A.
Campbell, a future Supreme Court justice from Alabama, agreed
with his antiwar views, others wrote of the rising temper among
Americans because of the breakdown of diplomatic negotiations.
In early October the disgusted president had issued orders to re-
call Trist. Barnard E. Bee, a Pendleton neighbor, warned that the
aroused public would no longer be satisfied with the Rio Grande.
"The Sierra Madre must now be your aim," he advised. Nor
would the public sanction paying millions for territory already
conquered.[13]

Calhoun was given another opportunity to urge caution when
Governor Johnson, in preparing his annual message to the legislature, sought his advice about the war. The governor was in-

11. Thompson to J. C. Calhoun, October 22, November 6, 1847, in Calhoun Papers,
    CU.
12. J. C. Calhoun to Thompson, October 29, 1847, in Jameson (ed.), *Correspondence
    of John C. Calhoun*, 738–39.
13. Quaife, *Diary of James K. Polk*, III, 185–86; Crallé to J. C. Calhoun, October 10,
    1847; Lumpkin to Calhoun, November 18, 1847; Campbell to Calhoun, November
    20, 1847; Bee to Calhoun, November 28, 1847, all in Calhoun Papers, CU. Camp-
    bell wished to annex no territory.

clined "to look with indulgence" on the origins of the war as a probable consequence of American annexation of Texas. But once Taylor had driven Mexican troops across the Rio Grande, a defensive strategy would have prevented further Mexican intrusion. Instead, the administration, ignoring the lessons of the Seminole War, had tried to "conquer a peace." Having failed in that, the government now seemed inclined to conquest and permanent occupation of Mexico. If true, Johnson proclaimed, "I protest against it from the bottom of my heart as unwise and unjust."

Calhoun advised the governor to say nothing more than "to do justice to our gallant army and especially our own regiment, which has so nobly done its duty, and to express, in general terms, your regret at the continuance of the war, and a hope for its speedy termination." He reminded Johnson of the vote of the South Carolina delegation for war. In addition, he doubted that the public would support a policy of no annexation. Calhoun feared such a proposal would tend "to divide and weaken the state; a thing that would be deplorable when union among ourselves is so desirable, in reference, to the other great subject [slavery]." It was fairly obvious that Calhoun would have been glad to adopt a "no territory" policy had such a course appeared politically feasible.[14]

In his message to the General Assembly on November 23, the governor prudently guarded his comments about the war. He reviewed its causes, its course, and America's efforts to "conquer a peace." Then he questioned: "When and how is this peace to be conquered? . . . What benefits are we to derive from this conquest?" His solution for the war was the withdrawal of American troops from the Mexican heartland and the imposition of a blockade. While admitting the need for communications between America's northwestern territory and the Pacific—a vague reference to California—the governor felt there was no further need for additional territory.

14. David Johnson to J. C. Calhoun, October 26, 1847, in Calhoun Papers, CU; Calhoun to Johnson, November 5, 1847, in Calhoun Papers, SCL; Fuller, *Movement for the Acquisition of All Mexico*, 101–102.

The answer of the South Carolina Senate to Johnson's message was the passage of William H. Gist's resolution: "Resolved, That the war waged against the Republic of Mexico by the United States is just and proper, and that South Carolina will sustain the Administration in prosecuting it with vigor to a successful termination." But the House, for reasons not clear, failed to concur. Probably some legislators, though desiring New Mexico and California, agreed with the *Mountaineer* that "no sane man" would want all of Mexico, and they therefore did not wish to give support to the more ardent imperialists.[15]

Johnson also called attention to Virginia's resolutions against the Wilmot Proviso and recommended legislative endorsement. The Senate approved but could not reconcile its version with that of the House. Failure of the General Assembly to reach agreement about the tenor of resolutions against the proviso seems strange in view of the great agitation in the state earlier in the fall. Apparently, events in the North had cooled the South Carolina hotheads somewhat. In mid-October the *Mountaineer* had noted that northern Democrats were changing their attitude about the Wilmot Proviso.

In New York, after Silas Wright's death, the pro-Wilmot Proviso Barnburners lost control of the Democratic party to the more moderate Hunkers. In addition, northern Democratic presidential candidates James Buchanan, Vice-President George M. Dallas, Supreme Court Justice Levi Woodbury, and Senator Lewis Cass sought to garner southern support by dissociating themselves from the Wilmot Proviso. Southerners were further heartened when in early 1848 northern state Democratic conventions—notably New York, Pennsylvania, Ohio, Michigan, and Indiana—played down or skirted the proviso for the sake of party solidarity in the upcoming election.

15. *South Carolina House Journal, 1847*, 21–23; *South Carolina Senate Journal, 1847*, 32, 77, 186; Greenville *Mountaineer*, December 3, 1847; Anderson *Gazette*, December 9, 1847; Charleston *Mercury*, November 29, 1847. See also DeSaussure to J. C. Calhoun, January 7, 1848, in Calhoun Papers, CU.

Northern propagandists for annexation insisted that the Wilmot Proviso was not needed to keep slavery out of the territory in question. If the propagandists were to be believed, the supporters of the proviso were not afraid of the extension of slavery but were using the bogey to forestall annexation. Calhoun was accused of doing the same thing. But now many northern Democrats were coming around to "popular sovereignty" in the territories, also an idea that was anathema to Calhoun and many southeasterners.[16]

On December 7 President Polk sent his annual message to Congress. He had worked on it for three or more weeks, had confidentially consulted his cabinet and other leaders, including Congressman Robert Barnwell Rhett. The South Carolinian agreed with its general disposition but advised the president to wait another year before establishing territorial governments over California and New Mexico.

In his message Polk made it clear that under no circumstance would the United States surrender New Mexico and California, and he warned that a continuation of the war might require additional territory. Yet, he avowed no desire "to make a permanent conquest" of Mexico or "to annihilate her separate existence as an independent nation." Then, with Calhoun obviously in mind, the president emphatically rejected the suggestion of withdrawing the army to a defensive line. Such a move would not terminate the war. It would only lead to Mexican harassment of isolated American army posts.[17]

Under increasing pressure from the Northeast and West to take all Mexico, the president may have been ready to do so if his peace efforts failed. To oppose such an eventuality, Calhoun, the leading antiimperialist Democrat in the Senate, began to prepare a counterattack. He was displeased with the president's message,

16. Charleston *Mercury*, January 14, 1848, quoting Philadelphia *Ledger; South Carolina House Journal*, 1847, 21–23; Georgetown *Winyah Observer*, December 1, 1847; Edgefield *Advertiser*, December 22, 1847; Greenville *Mountaineer*, October 15, 1847; Morrison, *Democratic Politics*, 79–88, 93–106; Fuller, *Movement for the Acquisition of All Mexico*, 74–75; Hamer, *Secession Movement*, 15–16.
17. *Congressional Globe*, 30th Cong., 1st Sess., 4–12; Quaife, *Diary of James K. Polk*, III, 225, 236.

which he privately called "very undignified & full of false assumptions. You will see," he told his son-in-law, "that things have progressed to a point, where it is difficult to advance or retreat." [18]

Prospects for stopping the annexation of Mexico seemed fair enough. A report from Washington indicated that the Whigs, who controlled the House of Representatives, looked to Calhoun's leadership to limit operations in Mexico and would attempt nothing without his concurrence. Moreover, from a number of sources came reports that General Taylor, Commodore Perry, and General W. O. Butler, soon to be Scott's successor in Mexico, favored Calhoun's defensive-line policy. It was even predicted that Congress would adopt such a policy. But before the South Carolinian could make his move, Daniel S. Dickinson, a Hunker Democrat from New York, dropped a bombshell in the Senate. In reference to a Mexican cession, he resolved that the question of "domestic policy therein" should be left to the legislatures chosen by the people of the territories. [19]

On December 15, the day following Dickinson's resolutions, Calhoun presented his own against the conquest and annexation of Mexico and against any military policy that might lead to "consequences so disastrous." Adhering to a position long held and previously explained, Calhoun was anxious for the American people to consider Mexican policy "with their eyes open" before embarking on a calamitous course.

At the same time his collaborator I. E. Holmes introduced similar resolutions in the House. However, the congressman from Charleston went much further than Calhoun. He proposed returning all Mexican territory beyond the Rio Grande, provided that Americans were permitted freedom of movement, the privilege to hold land, and freedom of religion and commerce in New

---

18. J. C. Calhoun to T. G. Clemson, December 10, 1847, in Calhoun Papers, CU; Fuller, *Movement for the Acquisition of All Mexico,* 99–102. Calhoun maintained the proper amenities by calling on the president. Quaife, *Diary of James K. Polk,* III, 245.

19. Charleston *Courier,* November 6, 1847; Pendleton *Messenger,* November 5, 1847; Charleston *Mercury,* January 26, 1848; Fisher to J. C. Calhoun, December 4, 1847, in Calhoun Papers, CU; *Congressional Globe,* 30th Cong., 1st Sess., 21.

Mexico and California "as fully as any of the Mexican citizens of these provinces." Holmes also demanded a railroad right-of-way to San Diego, and as a hostage to fulfillment of those requirements, the United States would hold the fort of San Juan de Ulúa at Vera Cruz.[20]

Calhoun's and Holmes's resolutions received an immediate and favorable response in the South Carolina press, and Waddy Thompson hastily sent Calhoun a lengthy letter that cataloged American-Mexican incompatibilities and difficulties the United States would encounter beyond the Rio Grande. If the United States should annex a large section of Mexico, Thompson feared it would furnish room for fifteen or twenty free states. "Woe to the Southern man who lends his aid to doing that," he added. Calhoun realized the difficulty before him; he saw that the movement to annex all Mexico was "exceedingly strong" and would become "overwhelmingly so" unless arrested by a vote in the Senate.[21]

As for Dickinson's resolutions, Calhoun was convinced that they had originated with the administration as a rallying point for the Democratic party. But with the Mexicans, who were all abolitionists, and northerners in the majority in the conquered territories, the popular sovereignty that Dickinson proposed would exclude slavery as effectively as the Wilmot Proviso. Calhoun was much upset and furthermore feared that Polk's policy would end the war in such a manner that America would have no choice but to hold Mexico as a conquered province or to incorporate it into the Union.

Calhoun therefore informed Henry S. Foote, the ardent Mississippi expansionist, that he would denounce Dickinson's resolutions. Foote, with the assistance of Senator Cass, persuaded Dickinson not to press his resolutions to a vote, and Calhoun

20. *Congressional Globe*, 30th Cong., 1st Sess., 26, 38; J. C. Calhoun to Conner, December 16, 1847, in Conner Papers.
21. Thompson to J. C. Calhoun, December 18, 1847; Calhoun to Mrs. T. G. Clemson, December 26, 1847, in Calhoun Papers, CU. See Columbia *Daily Telegraph*, December 20, 21, 28, 30, 1847, for its views and reports from other South Carolina papers.

acquiesced in the move when informed that a fight over Dickinson's resolutions would divide opponents of the Wilmot Proviso. In addition, the Senate agreed to make Calhoun's resolutions the special order of the day, January 4. Nevertheless, Calhoun urged the South Carolina press to attack Dickinson's resolutions, and the *Mercury* took the lead in doing so. Quoting Calhoun, its editor declared, "Mexico is to us the forbidden fruit; the penalty for eating it would be to subject our institutions to political death." [22]

Since Polk had no intention of changing his war policy, he was anxious to gain congressional approval for an additional ten regiments to aid the depleted ones already in Mexico. On December 30 and again on January 3 Senator Cass, acting for the administration, brought up his motion to increase the army by another 7,500 men. In reply, Calhoun expressed concern that further involvement would lead to the extinction of Mexican nationality, to which Cass strongly disagreed, saying that the president was "entirely opposed" to such a goal. "Sir," Calhoun cautioned, "we often get into situations which we never intended to get into." But because it was clear that Calhoun also favored retention of California and New Mexico, the administration forces, in an effort to mollify the influential Carolinian, agreed to postpone debate on the Ten-Regiment Bill until after his speech the following day. [23]

By midmorning on January 4, the Senate gallery, antechamber, and hallways were jammed "almost to suffocation" by diplomats, cabinet members, ladies, members of the House of Representatives, and others. One observer remarked that "such an audience, so crowded, so brilliant, so distinguished has never before graced the Senate Chamber." Shortly before one o'clock a hush fell over the chamber as Calhoun rose to make his much-heralded speech. For an hour and a half he held his audience so spellbound that "not a whisper broke the silence."

The gaunt and aged South Carolinian reviewed the causes of

22. *Congressional Globe*, 30th Cong., 1st Sess., 53–56; Morrison, *Democratic Politics*, 88–89; J. C. Calhoun to Conner, December 16, 1847, in Conner Papers; Charleston *Mercury*, December 30, 31, 1847.
23. *Congressional Globe*, 30th Cong., 1st Sess., 78–79, 86–92.

the war and how it might have been prevented, and he repeated his proposal for a defensive line as the "only certain mode" of ending the conflict successfully. Such a line would be neither expensive nor difficult to maintain. Recalling the president's policy of "conquering a peace" and recounting America's military successes, Calhoun queried: "Have we conquered a peace? Have we obtained a treaty? Have we obtained an indemnity?"

Calhoun next moved to the heart of the matter. For America to continue to build up its armed forces would not only cause a great financial crisis but would lead to the destruction of Mexico's army and civil government. He warned against the folly of attempting by force of American arms to establish a Mexican puppet regime in that chaotic situation. And for the United States to take over aliens of a different race and culture would conflict with "the genius and character" of American institutions. In opposing the annihilation of Mexico, Calhoun, though he did not mention it, had the antislavery movement uppermost in his mind.

In closing, the senator avowed a willingness to negotiate the exact location of his defensive line, and he made a special appeal to both parties. He told the Whigs that their policy of no indemnity was out of the question because "the voice of the country had decided irrevocably against it." And he asked the Democrats to put aside their pride and reverse their policy.[24]

Calhoun's speech was sensational and attracted nationwide attention. One senator was reported to have said, "I would rather be the author of that speech, than President of the United States." Another exclaimed, "I would rather have made that speech, than have gained all our victories in Mexico." And some politicos, wrote A. P. Butler, deemed Calhoun's speech "the highest effect of his life." The *Mercury* editor believed that posterity would characterize the fearless and independent South Carolinian as "the statesman of the age." Other Palmetto newspapers were also fulsome in their praise of the senator.[25]

24. *Ibid.*, 96–100; Charleston *Mercury*, January 10, 1848.
25. Charleston *Mercury*, January 10, 11, 31, 1848; Charleston *Courier*, January 12, 20, 1848; Columbia *Daily Telegraph*, January 13, 1848; Abbeville *Banner*, January 19, 1848; Greenville *Mountaineer*, January 21, 1848; Anderson *Gazette*, January 20, 1848; A. P. Butler to Elmore, January 5, 1848, in F. H. Elmore Papers, LC.

Elsewhere, Calhoun's speech received favorable comment from the Whig press, which applauded his antiwar sentiments but considered his defensive-line strategy only a temporary expedient in the right direction. They clung to their futile no territory, no indemnity principle. In Congress Calhoun's plan quickly became the subject of debate. Administration spokesmen, voicing Polk's views, termed a defensive line impractical and likely to prolong the war.

Privately, Calhoun received conflicting reactions and advice from various persons outside the state. Louis McLane, a former secretary of state from Maryland, while appreciative of Calhoun's efforts, believed that once the war had begun the administration was remiss in not prosecuting it with "utmost vigor." From Virginia came word that Calhoun's policy was unsuited to the present emergency. But a Mobile resident regarded Calhoun as "our *Pillar of Fire*." And aged Albert Gallatin wrote that he had a "most rooted aversion to the annexation of New Mexico to our Union."

On January 17 Senator Butler arose to defend his colleague and present a slightly different plan for peace. After restating some of Calhoun's views, Butler proposed holding the Rio Grande, sending "the most illustrious embassy" to Mexico, and negotiating the line to the Pacific. He was not averse to the 37th parallel, an ill-concealed effort to avoid an immediate fight over slavery below the Missouri Compromise line. In any case, he foresaw that American settlers moving west would "inevitably" bring the territory in question under American control. For the moment there was an urgent need to end the war.[26]

Butler's speech was likewise applauded in his home state, but Congressman R. F. Simpson doubted that such efforts could stop "this grasping wholesale robbery." The Pendleton *Messenger* observed that Polk was under heavy pressure from both southern and northern leaders, including Buchanan, Dallas, and Cass, to

26. *Congressional Globe*, 30th Cong., 1st Sess., 184–89; Schroeder, *Mr. Polk's War*, 151–52; Albert Gallatin to J. C. Calhoun, March 3, 1848; Lindsay to Calhoun, February 9, 1848; James Henry to Calhoun, February 5, 1848; Louis McLane to Calhoun, January 18, 1848; Crallé to Calhoun, January 17, 1848; Alexander Bowie to Calhoun, January 19, 1848, all in Calhoun Papers, CU.

annex all Mexico. The pressure was probably not for all Mexico, but Polk's diary reveals that he was subjected to pressure to annex more than California and New Mexico.[27]

From within South Carolina Calhoun received much commendation and advice. Some correspondents agreed entirely with his position, and they saw no need for a large army on the frontier. Others cautioned that it would be difficult to abandon Mexico City and Vera Cruz or advised that the United States should claim the entire Rio Grande Valley. But there was universal worry over the continuation of the war, rising militarism, and the movement to annex all of Mexico.

Colonel James Gadsden, the railroad promoter, wrote caustically about "mad designs of Conquest," "the whole pack of hungry land hounds," and "the spirit of military glory." He was convinced that conquest, not peace, was the object of the administration. He reported that he and General Shields, an avowed expansionist, had had "a very unpleasant argument" over the annexation of Mexico at a Charleston dinner party. And the infirm George McDuffie wrote, "I cannot see how we are going to terminate the Mexican War—if we fight and conquer till the *day of Judgment* or kill all the Mexicans." [28]

Meanwhile, Henry W. Conner, who had close *Mercury* connections, Henry Gourdin, *Mercury* editor John Carew, and F. H. Elmore, who was then in Columbia, were working to marshal additional upstate newspaper support for Calhoun's views. All the Charleston papers, even the *Courier*, supported Calhoun's defensive-line strategy in preference to Mexican annexation. The *Courier* ran two lengthy articles on the war by Waddy Thompson, alias "Lowndes," and commended them to its readers.[29]

The former diplomat at great length repeated much of his ear-

27. Charleston *Mercury*, January 28, 1848; Columbia *Daily Telegraph*, January 31, 1848; Simpson, in Pendleton *Messenger*, January 28, 1848; Quaife, *Diary of James K. Polk*, III, 277.
28. D. J. McCord to J. C. Calhoun, January 23, 1848; Henry Gourdin to Calhoun, January 17, 19, 1848; Gadsden to Calhoun, December 28, 1847, January 8, 17, 23, 1848, all in Calhoun Papers, CU; Paul Quattlebaum to Burt, February 18, 1848, in Burt Papers; G. McDuffie to Burt, January 13, [1848], in George McDuffie Papers, DU.
29. Conner to J. C. Calhoun, January 17, 1848; Gourdin to Calhoun, January 17,

lier argument against America's legal claim to land beyond the Nueces. He preferred that the territory between the Nueces and the Rio Grande be kept a no man's land as a discouragement to runaway slaves. On the other hand, he favored the acquisition of Upper California and would pay liberally, if Mexico was willing to sell; but he would not continue the war for one day in order to acquire it. Then touching on the issue of slavery, he declared that surely "no sane man" could suppose it would ever exist in California, but more to the point, he solemnly warned against the annexation of Mexico. Such a move would be "a fatal blow to the institution of slavery" and lead quickly to abolition.

Not only did Thompson furnish Calhoun strong support, but Poinsett, long silent about the war, also entered the fray. Well informed about conditions south of the border, he sent three letters to Senator Butler explaining his objections to the administration's aggressive war policy. The senator in turn released the letters to the *National Intelligencer* for publication, and during late January and February they were widely reprinted with favorable comment in the South Carolina press. In them Poinsett proclaimed: "I firmly believe that if the United States would act with justice toward her weaker sister republic peace might be made upon advantageous terms. But if the war is to be continued and prosecuted with vigor, ten thousand additional troops will not be enough. . . . I believe that the Mexicans will display the same pertinacity in maintaining their national existence that they did in achieving it, and with the same result."[30]

By mid-February, with peace still seemingly distant, the *Winyah Observer* noted that the defensive plan recommended by Calhoun and Poinsett was daily gaining strength and might ultimately be adopted as the only road to peace. That the plan was gaining strength was certainly true in South Carolina. The Greenville

1848, in Calhoun Papers, CU; Conner to Burt, January 26, 1848, in Burt Papers; Charleston *Courier*, January 7, 14, 1848.

30. Poinsett's letters were written December 12, 1847, January 28, and February 11, 1848. For reprints see Columbia *Daily Telegraph*, January 27, February 10, 26, 1848. For further editorial comment see Charleston *Mercury*, January 25, February 8, 12, 1848; Georgetown *Winyah Observer*, February 2, 16, March 1, 1848.

Mountaineer and the Camden *Journal* both announced support of the defensive-line strategy, leaving the Abbeville *Banner* as the only newspaper in South Carolina still an avowed supporter of Polk's war policy.

In addition, Calhoun's longtime political foe, Benjamin F. Perry, admitted that the war had continued too long; the army and the country had won enough glory. He was now "more & more convinced of the wisdom" of Calhoun's policy and, requesting a more detailed plan for peace, was soon in touch with the senator. He also supported Senator Butler's proposal to send a team of ambassadors on a final peace mission. But still retaining a warlike fervor, Perry suggested an ultimatum to Mexico. "If you do not treat with us, we shall destroy our fortresses & castles & the walls of your cities, carry off all your public property, & occupy the Californias, New Mexico & the country east of the Sierra Madre."[31]

Calhoun seemed reasonably well pleased with the shape of events in late January and early February. He claimed for himself much of the credit for having killed the Wilmot Proviso, though not unmindful of the danger of popular sovereignty in a Mexican cession. He believed his speech of January 4 had been "exceedingly well received" and had awakened the public to the dangers of annexing all Mexico, which otherwise would have resulted. Now the American people were "beginning to recover from the intoxicating dose of glory, & come to their senses." In his opinion nothing short of a treaty or the adoption of his policy could save the administration, but he wished to give them "a fair opportunity" to make peace before pushing his plan to a vote.[32]

With each passing day there were no sure signs, only rumors,

31. Georgetown *Winyah Observer*, February 16, 1848; Greenville *Mountaineer*, February 4, 11, 1848; Camden *Journal*, February 16, 1848; Abbeville *Banner*, February 9, 1848; Perry to Burt, February 11, 1848; to J. C. Calhoun, February 21, 1848, in Benjamin F. Perry Papers, Alabama Department of Archives and History, Montgomery.
32. J. C. Calhoun to Conner, January 8, 1848; to Gourdin, January 8, 1848, in Conner Papers; Calhoun to James Calhoun, January 22, 1848; to T. G. Clemson, February 4, 1848, in Calhoun Papers, CU; Calhoun to Francis Lieber, February 6, 1848, in Calhoun Papers, SCL; Calhoun to Lesesne, February 11, 1848, in Duff Green Papers, SHC.

that the discredited Nicholas Trist had persuaded the recalcitrant Mexicans to come to terms. Peace efforts seemed further complicated by a squabble among the generals in Mexico. Scott had brought charges of insubordination against politically ambitious General Pillow and had hassled with the president over that and other matters. Polk considered the difficulties in Mexico due mainly to "the vanity and tyrannical temper of Gen'l Scott, & his want of prudence and common sense." The irate president relieved his commander on January 13 and placed General William O. Butler in charge.[33]

Meanwhile, in Congress on February 7 Senator R. M. T. Hunter, a Calhoun supporter from Virginia, urged the adoption of a defensive-line strategy, and two days later Senator John Niles, a Democrat from Connecticut, echoed much of Calhoun's sentiment when proposing another attempt at negotiations. A report emanating from a Whig journal in New York indicated a belief that the Whigs were preparing to unite on Calhoun's plan. The senator himself, though uncertain of his strength, felt that in a showdown the Whigs would rally to his position. Many probably would have, to embarrass Polk, but few openly endorsed his plan. The question remained, whether Calhoun's defensive strategy would gain sufficient public approval to force Polk's hand.[34]

Calhoun's hopes for Whig support were hardly encouraged by a lengthy speech of Robert Barnwell Rhett in the House on February 1. Rhett, now cool to his elder colleague, defended the president against a Whig resolution that he had acted unconstitutionally in making war on Mexico. In turn, he accused the Whigs of violating the Constitution in an effort to build up the powers of Congress for the benefit of the North, the majority region. He further accused the Whigs of having no desire to end the war; they looked to it "as the grand instrument" for success in the forthcoming presidential election.

Two weeks later Calhoun received another blow when Con-

33. Quaife, *Diary of James K. Polk*, III, 266–67, 278–80, 293; Bauer, *Mexican War*, 371–74.
34. Schroeder, *Mr. Polk's War*, 152–53; J. C. Calhoun to Lesesne, February 11, 1848, in Green Papers; Charleston *Mercury*, February 11, 1848, citing New York *Commercial Advertiser*.

gressman A. D. Sims denounced his defensive-line plan. Never one to yield to Calhoun's dictation, the representative from the Pee Dee loudly called for "a vigorous prosecution" of the war. James H. Hammond, one of Calhoun's silent critics, was also still of the opinion that the United States should give Mexico "a *thorough* drubbing." And from Mexico itself, H. Judge Moore informed the *Mountaineer* that he and a majority of the remaining Palmettos objected to Calhoun's plan. The only way to end the war, wrote Moore, was "to *advance* or *recede*; and where is the man who loves his country, and is willing to peril his life in defense of her honor, who would hesitate a moment in choosing between the two." [35]

As matters stood in mid-February, 1848, the president was buffeted by Democrats who wished to annex all Mexico, by Whigs who wished no annexation, and by some members of both parties who supported Calhoun's policy. Calhoun, despite some objection in his own state, believed his plan was gaining additional support. On the twentieth he wrote, "I am of the impression, if peace is not made in a reasonable time, there will be a majority for [my plan] in both Houses and the Union." Perhaps so, but on the previous evening the president glimpsed a ray of hope when a special courier arrived in the capital with a treaty illegally negotiated by Trist but drawn along lines of Polk's earlier instructions.

Unofficial reports of the treaty reached Charleston on the seventeenth, and the South Carolina press hailed the news with joy. The Sumter *Banner* was pleased that "the lust and pride of domination so apt to attend conquerors has not yet corrupted us as a nation." The *Mercury* admitted that if Polk could gain Senate approval of the treaty, it would be "the crowning glory" of his administration. Calhoun foresaw strong opposition but predicted approval, which would be "a fortunate deliverance." [36]

35. *Congressional Globe*, 30th Cong., 1st Sess., appendix, 239–42, 347–48; J. H. Hammond to Col. [D. J.] McCord, February 25, 1848, in Hammond Papers, SCL; Moore, in Greenville *Mountaineer*, January 28, March 3, April 7, 28, 1848.
36. Quaife, *Diary of James K. Polk*, III, 344–46; Sumter *Banner*, February 23, 1848; Charleston *Courier*, February 18, 1848; Charleston *Mercury*, February 24, 1848; J. C. Calhoun to Mrs. T. G. Clemson, February 20, 1848, in Calhoun Papers, CU; Calhoun to A. P. Calhoun, February 23, 1848, in Jameson (ed.), *Correspondence of John C. Calhoun*, 744.

The president was worried. He feared that all-Mexico Democrats and no-territory Whigs would combine to defeat the treaty for opposite reasons. The upcoming presidential contest had, he recorded, "too much to do with the question of ratification of the Treaty." Moreover, two members of his own cabinet and four of five members on the Senate Foreign Relations Committee voiced objection for various reasons. Polk likewise preferred a larger indemnity, and he considered Trist to be "an impudent and unqualified scoundrel"; but to reject the treaty would cause great political difficulties in both countries. He therefore decided to push it with one major amendment—the deletion of the clause validating Mexican land titles in Texas.

From February 23 to March 10 the Senate debated in executive session, while the administration pressured waverers wherever it could. On the tenth the Senate voted 38 to 14 to approve the treaty. The opposition was evenly divided between Whigs and Democrats. Calhoun's role was crucial, and the historian of the movement for all Mexico concluded that "there might have been sufficient demand for annexation in February and March, 1848, to have wrecked the Treaty of Guadalupe Hidalgo had it not been for the opposition of pro-slavery Democrats led by Calhoun."[37]

Sufficient demand to wreck the treaty perhaps, but not to annex all Mexico. Frederick Merk has shown that the American people were reluctant to absorb eight million people of a mixed race. Could these so-called inferior people be granted citizenship? Merk contends that the strength of the all-Mexico movement was overrated, and most of the nation's intellectual leaders were opposed to it. Nevertheless, once the Senate approved, Polk still fretted, and Calhoun more so, lest Mexico should reject the amended treaty. The latter could envision the government's collapse and anarchy prevailing. Several South Carolina newspapers expressed the same fears, but all were hopeful that the war had ended, and in general they commended the president.[38]

37. Quaife, *Diary of James K. Polk*, III, 346–77; Fuller, *Movement for the Acquisition of All Mexico*, 163; *Congressional Globe*, 30th Cong., 1st Sess., 384. Original news reports listed the vote 37 to 15. Charleston *Mercury*, March 16, 1848.
38. Charleston *Mercury*, March 14, 1848; J. C. Calhoun to T. G. Clemson, March 7, 1848, in Calhoun Papers, CU; Sumter *Banner*, March 8, 1848; Greenville *Moun-*

Although he approved the treaty, Calhoun did not cement allegiance to the administration. He joined the Whig senators in an unsuccessful effort to block the Ten-Regiment Bill and delivered a major assault against it on March 16. Neither force nor intimidation was necessary toward Mexico; its government existed only by American forbearance. If it should collapse without approving the treaty, the United States could take the boundary and pay nothing. Above all, Calhoun wished to dampen the spirit of aggressive war. His speech was anticlimatic. His home state press dutifully reported it but with little enthusiasm. By late March most South Carolinians regarded the war as finished. They turned their attention to news of the recent French revolution and increasingly to the approaching presidential contest.[39]

Calhoun's mood varied. During late March and throughout April he felt reasonably confident that Mexico would approve the treaty. If not, America would effectively terminate the war anyway by taking a defensive line. Nonetheless, the faction-ridden Mexican Congress dallied, and the nation was beset with a revolt in Yucatan. In May reports reached Charleston that Mexico had rejected the treaty, and there was "no prospect of peace." Again Calhoun had doubts. Perhaps deep down he yet hoped the administration would be forced to accept his defensive line. That was not to be, for in early June news arrived that the Mexican Congress had accepted the treaty with America's modifications. There was nothing left for the United States to do but bring the troops home, including the remaining Palmettos.[40]

---

taineer, March 24, 1848; Pendleton *Messenger*, March 25, 1848; Columbia *Daily Telegraph*, March 17, 1848; Merk, *Manifest Destiny*, 121, 187–94; Edgefield *Advertiser*, March 22, 1848.

39. Charleston *Courier*, March 20, 1848; Georgetown *Winyah Observer*, March 29, 1848; *Congressional Globe*, 30th Cong., 1st Sess., 467, 477–80, 483–503. Butler joined Calhoun in trying to amend the Ten-Regiment Bill. Failing in that, he voted for its passage, but the bill died in the House. The Greenville *Mountaineer*, March 24, 1848, was filled with news of events in France.

40. J. C. Calhoun to T. G. Clemson, March 22, April 1, 13, May 13, 26, 1848, in Calhoun Papers, CU; Charleston *Mercury*, May 22, 24, June 3, 9, 1848. The Mexican lower house approved 51 to 35, the Senate 33 to 4.

Epilogue

IN THE LONG MONTHS between the capture of Mexico City and the conclusion of peace, the Palmettos had not been forgotten back home. In the late fall of 1847, there was even talk of relieving them. The Abbeville *Banner*, observing that the war might continue indefinitely, asked, "Shall they be required to remain in service until the last man shall perish and the Palmetto Regiment become extinct?" From General Scott's headquarters came reports that the volunteers would be relieved no sooner than the regulars. In late February, 1848, as the Ten-Regiment Bill became enmeshed in a political row, General A. C. Jones, a Laurens District militia officer, recommended recruitment of another regiment to replace the Palmettos, reduced to less than three hundred men. He vowed that he could raise a company within two days. His generous proposal received editorial applause, but nothing came of it.[1]

The volunteers kept the folks back home informed of their activities. In December they were moved from the National Palace to the nearby village of San Angel, too calm a place for some. Major Gladden was promoted to lieutenant colonel, and there were promotions down the line, some of which not unexpectedly rankled the privates. Daily routine was easy, though the volun-

---

1. Abbeville *Banner*, November 10, 1847; Anderson *Gazette*, January 20, 1848; Greenville *Mountaineer*, January 28, February 25, March 3, 31, 1848; Edgefield *Advertiser*, March 1, 1848.

teers had to remain on guard against brigands. The health of the
regiment improved; only an occasional death from disease and
one from murder by a fellow volunteer were reported.

Captain Preston Brooks firmly denied a desire to leave Mexico
before peace was concluded, but others indicated a longing for
home. One lieutenant requested Major Eaves to "keep the younger
ladies from marrying untill we do return—and inform us by some
means what you are doing with them for us." After the preliminary treaty was signed in early February, the Palmetto volunteers,
like other American troops, fraternized more freely with the Mexicans. In fact, the fraternization went much further than some
thought proper. Calhoun received a report from Mexico City denouncing the legalized gambling and prostitution permitted by
American authorities. The writer was appalled at the corruption
and profligacy of the American soldiers, from gray-bearded men
to beardless youths.[2]

In May there were new promotions: Gladden to colonel, Dunovant to lieutenant colonel, and Keith Moffatt, commander of
the Kershaw Company, to major. By that time, however, the Palmettos were little interested in promotions; they were anxious to
go home. One volunteer remarked, "We are fairly worn out with
the ennui and dullness—there is nothing at all new." Hence, when
Mexico approved the treaty later in May, the happy Palmettos
evacuated San Angel on the thirtieth with "willing hearts and
limbs." They arrived at Vera Cruz on June 17 and embarked the
next day for Mobile, where they were mustered out of service.
Unfortunately for them, War Department orders reached Mexico
too late for them to be transported to Charleston. From Mobile
they made their way in small groups back to South Carolina. Most
arrived in early July.[3]

2. Lt. J. T. Walker to Eaves, March 21, 1848, in Eaves Papers; Charleston *Courier*,
  December 8, 1847, January 6, 1848; Preston Brooks, in Edgefield *Advertiser*, April
  19, 1848; Moore, in Greenville *Mountaineer*, April 21, May 26, 1848; Charleston
  Mercury, May 4, 1848; J. G. Tod to J. C. Calhoun, April 5, 1848, in Calhoun Papers, CU.
3. Gettys, "To Conquer a Peace," 327, 335–58; John Hammond Moore (ed.), "Private Johnson Fights the Mexicans," 226–28; Charleston *Mercury*, May 30, 1848;
  Charleston *Courier*, July 8, 1848; Sumter *Banner*, July 5, 1848.

The Palmettos paid heavily for their part in the Mexican War. Altogether 1,019 men served in the regiment at some time. Of that number 429 died, 43 deserted, and 547 returned home; but of the returnees 160 had been discharged earlier, mainly because of wounds or disability. Several companies had been reduced to no more than 30 or 35 men. The Palmettos' death rate of almost 43 percent compared dismally with the army's overall average of about 15 percent of those who served in Mexico, and it was probably higher than that of any other regiment.[4]

The state held the survivors in high esteem and honored them in their respective districts. The ceremonies, held in late July and August, were much like those that sent the companies off to war, with band music, banners, parades, speeches, toasts, dinners, and large crowds. Some three thousand persons attended the Edgefield dinner, and four thousand were present in Abbeville, where there was "most perfect order" due largely to the absence of liquor. At least one happy festival ended on a sour note. Six months after the Sumter celebration, the financially embarrassed proprietor of China's Hotel, scene of the dinner for "the Sumters," published an urgent request for the arrangements committee to pay $175.61 still due him.[5]

Thus ended a great adventure in which South Carolina played no small part. It is true that the state encountered difficulty in recruiting a regiment, that the volunteers suffered unduly from hardship and disease, and that all soon tired of the onerous service. But in the end the Palmettos, though ill fated, performed nobly and earned their glory. The headstrong Mexicans had deserved chastisement, so it was felt, and America had administered it in full measure. Nevertheless, the cause of the war and Polk's policy

4. For Palmetto casualties I have relied on Gettys, "To Conquer a Peace," 389–91. Slightly different numbers are found in "Documents of the Palmetto Regiment," 256–77. W. W. Dudley, commissioner of pensions in 1884, listed 90,582 regulars and volunteers who served in Mexico. Of these, deaths from all causes totaled 12,878. *Congressional Record*, 48th Cong., 1st Sess., 4505–506. See also Bauer, *Mexican War*, 397; Smith, *War with Mexico*, II, 511–12.
5. Charleston *Courier*, June 30, July 31, 1848; Edgefield *Advertiser*, August 2, 1848, and quoting Abbeville *Banner*; Sumter *Banner*, August 23, 1848; Gregorie, *History of Sumter County*, 160.

"to conquer a peace" had caused qualms among many South Carolinians.

Some felt that Taylor's march to the Rio Grande had been unnecessarily provocative. As the war became prolonged, there was mounting criticism of the president's having sent American troops deep into anarchy-prone Mexico to face "unconquerable" guerrillas. The long, drawn-out Seminole War, they believed, should have taught him better. There were others who felt that the United States had no right to despoil Mexico of territory beyond the Rio Grande, perhaps beyond the Nueces. Then, there was concern about the effect of the war on the national debt, the tariff, the centralization of authority in Washington, and the move to annex a land with eight million aliens of mixed blood. Above all, South Carolinians, and many southerners, were gravely worried over the growing sentiment in the North to restrict slavery in the newly conquered territory.

With exceptions, the South Carolina press was wishy-washy in its support of the administration. At the time of American victories, most of the Palmetto newspapers commended the president, and they were ever effusive in their praise for the Palmettos. At other times many, led by the Charleston *Mercury*, were critical, but none was as caustic or bitter as Horace Greeley's New York *Tribune* and some other northern journals. Only in the winter of 1848, when peace seemed elusive, did the South Carolina press almost unanimously come to endorse Calhoun's defensive-line policy.

The outspoken South Carolina critics of the Polk administration were Waddy Thompson, Joel R. Poinsett, John C. Calhoun, and David Johnson. Thompson and Poinsett openly sympathized with Mexico, questioned the justice of American claims, and warned of the disastrous consequences of the war. Calhoun and Johnson held similar views, but as officeholders they were more sensitive to public opinion than were the two former diplomats with no further political ambition.

Early in the war Calhoun comprehended a strong public demand to keep the Rio Grande, New Mexico, and California—sparsely populated areas that American forces had overrun. He himself may have sincerely desired that territory; and in view of Mexican intransigence toward American peace overtures, his defensive-line strategy seemed to be an ideal solution, that is, until the Wilmot Proviso's popularity in the North clearly revealed to all thinking southerners the dilemma they faced in absorbing any Mexican territory.

Calhoun understood as well as Thompson that slavery would not prosper in the proposed cession, and after further reflection he may have desired no territory beyond the Rio Grande; but politically he could not subscribe to the Whigs's no-territory doctrine. The war spirit had been aroused, the nation's honor was involved, heavy expenses had been incurred, and American lives lost. "The voice of the country," as he had told the Senate, "had decided irrevocably" in favor of an indemnity. This view was clearly seen at the numerous anti-Wilmot Proviso rallies held in South Carolina in the fall of 1847. Although several editors and political leaders, including Senator Butler, desired no territory west of the Rio Grande or south of 36°30' as a means of heading off the Wilmot Proviso, most South Carolinians, however reluctantly, were unwilling to return the coveted Mexican provinces only to avoid a confrontation with the abolitionists. There was a matter of principle involved; their constitutional rights in the territories were at stake.

For the sake of unity within his home state, Calhoun subscribed to an imperialist grab that he knew was fraught with danger for his region. Yet, the boundary called for in the Treaty of Guadalupe Hidalgo was almost identical with his proposed defensive line. How could he vote against it? Moreover, if the Senate failed to approve the treaty, he feared that such action would give the all-Mexico movement momentum that would surely deal a death blow to slavery. In any case, the results of the war augured ill for the South Carolinians, but many probably agreed with editor William J. Francis, who commented that regardless of Polk's action in the spring of 1846, "there can be but little doubt that war between the United States and Mexico, in the course of a few years, could not be avoided." [6]

Whether the war was foreordained, the Polk administration and the American people were fortunate that the Mexican government in early 1848 pulled itself together and decided to accept the American terms for peace. There was much sentiment in Mexico for continued guerrilla warfare, and had the government decided on such a policy, as the Vietnamese did in later years, the war would have been prolonged indefinitely with possible disastrous political and military consequences to both nations. Calhoun, Thompson, and many others foresaw such a danger. But the advent of a greater conflict in 1861 overshadowed the Mexican War ("a rehearsal") and obscured lessons that might have been learned from that experience.

6. Sumter *Banner*, June 15, 1848.

Bibliography

PRIMARY SOURCES

Manuscript Collections

Barrow Papers (microfilm), Southern Historical Collection, Chapel Hill, N.C.
Preston Brooks Papers, South Caroliniana Library, Columbia, S.C.
Armistead Burt Papers, Duke University, Durham, N.C.
P. M. Butler Papers, South Caroliniana Library
John C. Calhoun Papers, Clemson University, Clemson, S.C.
John C. Calhoun Papers, Duke University
John C. Calhoun Papers, South Caroliniana Library
John P. Cantwell MS, South Carolina Historical Society, Charleston, S.C.
Henry W. Conner Papers (microfilm), Library of Congress, Washington, D.C.
Dickson Family Papers, Southern Historical Collection
N. R. Eaves Papers, South Caroliniana Library
F. H. Elmore Papers, Library of Congress
Joseph A. Gamewell MS, South Caroliniana Library
James Gadsden Papers, South Caroliniana Library
Duff Green Papers, Southern Historical Collection
John B. Grimball Diary (typescript), Southern Historical Collection
James Hamilton, Jr., Papers, Southern Historical Collection
James H. Hammond Papers, Library of Congress
Hammond Papers, South Caroliniana Library
W. S. Johnson Papers, South Caroliniana Library
J. W. Lesesne Papers, Southern Historical Collection
George McDuffie Papers, Duke University
Mary E. Moragne Papers, South Caroliniana Library
Benjamin F. Perry Diary, Southern Historical Collection
Benjamin F. Perry Papers, Alabama Department of Archives and History, Montgomery, Ala.
Francis W. Pickens Papers, Duke University
James K. Polk Papers, Library of Congress

Quitman Family Papers, Southern Historical Collection
E. G. Randolph Papers, South Caroliniana Library
John R. Shurley Diary (microfilm), Southern Historical Collection
Townes Family Papers, South Caroliniana Library
Beaufort T. Watts Papers, South Caroliniana Library
Williams-Chesnut-Manning Papers, South Caroliniana Library

Newspapers

Abbeville *Banner*, 1846–1848
Anderson *Gazette*, 1846–1848
Camden *Journal*, January 5, 1848–August 2, 1848
Charleston *Courier*, 1846–1848
Charleston *Mercury*, 1846–1848
Columbia *Daily Telegraph*, October 19, 1847–1848
Columbia *South Carolinian*, May 14, 1846–1848
Edgefield *Advertiser*, 1846–1848
Georgetown *Winyah Observer*, 1846–1848
Greenville *Mountaineer*, 1846–1848
Pendleton *Messenger*, 1846–1848
Sumter *Banner*, November 6, 1846–1848

Public Documents

Biographical Directory of the American Congress, 1774–1971: The Continen-
    tal Congress, September 5, 1774, to October 21, 1788, and the Congress of
    the United States from the First Through the Ninety-First Congress, March
    4, 1789, to January 3, 1971, Inclusive. Washington, D.C.: Government
    Printing Office, 1971.
Congressional Globe. 1st Session of the 29th Congress. Washington, D.C.:
    Blair & Rives, 1846.
Congressional Globe. 2nd Session of the 29th Congress. Washington, D.C.:
    Blair & Rives, 1847.
Congressional Globe. 1st Session of the 30th Congress. Washington, D.C.: Blair
    & Rives, 1848.
"Documents of the Palmetto Regiment, 1846–1849." Manuscript in South Caro-
    lina Department of Archives and History, Columbia.
Journal of the House of Representatives of the State of South Carolina. Being
    the Annual Session of 1847. Columbia, S.C.: A. G. Summer, 1847.
Journal of the Senate of the State of South Carolina. Being the Annual Session of
    1847. Columbia, S.C.: A. G. Summer, 1847.
Reports and Resolutions of the General Assembly of the State of South Caro-
    lina, Passed at the Annual Session of 1847. Columbia, S.C.: A. G. Summer,
    1847.
Reynolds, Emily B. and Joan R. Faunt, comps., *Biographical Directory of the*
    Senate of the State of South Carolina, 1776–1964: Compiled under the Di-
    rection of the Senatorial Research Committee. Columbia: South Carolina
    Archives Department, 1964.

Published Manuscript Collections

Benton, Thomas Hart. *Thirty Years' View: Or, a History of the Working of the American Government for Thirty Years, From 1820 to 1850.* 2 vols. New York: D. Appleton, 1856.

Boucher, Chauncey S. and Robert P. Brooks, eds. "Correspondence Addressed to John C. Calhoun, 1837–1849," in *Annual Report of the American Historical Association for the Year 1929.* Washington, D.C.: Government Printing Office, 1930, pp. 125–533.

Carson, James Petigru. *Life, Letters and Speeches of James Louis Petigru: The Union Man of South Carolina.* Washington, D.C.: W. H. Lowdermilk, 1920.

Claiborne, J. F. H. *Life and Correspondence of John A. Quitman: Major-General, U.S.A., and Governor of the State of Mississippi.* 2 vols. New York: Harper & Brothers, 1860.

Dunovant, R. G. M. *The Palmetto Regiment, South Carolina Volunteers, 1846– 1848. The Battles in the Valley of Mexico, 1847.* [Part 1]. Columbia, S.C.: Bryan Printing, 1895.

———. *The Palmetto Regiment, South Carolina Volunteers, 1846–1848. The Battles in the Valley of Mexico, 1847.* Part 2. Charleston, S.C.: Walker, Evans & Cogswell, 1897.

Jameson, J. Franklin, ed. *Correspondence of John C. Calhoun.* Vol. II of *Fourth Annual Report of the Historical Manuscripts Commission of the American Historical Association.* Washington, D.C.: Government Printing Office, 1900.

Manigault, A. M. "A Letter from Vera Cruz in 1847." *Southwestern Historical Quarterly,* XVIII (October, 1914), 216–17.

McGowan, Samuel. *An Address on the Occasion of the First Anniversary of the Palmetto Association, Delivered in Columbia, S.C. May 14th, A.D. 1857.* Columbia, S.C.: I. C. Morgan, 1857.

Moore, H. Judge. *Scott's Campaign in Mexico: From the Rendezvous on the Island of Lobos to the Taking of the City, Including an Account of the Siege of Puebla, with Sketches of the Country, and Manners and Customs of the Inhabitants.* Charleston, S.C.: J. B. Nixon, 1849.

Moore, John Hammond, ed. "Private Johnson Fights the Mexicans, 1847– 1848." *South Carolina Historical Magazine,* XLVII (October, 1966), 203– 28.

Oliphant, Mary C. Simms, Alfred Taylor Odell, and T. C. Duncan Eaves, eds. *The Letters of William Gilmore Simms.* 5 vols. Columbia: University of South Carolina Press, 1952–1956.

Phillips, Ulrich B., ed. *The Correspondence of Robert Toombs, Alexander H. Stephens, and Howell Cobb.* Vol. II, in *Annual Report of the American Historical Association for the Year 1911.* Washington, D.C.: Government Printing Office, 1913.

Poinsett, Joel R. "Our Army in Mexico." *Commercial Review of the South and West,* II (December, 1846), 426–30.

———. "War in Mexico." *Commercial Review of the South and West,* II (July, 1846), 21–24.

Quaife, Milo Milton, ed. *The Diary of James K. Polk: During His Presidency, 1845 to 1849.* 4 vols. Chicago: A. C. McClurg, 1910.

Simms, W. Gilmore. *Lays of the Palmetto: A Tribute to the South Carolina Regiment, in the War with Mexico*. Charleston, S.C.: John Russell, 1848.
Thompson, Waddy. *Recollections of Mexico*. New York and London: Wiley and Putnam, 1847 [1846].

SECONDARY SOURCES

Dissertations

Edmunds, John Boyd, Jr. "Francis W. Pickens: A Political Biography." Ph.D. dissertation, University of South Carolina, 1967.
Gettys, James W., Jr. "'To Conquer a Peace': South Carolina and the Mexican War." Ph.D. dissertation, University of South Carolina, 1974.
Glen, Virginia Louise. "James Hamilton, Jr., A Biography." Ph.D. dissertation, University of North Carolina, 1964.
Hrumeni, George Anthony. "Palmetto Yankee: The Public Life and Times of Joel Roberts Poinsett: 1824–1851." Ph.D. dissertation, University of California, 1972.
Tucker, Robert C. "James Henry Hammond, South Carolinian." Ph.D. dissertation, University of North Carolina, 1958.

Articles

Crowson, E. T. "Manifest Destiny, Mexico, and the Palmetto Boys." *Sandlapper*, V (January, 1972), 32–34, 66–69.
Foreman, Carolyn T. "Pierce Mason Butler." *Chronicles of Oklahoma*, XXI (Spring, 1952), 6–28.
Franklin, John H. "Southern Expansionists of 1846." *Journal of Southern History*, XXV (August, 1959), 323–38.
Lander, Ernest M., Jr. "The Calhoun-Preston Feud, 1836–1842." *South Carolina Historical Magazine*, LIX (January, 1958), 24–37.
———. "General Waddy Thompson, a Friend of Mexico During the Mexican War." *South Carolina Historical Magazine*, LXXVIII (January, 1977), 32–42.
Lord, C. W. "Young Louis Wigfall: South Carolina Politician and Duelist." *South Carolina Historical Magazine*, LIX (April, 1958), 96–112.
McCrary, Royce C. "Georgia Politics and the Mexican War." *Georgia Historical Quarterly*, LX (Fall, 1976), 211–27.
Rayback, Joseph G. "The Presidential Ambitions of John C. Calhoun, 1844–1848." *Journal of Southern History*, XIV (August, 1948), 331–56.

Books

Bauer, K. Jack. *The Mexican War, 1846–1848*. New York: MacMillan, 1974.
Capers, Gerald M. *John C. Calhoun, Opportunist: A Reappraisal*. Gainesville, Fla.: University of Florida Press, 1960.
Chapman, John A. *History of Edgefield County: From the Earliest Settlements to 1897*. Newberry, S.C.: Elbert H. Aull, 1897.

Cole, Arthur C. *The Whig Party in the South*. Gloucester, Mass.: Peter Smith, 1962.

Coit, Margaret. *John C. Calhoun: American Portrait*. Boston: Houghton Mifflin, 1950.

Donald, David. *Charles Sumner and the Coming of the Civil War*. New York: Alfred A. Knopf, 1961.

Freidel, Frank. *Francis Lieber: Nineteenth-Century Liberal*. Baton Rouge: Louisiana State University Press, 1947.

Fuller, John D. P. *The Movement for the Acquisition of All Mexico, 1846–1848*. Baltimore: Johns Hopkins Press, 1936.

Gregorie, Anne King. *History of Sumter County, South Carolina*. Sumter, S.C.: Library Board of Sumter County, 1954.

Hamer, Philip M. *The Secession Movement in South Carolina, 1847–1852*. Allentown, Pa.: H. Ray Haas, 1918.

Henry, Robert S. *The Story of the Mexican War*. Indianapolis and New York: Bobbs-Merrill, 1950.

Hollis, Daniel W. *South Carolina College*. Vol I of 2 vols., in *University of South Carolina*. Columbia: University of South Carolina Press, 1951.

Jones, Oakah L., Jr. *Santa Anna*. New York: Twayne, 1968.

Kibler, Lillian. *Benjamin F. Perry: South Carolina Unionist*. Durham, N.C.: Duke University Press, 1946.

King, Alvy L. *Louis T. Wigfall: Southern Fire-eater*. Baton Rouge: Louisiana State University Press, 1970.

King, William L. *The Newspaper Press of Charleston, S.C.: A Chronological and Biographical History, Embracing a Period of One Hundred and Forty Years*. Charleston, S.C.: Edward Perry, 1872.

Kirkland, Thomas J., and Robert M. Kennedy. *Historic Camden: Part Two, Nineteenth Century*. Columbia, S.C.: State Company, 1926.

Lesesne, J. Mauldin. *The Bank of the State of South Carolina: A General and Political History*. Columbia: University of South Carolina Press, 1970.

Meigs, William M. *The Life of John Caldwell Calhoun*. 2 vols. New York: Neale, 1917.

Merk, Frederick. *Manifest Destiny and Mission in American History: A Reinterpretation*. New York: Alfred A. Knopf, 1963.

Morrison, Chaplain W. *Democratic Politics and Sectionalism: The Wilmot Proviso Controversy*. Chapel Hill: University of North Carolina Press, 1967.

Pletcher, David M. *The Diplomacy of Annexation: Texas, Oregon, and the Mexican War*. Columbia: University of Missouri Press, 1973.

Pope, Thomas H. *The History of Newberry County, South Carolina: Volume One, 1749–1860*. Columbia: University of South Carolina Press, 1973.

Rayback, Joseph G. *Free Soil: The Election of 1848*. Lexington: University of Kentucky Press, 1970.

Rippy, J. Fred. *Joel R. Poinsett: Versatile American*. Durham, N.C.: Duke University Press, 1935.

Schroeder, John H. *Mr. Polk's War: American Opposition and Dissent, 1846–1848*. Madison: University of Wisconsin Press, 1973.

Sellers, Charles G. *James K. Polk: Continentalist, 1843–1846*. Princeton, N.J.:

Princeton University Press, 1966.

Smith, Justin H. *The War with Mexico.* 2 vols. Gloucester, Mass.: Peter Smith, 1963.

Wakelyn, Jon L. *The Politics of a Literary Man: William Gilmore Simms.* Westport, Conn.: Greenwood Press, 1973.

Weems, John E. *To Conquer a Peace: The War Between the United States and Mexico.* Garden City, N.Y.: Doubleday, 1974.

White, Laura A. *Robert Barnwell Rhett: Father of Secession.* New York and London: Century, 1931.

Wiltse, Charles M. *John C. Calhoun: Sectionalist, 1840–1850.* New York: Bobbs-Merrill, 1951.

Index

Butler, A. P.: elected to Senate, 60; supports Calhoun, 60–61, 74, 78, 162, 163, 165; on Wilmot Proviso, 71; and brother's death, 122; on South Carolina Regiment, 138; and plan of peace, 163, 166, 175; mentioned, 73, 112

Butler, Pierce M.: organizes South Carolina Regiment, 28, 36–37, 39, 41, 44, 49, 137; and Mason, 37–38, 122; on way to Mexico, 50–51, 54–55, 56; at Vera Cruz, 82, 83, 85; and hardships of South Carolina Regiment, 88–89, 92, 94, 95, 96–98, 103, 105, 106; on peace, 90, 96; at Contreras, 117–18; death of, 119–20, 121; eulogies and burial of, 121–22, 132, 136, 138, 139, 141, 144, 145, 146–47; mentioned, 58, 60

Butler, Sampson H., 17–18

Butler, Thomas P., 26, 44, 107

Butler, William O., 159, 167

Cain, William, 60

Calhoun, Andrew, 56

Calhoun, John C.: and Texas annexation, 1, 72; on Oregon question, 3, 4, 10, 11; opposes war, 3, 6–7, 8–11, 23, 30, 32, 34, 58, 62–64, 88, 108–109, 111, 113–14, 154, 155, 156, 158, 161, 163, 174, 176; South Carolina press supports, 12–14, 15, 69, 72, 160, 164, 165–66; opposed, 14–15, 16–21, 168; evidence of South Carolina support of, 17, 22–23, 33, 73, 74, 76, 110, 112, 164–65, 174; and internal improvements, 19, 20, 21, 29–30; and Pickens, 20–21, 33–34, 61; and tariff, 29–30, 63; defensive-line policy of, 32, 36, 59, 64–65, 66, 67–68, 71–72, 110, 159, 161–62, 163, 165, 167, 168, 170, 174–75; and recruitment, 46; presidential aspirations of, 61–62, 63, 65, 66, 74–76, 77–78, 79, 109; and southern unity, 73–74, 76, 77, 79, 80, 152; and Wilmot Proviso, 152, 160–61, 166; and Treaty of Guadalupe Hidalgo, 169, 170; mentioned, 36, 56, 172

Calhoun, Patrick, 109

Camden *Journal*, 166

Campbell, John A., 155

Camp Deas, 54–56

Camp Magnolia, 48

Cantey, James W.: and South Carolina Regiment, 25, 48, 49; on supplies, 82; on regiment's health, 89, 117, 118, 122; at Chapultepec, 124–25

Cantwell, John P., 137

Carew, John E., 70, 116, 152, 164

Carroll, B. R., 14, 35

Cass, Lewis: and war bill, 9; criticized, 69; opposes Calhoun, 72; opposes Wilmot Proviso, 157, 160; and Ten-Regiment Bill, 161; on annexation, 163–64

Caughman, H. J., 145

Cerro Gordo: and South Carolina Regiment, 89–90, 93, 100, 101; mentioned, 115, 117

Chapultepec, 124–25, 132, 137, 140

Charleston Company: organized, 26, 41–42; and war, 29, 90, 91

Charleston *Courier*: on war, 3, 5, 13, 14, 99–100, 119, 150, 153–54; on Calhoun, 20, 22, 69, 164; on recruitment, 26, 39, 40–41; on Santa Anna, 31; on Butler, 122, 132, 147; mentioned, 144

Charleston *Evening News*: on war, 13, 59; on Calhoun, 66, 69; on South Carolina Regiment, 134; on southern unity, 152

Charleston *Mercury*: criticizes Polk, 4, 5–6, 31; on war, 11–12, 13, 35–36, 59, 112, 168, 174; opposes Calhoun, 16, 18–19; supports Calhoun, 22, 66, 69, 70, 71, 110, 162, 164; on South Carolina Regiment, 95, 97, 127, 139; on Wilmot Proviso, 116, 152, 154, 161; mentioned, 144

Charleston *Patriot*, 13

Chester Company: organized, 26, 44; on way to Mexico, 46–47; mentioned, 139, 140

Childs, Thomas, 117, 128, 129

Churubusco: South Carolina Regiment at, 118–19, 120–21, 127, 131, 133, 140, 142, 143

Clapp, J. Milton, 4, 59, 70

Clark, Dr. C. J., 105

Clark, J. L., 44

Clark, James R., 148

Clayton, John M., 9

Clemson, Thomas G., 34, 77

Cobb, William, 104

Columbia *Daily Telegraph*, 147, 151

Columbia *South Carolinian*: on war, 14,

Palmetto regiment. *See* South Carolina
Regiment
Palo Alto, 12
Paredes, Mariano, 2, 3, 31
Patterson, Robert, 80
Pendleton *Messenger*: on war, 2, 3, 13,
35, 59, 90, 163–64; on Santa Anna,
31; supports Calhoun, 69; on South
Carolina Regiment, 134; on Wilmot
Proviso, 152
Perrin, J. M., 104, 123, 127
Perry, Benjamin F., 47, 58, 101, 151, 166
Perry, Matthew C.: and expedition to Al-
varado, 83, 84, 86–87; and P. M. But-
ler, 85; supports Calhoun, 159
Petigru, Daniel, 108
Petigru, James L., 108
Pickens, Francis W.: on war, 15, 16, 33,
151; and Calhoun, 16–17, 18, 20–21,
33–34, 61; supports Polk, 18, 19, 21,
61, 151; and South Carolina Regiment,
46, 138; mentioned, 43, 76
Pickens, Susan, 43
Pillow, Gideon: and assault on Mexico
City, 116, 117, 118, 124, 125; and
Scott, 167
Pinckney, R. Q., 25
Poinsett, Joel R.: on war, 23, 41, 42, 155,
166; supports Calhoun, 23, 109, 110,
165, 174
Point Isabel, Texas, 50
Polk, James K.: war policy of, 2–3, 4, 5,
8, 30, 31, 32, 58, 62–63, 65–66, 77,
109–11, 113, 150–51, 155, 158, 161,
163, 164, 167, 169, 173–74, 175, 176;
criticized, 4, 5–6, 66–67, 108–10,
113, 114, 153–54, 158–59, 160, 162,
163, 165, 168, 174; and Calhoun, 10–
11, 66, 70, 74, 75, 77; supported in
South Carolina, 13–14, 17, 18, 39,
151–52, 166, 167, 168, 169, 174; and
domestic legislation, 29–30; mentioned, 25, 35, 46, 112
Popular sovereignty, 158, 159, 160, 166
Posey, Ben L., 54, 96
Press, South Carolina: influences recruitment, 45; supports Polk, 58, 59, 111,
168, 169, 174; opposes Wilmot Proviso, 72–73, 161; on U.S. victories,
99–100, 101–102, 111, 174; on South
Carolina Regiment, 135, 138; supports
antiadministration views, 153, 162,
164, 165, 170, 174

Preston, William C., 18, 146
Puebla: expedition to, 92, 93–95, 96,
108; South Carolina Regiment at, 102–
106, 107, 113, 116–17, 128–29, 131

Quitman, John A.: at battle of Vera Cruz,
80, 81, 83; on march to Alvarado, 83,
84, 86, 87; on march to Jalapa, 89, on
war, 90, 96, 123, 130; on march to
Puebla, 93, 94–95; at Puebla, 102,
103, 106; and assault on Mexico City,
116–17, 117–18, 120, 124, 125–26,
126–27, 128; on South Carolina Regiment, 144

Rayback, Joseph, 79
Rea, Joaquin, 129
Recruitment: enthusiasm for, 25, 26, 40–
41, 42, 43–45; difficulties in, 27, 41,
42, 44–46, 106–108, 131, 173; to re-
place South Carolina Regiment volun-
teers, 171
Resaca de la Palma, 12
Rhett, James, 140
Rhett, Robert Barnwell: on war, 6, 7, 8,
30; and Calhoun, 17, 18–19, 20, 110,
111; supports Polk, 158, 167
Richardson, J. P., 17
Richland Company, 43–44, 132, 148
Richmond *Whig*, 76, 127
Ritchie, Thomas, 69–70, 75
Robertson, L. F., 90
Ross, Dr. F. A., 89
Ross, John, 37

Saluda Company, 26
San Agustín, 117, 121
Santa Anna, Antonio López de: and Mexican politics, 2, 31, 59, 62, 111–12,
128, 130; South Carolina press on, 4,
31–32, 113; negotiates with Polk, 30,
31, and Cerro Gordo, 90; at Amozoc,
94, 104; at Buena Vista, 99; negotiates
with Scott, 112–13, 116; and Scott's
assault on Mexico City, 117, 118, 123,
126, 127, 128, 129; mentioned, 58, 67,
90, 112
Scott, Winfield: and assault on Vera Cruz,
56, 57, 80, 81, 82–83, 99; Polk on, 63,
159, 167; on march to Puebla, 93, 95;
at Cerro Gordo, 100; at Puebla, 102,
103, 108, 113; and Santa Anna, 112–
13, 116; and assault on Mexico City,

92, 95, 97, 100, 103, 172; mentioned, 55, 88, 99, 107, 109, 110, 115, 129, 130, 136, 160, 164

Walker, N. G., 145
Walker Tariff, 29
War of 1812, pp. 10, 137
Washington *Union*, 69, 70, 75, 79, 112
Watts, B. T., 37, 100
Weir, Samuel, 137
Whitaker, Daniel K., 20–21
Wigfall, Louis T., 15–16, 17, 33
Williams, James, 52
Williams, Robert W., 121, 148
Wilmot, David, 30–31
Wilmot Proviso: as opposition to Polk's

peace plan, 30–31, 154, 157, 158; as evil arising from war, 59, 71, 72, 73, 78, 112, 116, 153, 175; feared by Calhoun, 63–64, 70, 71, 73, 75, 114, 160, 161, 166; as denial of southern equality, 64, 71, 73, 78, 152, 157, 175
Woodbury, Levi, 157
Woodward, Joseph A., 6, 37
Worth, William J.: at battle of Vera Cruz, 80; captures Jalapa, 90; captures Fort San Carlos de Perote, 92–93; at Puebla, 94, 102; at assault on Mexico City, 116, 117, 120, 122, 124, 125, 126
Wright, Silas, 62, 64, 75, 79, 157

Yulee, David L., 70